A Framework for
Discourse Analysis
II

A FRAMEWORK
FOR
DISCOURSE ANALYSIS
II

Wilbur N. Pickering, ThM PhD

ISBN Print: 979-0-9898273-4-8

Cover photo: a rural scene in Goias, Brazil, courtesy of Dan Jore

CONTENTS

Contents

NOTICE TO THE READER

This is the PhD dissertation that I submitted to the University of Toronto in 1976, and reflects the literature available at that time. This reprinting includes a few retouchings, but no effort has been made to account for subsequent literature.

PREFACE

To begin, I wish to acknowledge the contribution that my thesis supervisor, H.A. Gleason, Jr., made to my thinking and so to this publication. I have tried to acknowledge overtly in the text the major ideas I owe to him, but during five years of interaction, he influenced my thinking in so many ways that I am at a loss to specify the full extent of his contribution. While I take full responsibility for the content of this study, it is only fair to say that Gleason's contribution extends far beyond the places that have been documented. I also wish to express my thanks to the other two members of my thesis committee, P.A. Reich and H.G. Schogt, for their help. While many people have stimulated my thinking, directly or indirectly, the following deserve individual mention: J. Beekman, K. Callow, J.E. Grimes, M.A.K. Halliday, R.E. Longacre, and K.L. Pike.

I wish to acknowledge the financial assistance I received from the School of Graduate Studies of the University of Toronto in the form of two Open Fellowships. I also thank the taxpayers of the Province of Ontario for subsidizing my tuition. I must also mention those faithful persons who, in the long-range interest of Bible translation for the minority peoples of the world, have sustained us financially through thick and thin.

My wife, Ida Lou, deserves special mention of appreciation. Not only did she type three drafts of this treatise, she cared for me in all the ways that spell 'home', and without her help this study probably would not have been undertaken.

Last, and perhaps above all, I wish to acknowledge the unique help of my Lord and Savior, Jesus Christ, on two counts: 1) He has given meaning and direction to my life; 2) He is the ultimate source of the original insights presented herein (Colossians 2:3).

v

1 INTRODUCTION

The aim of this treatise is to present a framework for discourse analysis. The use of the term 'analysis' rather than 'structure', and 'framework for', rather than 'model of', reflects its orientation—it is more practical than theoretical. The use of the term 'framework', rather than 'method', reflects an aspiration to general or universal validity or usefulness, whereas 'method' might more appropriately be used of the more precise and detailed roster of considerations that one might develop for a specific language or a certain genre of discourse.

The practical orientation of this presentation reflects my conviction that the main purpose of theory is to make us more efficient by increasing our understanding of reality. If our discipline is not useful, or does not have practical applications (direct or indirect), how can we continue to justify its place in society?[1] But theory is an indispensable component of any discipline and I hope that this discussion will prove to be of some theoretical consequence.

As suggested by the use of the term analysis in the title, I have adopted a decoding perspective. This is in line with my desire to contribute to the efficiency of ordinary working linguists as they seek to understand the workings of real languages. Although one might gather from a glance at the contemporary linguistic scene that theoretical relevance calls for an encoding perspective, I question the validity of that assumption. How does a child learn a language? Since children invariably learn only the language(s) to which they are exposed, and when artificially isolated from language contact, learn or develop none

---

[1] I am in essential agreement with H.A. Gleason's thoughts on this subject (1976). In a world which is going to hell in every possible sense of the expression, theory for theory's sake, a theorizing which is not constrained by reality and which has no interest in being useful, I hold to be reprehensible.

1

at all, the child must learn by decoding. He learns the language that he hears. What he hears is a welter of sound, and he must learn to abstract meaning from that sound. Such abstraction is possible because the sound is organized and the child learns the organizing system through a decoding process. Similarly, a linguist attempting to learn an unwritten language must use a decoding process.

My own introduction to linguistics was solidly tagmemic, and I follow that general orientation here—at least in the sense that I view language as form-meaning composite and feel that form and meaning must be analyzed as a composite. I accept a deep-surface distinction in the sense of abstraction versus organized sound (or symbol), but not as poles of a continuum with intermediate stages which the human mind actually uses. The mind has to juggle all the variables at once, because they are interrelated, and produce the result in linear sequence. Or, when decoding, the final verdict on the phonology often waits for an interpretation that makes sense. The analysis of ancient manuscripts furnishes an analogy. It is a convention among papyrologists not to publish a reconstruction of a text unless they can furnish a translation or identification—holes in the text (missing letters or parts of letters) are filled in on the basis of interpretation. The variables are interrelated and must be processed simultaneously.

H.A. Gleason's discovery in 1962 (first mentioned in print in 1964) that a discourse grammar of Kâte (Papua New Guinea) seemed to be more insightful and economical than a sentence grammar may prove to be one of the major watershed or milestone events in the development of our discipline. It furnished an impetus for the study of discourse. Robert Longacre, after two recent workshops (Fall 1974 and Spring 1975) concentrating on discourse structure in a number of languages in Colombia and Panama, is now affirming that it is impossible to achieve a correct grammatical analysis of a language without accounting for its discourse level conventions. I quote from his introduction to the first volume of a three-volume work containing a number of articles resulting from those workshops.

> *In earlier work, discourse analysis was regarded as an option open to the student of a language provided that he was interested, and provided that he had a good start on the structure of lower levels (word, phrase, clause). But early in the first workshop it was seen that all work on lower levels is lacking in perspective and meets inevitable frustration when the higher levels—especially discourse and paragraph—have not been analyzed. One can describe the verb morphology of a language but where does one use a given verb form? One can describe a transitive clause in terms of obligatory and optional parts but under what conditions do 'optional' time and location expressions get used? One can describe linear permutations of predicate, subject, and object, but what factors control alternative word orderings? One can call the roster of sentence-initial conjunctions, but where does one use which? Furthermore, what about certain mysterious verb or noun affixes or certain particles that defy analysis and for which the informant can give no meaning? To answer these and other problems one needs discourse perspective.*
>
> *In view of these considerations, discourse analysis emerges not as an option or as a luxury for the serious student of a language but as a necessity (Longacre 1976b:2).*

Longacre is not the first to say something of this sort. Joseph Grimes agrees with Gerald Sanders (1970) that a sentence grammar will not work unless it is part of a discourse grammar (1975:8). He says further:

> *Our grasp of grammar has changed sufficiently in the past decade that instead of simply saying that a language has, for example, thirty-two clause types, we can now ask legitimately what the various clause types are for, and by tracing their pattern of use within a discourse we can get an answer (1975: 97).*

And only by studying discourse can we answer such questions. Already in 1949 Kenneth L. Pike found it necessary to include hierarchy in grammatical theory, since the definition of a unit depends upon its including structures as well as its internal structure. This led him to levels above the sentence and to a cultural-behavioral setting for language. Pike's present feelings about the importance of discourse may be guessed from the circumstance that he now starts his beginning grammar course at the discourse level (Pike and Pike 1977).

I owe to Gleason an insight which I consider to be powerful and far-reaching. There is a difference between citation forms and context forms. A citation form is produced in isolation in response to elicitation; a context form occurs naturally in a linguistic and situational context. Further, elicitation produces only citation forms, not context forms, and nothing above a sentence has a citation form. Also, careful reflection makes clear, I think, that an appeal to intuition is a form of elicitation (producing citation forms). (With reference to intuition, I am reminded of William Labov's [1973a:114] statement: "The student of his own intuitions, producing both data and theory in a language abstracted from every social context, is the ultimate lame.") It follows that any theory or procedure that is based on elicitation and/or intuition will find itself bound to the sentence. Any resulting grammar will be less than fully valid. I think the moral is inescapable: only a discourse grammar has a chance of being fully valid. (A sentence grammar based on context forms would be partly invalid because a large part of the relevant context would have been ignored.)

One wonders how long a sentence grammar can continue to be theoretically defensible. Happily, the accumulated knowledge that forces us to raise our sights to discourse grammar also renders the enterprise feasible. Among them Gleason, Grimes, Longacre, and Pike have supervised the writing of discourse related articles for well over 100 languages from around the world. The main successes and advances in discourse analysis up to this point have been with participant orientation in particular and narrative type discourse in general. In both second language learning and translation, competence

4

is achieved in narrative type discourse well before expository and hortatory type discourse, and so it has been assumed that the discourse structure of the former would be easier to analyze than that of the latter. Accordingly, narrative discourse was tackled first. I believe the time has come to attempt to devise a framework adequate for the analysis of expository discourse. (If the assumed greater complexity of expository discourse structure is substantiated, then such a framework should also prove adequate for narrative discourse. If the assumption proves to be invalid, such a framework should still provide insights or analogies to enhance our understanding of narrative structure.) A wealth of ideas and studies lies ready to hand. In attempting a synthesis, I have tried to incorporate such valid insights (in my judgment) as have come to my attention, from whatever source, adding a few of my own. It is my conviction that all valid insights into reality must be compatible and will ultimately fit into a coherent model.

Since my purpose is to be suggestive and to present a synthesis of existing ideas, I am not concerned to be exhaustive either in exposition or documentation. With respect to the latter, I have generally based my discussion on current works of scholars, particularly the ones to whom I happen to be directly indebted. In almost all cases the history of the ideas included in my synthesis goes back several generations; e.g., I refer to Halliday's use of *theme* and *rheme* because in the English-speaking linguistic world the terms are associated with him, but I do not intend to imply thereby that the notion is original with him; Vilém Mathesius and the Prague School were using it several decades before, and something of the sort was mentioned by scholars like G. von der Gabelentz and A.M. Bell in the nineteenth century (Vachek 1966:111; Firbas and Golková 1976:11).

What got me started on the train of thought which has resulted in the following framework was the effort to organize the roster of topics discussed by Grimes in his *Thread of Discourse* (1975) in a way that I could understand. That effort resulted in three "systems" with several pieces left over, which eventually found their way into the five "macrosystems" offered below. Although Grimes may not recognize any family resemblance and may even renounce his offspring, I wish to thank him for getting me started. The first part of the discussion consists of a presentation and exposition of my framework for discourse analysis. I then apply the framework to a linguistic corpus by way of illustrating how and to what extent it works.

I have felt rather like someone trying to put together a complicated jigsaw puzzle with over half the pieces missing. As Grimes says, "what we do not know is more important at this stage than what we have found" (1975:359). I do not claim to have solved the language puzzle, but I believe this approach represents a forward step.

When I speak of a 'framework for discourse analysis', I am thinking of a means to get at, discriminate, and describe all of the factors that contribute to the abstraction, or total meaning, evoked by a spoken (or written) discourse of whatever size. For centuries men have spoken of the general impact or effect of a speech, but I believe the time has come to isolate the individual components that combine to produce the effect. If a number of listeners react in essentially the same way to a nuance in a speech, there must be a specific signal, or combination of signals, to account for it. But before trying to match cause with effect in a particular language, it would be helpful to have as nearly complete a roster as possible of the factors that may reasonably be expected to contribute to the abstraction that a discourse is designed to evoke. The framework which is presented in Figure 1 aspires to be such a roster. It is important that the roster be complete because the presence of any unlooked-for factors will skew our interpretation of the rest, since we will not be taking any account of their influence. For example, I have included idiolect as a factor, not because it is a part of the organizing system of a language (by definition it cannot be), but because any truly idiosyncratic elements that are not skimmed off will get in the way of the analysis.

First the framework is presented in outline form (fig. 1) to give an idea of its scope, and then it is discussed in detail. I call the major sections in the outline 'macrosystems', but not as a technical term *à la* Halliday. I see the systems as being simultaneous and overlapping, but distinct (like Halliday's "macrofunctions", except that I slice the pie differently). My present feeling is that systems A-E dictate the discourse structure of a text, as such, whereas F and G represent factors that must be taken into account but which form the background upon which A-E are superimposed; or, to put it more precisely, F and G represent restrictions or boundaries which condition or limit what can be done with systems A-E.

The comments in parentheses—outline perspective, linear perspective, etc.—reflect my feeling that each of the first five macrosystems gives expression to an organizational perspective which is clearly distinct from the others and which can be clearly characterized. Discourse structure is the result of the interplay among these organizational perspectives. I suppose that no two languages will have identical rosters of possible combinations; nor will any two discourses have identical rosters of actual combinations. I deliberately avoid speaking of the discourse structure of a language; the phrase is appropriate only to specific discourses. I will use 'discourse system' to speak of the totality of expectations shared by the members of a speech community. I proceed to discuss each macrosystem in detail.

A. Hierarchy (outline perspective)
  1. Constituent structure
  2. Taxis
  3. Span

B. Cohesion (linear perspective)
  1. Grammatical agreement
  2. Phoric reference
  3. Conjunction
  4. Lexical association
  5. Given information

C. Prominence (thematic perspective)
  1. Theme
  2. Focus
  3. Emphasis

D. Style (social perspectlve)
  1. Register
  2. Code
  3. Dialect
  4. Idiolect

E. Strategy (pragmatic perspective)
  1. Content
  2. Genre
  3. Information rate
  4. Modality
  5. Sincerity

F. Medium

G. Language and Culture

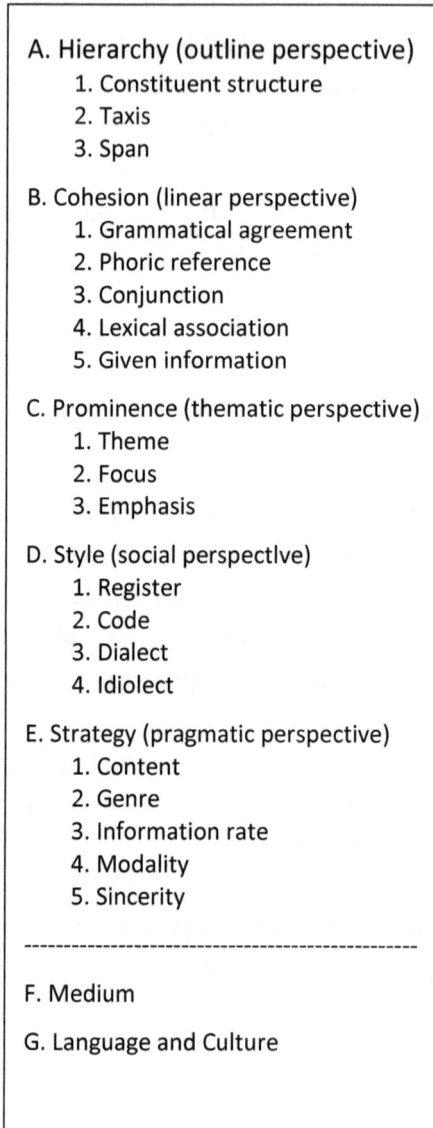

Fig. 1: A Framework for Discourse Analysis

PART I:
THE FRAMEWORK

2 Hierarchy

Whether one speaks of tree structure or phrase structure or constituent structure or grammatical structure or outline or hierarchy, I believe linguists of all persuasions recognize that there is some such organizational perspective in language. I would say that this organizational system is a consequence and reflection of the basic limitation in human short-term memory which George Miller characterized as 7 ± 2 (1956). (The average human mind can only keep track of up to seven random or unrelated chunks of information at a time.) Hierarchy is the result of the human necessity to package and repackage the linear flow of language so as to keep the number of bundles on the short-term memory tray within the magic number—or else pieces get pushed off and 'lost'.

Hierarchy, then, is fundamentally a packaging view, and since packaging is indispensable to human communication, hierarchy must be fundamental, perhaps the most fundamental of the macrosystems. At any rate, most of the grammatical analysis done through the ages has concerned itself with hierarchy in one way or another, if only up to the sentence level. Similarly, most of the work so far done in discourse analysis has really focused on hierarchy, wittingly or not. I believe that hierarchy must continue to have a prominent place in discourse analysis. How then can we determine the hierarchical structure of a discourse? I suggest that Hierarchy is signaled by three organizing factors: constituent structure, taxis, and span. They will be discussed in that order.

2.1 **Constituent Structure.** The best known analytical approach is probably immediate constituent (IC) analysis. Given an utterance, e.g., a sentence, a binary cut is made; the resulting pieces in turn are subjected to binary cuts, and so on until each word (or morpheme) has been isolated. By way of illustration I will attempt an IC analysis of the sentence, "John ate his piece of pie with a spoon".

John / ate his piece of pie with a spoon
     ate / his piece of pie with a spoon
          his piece of pie / with a spoon
          his piece / of pie   with / a spoon
          his / piece   of / pie   a / spoon

The decision of where to cut is based partly on convention (separate subject from predicate first) and partly on a subjective feel for the relative degree of intimacy or attachment between words; the cut at each level is made between the two words judged to have the least attachment. Thus the words, "his piece" were judged to be more intimately related than "ate his" with the result that the cut between "ate" and "his" was made at a higher level than that between "his" and "piece".

It is evident that some of the decisions are quite arbitrary, giving rise to endless arguments among practitioners, but a more serious problem has been well stated by Longacre.

> *Immediate constituent analysis yielded ad hoc hierarchies built anew in every separate sentence which was analyzed. It did not yield genuinely comparable constructions because of its binary bias whereby breaks of considerable importance were confused with comparatively trivial layering tendencies (1976a:255-56).*

In short, IC analysis obscures the hierarchical structure because it fails to recognize that there may be more than two constituents of equal rank at a given level. (Well, perhaps my description of IC analysis has some straw in it. Gleason says that three equal constituents will occur "only occasionally" and four "very seldom" [1961:144]. And there are some constructions that IC analysis handles best; e.g., the complex filler of the Head slot in an English noun phrase: the *I* state *II* land *III* tax

IIII office *IIIII* furniture.) A simple solution to these problems lies ready to hand. We need only switch to string constituent analysis, following the example of the tagmemicists. (The various tests Gleason suggests for ICs apply equally well to string constituents.)

The problem of arbitrary cuts is alleviated in two ways: the simultaneous recognition of all the constituents at a given level removes the obligation to assign an arbitrary order to cuts between equal constituents; the notion of slot plus filler class[2] removes some of the subjectivity in determining the boundaries of a constituent. To illustrate the first point I will give a string constituent analysis of the sample sentence used above.

John / ate / his piece of pie / with a spoon
              his / piece / of pie   with / a spoon
                       of / pie   a / spoon

In the IC analysis I ordered the first three cuts arbitrarily, although the first one is dictated by convention; here I recognized in a direct way that there are four constituents at the clause level. (Or three, should anyone prefer to take 'ate . . . with a spoon' as a constituent.) To illustrate the second point, that 'his piece of pie' may be replaced by 'two buns' or 'all he could possibly hold' without destroying the basic structure of the clause supports our intuition that 'his piece of pie' is a constituent. At the clause level we have the added help of the so-called deep-structure cases or roles. If we analyze the sample sentence as having a predicate with three roles (e.g., agent, patient, and instrument), this confirms our judgment that there are four clause-level constituents. If we judge 'his piece of pie' to correspond to the role

---

[2] The combination of a slot with its set of fillers is the original definition of a tagmeme. I believe it represents a fundamental insight into the organization of language. It is part of how a child organizes language and how adults organize a second language.

'patient', this confirms our conclusion that it is a clause-level constituent.

The notion of slot-plus-filler class is especially useful because such a composite can be assigned both a level and a function—and the functions are different at each level (see especially Pike and Pike 1977, Appendix 3; and also Fries 1974; Longacre 1976a:272-76; Wise 1971:9). I believe this is how we keep track of recursion and back-looping. Consider the noun phrase 'those two nice Canadian tourists standing at the rail who helped me with my luggage'. Based on my own tagmemic analysis of the English noun phrase, I would divide the sample phrase into constituents as follows:

those / two / nice / Canadian / tourists / standing at the rail / who helped me with my luggage

(I decline to attempt an IC analysis.) I wish to focus attention on the relative clause that is serving as a constituent within a phrase. The relative clause, in predictable relative position, is functioning as a modifier of the head noun. Its own constituents, having been packaged into a clause, find themselves repackaged into a phrase-level constituent where they join the other phrase-level constituents in being repackaged into a phrase, etc. Longacre has a good discussion of both back-looping and level-skipping (1976a:262-71).

2.1.1 Although most linguists evidently consider role or case to be part of deep (as opposed to surface) structure,[3] I agree with Longacre that it should be considered as part of grammatical structure (1976a).[4] I

---

[3] At the moment a precise definition of "deep" is not necessary, just so that it is distinct from "surface". I am aware that the term means different things to different people.

[4] The reader of Longacre may be misled by his terminology, as I was until I checked with him personally. When he speaks of "deep" and "surface" as poles of a continuum with intermediate forms, he does not mean it in a transformational sense; it is his way of trying to express what Halliday calls delicacy of choice (I think Halliday's use of a system network to talk about delicacy is more efficient).

believe case is an integral part of constituent structure at the clause level,[5] and just as much on the surface as anything else. Why is Agent thought to be deeper than Subject? Consider the word 'John' in 'John hit Bill'. Will a native speaker of English naturally identify it as Subject, or as Agent? I think the latter. What might Subject really mean in English grammar? I think little more than relative linear position and the thematic value attached to that position (along with the restrictions as to what sorts of things can occur there). It seems to me that the facts of linear position and thematic value are just as much universals of language as the fact of case or role. We can posit an etic reservoir of possible linear arrangements and ways of marking theme just as well as of possible roles. Each language has its own selection and combination of these variables, plus their possible arrangements. In other words, I would say that grammar includes not only the identity and possible arrangements of linear slots, but also the identity and possible arrangements of roles, and particularly the possible combinations of role and slot plus their arrangements.[6] Both combination and

---

[5] Case comes in only when a predication is made, so it will not be a factor at lower levels (phrase, word), except where embedded (including nominalized) clauses occur. It is partly for this reason that I view with concern the recent trend among tagmemicists to abandon the original two-cell tagmeme for a four-cell tagmeme which accommodates case. At any level other than clause, the extra cells tend to get in the way, and even at the clause level the fourth cell has seemed to me to be excess baggage; in fact, in a very recent work (K.L. Pike and E.G. Pike 1977), with many examples of four-cell tagmemes, the fourth cell is left vacant as often as not. I would simply add case as a third component to the tagmeme at the clause level. Since the threshold between nonpredication and predication is a crucial one, it should not be surprising that added complexity is introduced.

[6] Longacre devotes a whole chapter to a presentation of an etic list of forty-five case frames (1976a:38-96), which could well prove to be a valuable heuristic tool. I suspect that we must distinguish between conceptually possible case frames and realizable (or realized) case frames. For instance, I suppose it will be generally agreed that the predicate (verb) 'hit' implies the obligatory existence of an agent and a patient, but there must also be an instrument, really (it is a logical necessity)—and I suppose also Location, Time, and Manner (the hitting would necessarily occur some time and place, and be hard or soft, etc.)—although any or all may be suppressed on

arrangement are needed in order to properly understand the constituent structure. Nor is that all.

How do we distinguish role in 'the boy broke the window' versus 'the ball broke the window'? Evidently we must appeal to the lexicon: 'ball' is not among the fillers that may occur in the subject-as-agent slot, so it must be acting in a different role.[7] We do not need to know the denotation of 'ball', just that it is –Animate (minus animate), or some such thing.[8] But is not the difference between 'boy' and 'ball' just as much on the surface as anything else? In fact, 'boy' signals its denotation directly, whereas it must join with an appropriate slot and an appropriate selection and arrangement of other slot-role combinations in order to signal Agent. Denotation appears to be more accessible than role. In any case, must we not say that constituent structure includes lexicon (or lexical appropriateness) as well as role and slot (at the clause level)? Well, yes and no; I will embark on a digression in hopes of explaining what is involved.

2.1.1.1 It is necessary to distinguish between constituent structure as part of the abstract system of a language that we may call its grammar and the constituent structure of a particular text. Linguists are generally agreed that it is possible (whether or not it is useful) to factor out from a language three abstract systems—call them phonological, grammatical, and semantic—variously viewed as components, strata, levels, or hierarchies. In tagmemic terms (my preference), the

---

the surface. The speaker's decision as to how much to suppress enters into the discourse structure.

[7] In tagmemic theory the list of possible fillers is crucial to the definition of a specific tagmeme.

[8] Grimes (1975:126) follows Bruce Hollenbach in arguing that "ball" should be called Agent because otherwise there are "messy consequences" for the rules that relate "deep" to "surface". It seems to me that their difficulty is simply an artifact of their model and need not detain us. The real semantic relationships should be determined in their own right.

phonological hierarchy seems to be essentially self-contained: one can describe phonemes, syllables, stress groups, pause groups, breath groups, intonation, etc., solely in phonetic terms, given that the sound stream is produced deliberately as part of a communication system (we have to know that it is not random or meaningless). The grammatical hierarchy is a form-meaning composite, depending upon meaning in a far more explicit way than does the phonological hierarchy. The meaning part of the composite becomes more complicated the higher up the ladder one goes (as does the form, for that matter). To illustrate, I will discuss five levels: word, phrase, clause, sentence, and paragraph.

Word (or morpheme) equals a combination of sound (or symbol) plus meaning. In the case of a given example, like 'boy', we have the denotation, but as a level in the abstract system we only need to know that it has a denotation and not what it is. 'Boy' and 'yob' are each one syllable composed of three phonemes, but only one is a word in English.

Phrase equals a combination of sound plus meaning plus attribution, by which I mean the ascribing of a quality or characteristic (or several) to a central item.[9] Attribution starts to involve different classes of words whose relationship is signaled by their arrangement (in English). A random selection of words does not equal a phrase; they must be the right kind of words and in the right arrangement. Again, for purposes of the abstract system we do not need the identity of the words, just the right kind.

Clause equals a combination of sound plus meaning plus attribution plus role. The signaling of role requires not only an appropriate slot-role combination for the constituent in focus but an appropriate selection and arrangement of other slot-role combinations, plus what we might call 'category' or lexical appropriateness. In the case of 'ball' versus

---

[9] I borrow this use of attribution from John Beekman and John Callow. They have contributed to my thinking in various ways. Charles Hockett also uses attribution in this way (1968:99).

'boy', discussed above, we know that the role of 'ball' is not Agent because it is not animate. For the abstract system we do not need to know the full denotation of 'ball' (numerous other nouns could be substituted for it), just its category.

Sentence equals a combination of sound plus meaning plus attribution plus role plus 'attitude', by which I mean the choice between affirming, questioning, commanding, etc., the proposition encoded in a clause.[10] Attitude includes at least part of what Halliday calls 'mood'.

> Mood represents the organization of participants in speech situations, providing options in the form of speaker roles: the speaker may inform, question or command; he may confirm, request confirmation, contradict or display any one of a wide range of postures defined by the potentialities of linguistic interaction (1967, 3:199).

Attitude may be signaled by a variety of things, including intonation. Where a specific lexical item is used as a signal of attitude, the form-meaning composite might be said to actually include lexical meaning, even for the abstract system.

Paragraph equals a combination of sound plus meaning plus attribution plus role plus attitude plus 'relation'. By relation I mean something similar to Grimes' rhetorical predicates (1975, chap. 14), but I prefer the treatment of the subject in Beekman and Callow (1974, chap. 18) and follow them in using the term 'relation'. Relations are often signaled by conjunctions. I am aware that sentences, as usually defined, contain relations, so that relation is not diagnostic of paragraph unless I redefine the terms. Rather than do that, I simply wish to maintain that there is a fundamental difference between 'attitude' and 'relation', and that they operate at different hierarchical levels. I do feel that 'relation' is that which distinctively characterizes 'paragraph', and that when a

---

[10] For a thorough discussion of sentence structure, as distinct from clause, see Longacre (1970b).

sentence contains relations, it is partaking something of the nature of a paragraph. It will be observed that analogous to my treatment of role, I consider relation to be part of constituent structure and therefore on the surface.

The progressive complication of the form-meaning composite (which is the grammatical hierarchy) may be clearly seen in the following summary:

word = sound + meaning

phrase = sound + meaning + attribution

clause = sound + meaning + attribution + role

sentence = sound + meaning + attribution + role + attitude

paragraph = sound + meaning + attribution + role + attitude + relation

But to return to the point of this digression, constituent structure as an abstract system does not include denotation or reference, but it does include attribution, arrangement, role, appropriateness, attitude, and relation—which means it is a real workhorse. In decoding a text, however, the lexical items are present and it would be silly to ignore them, which brings up another matter.

2.1.1.2 It is possible and useful (for some purposes) to speak of a language as having the three abstract systems (phonological, grammatical, and semantic), but our decoding of a particular text involves reacting simultaneously to all three of them as they are interwoven in that text. We are confronted with a form-meaning composite in the fullest sense (this is distinct from the grammatical hierarchy I have been discussing): a stretch of organized sound (or symbol) designed to evoke a certain abstraction (total meaning). So what is the organizing agent or system that orients the construction of the text? I submit that it is what I will call the 'discourse system', the conventions in the language in question for handling all the factors listed in my framework. The constituent structure of the text will be an exponent of the grammatical hierarchy (of the language) and an important part of the discourse structure of the text, but only a part. The discourse structure of the text will be the specific selection of options from the discourse system which that text embodies.

In decoding a given clause, for example, what we have to work with is the specific selection of lexical items within the constituent structure of that clause. A lexical item, often a word, is a form-meaning composite in a direct way, what Saussure called a 'sign' (1959). I take it that each word will evoke one or more atoms (features, components) of meaning, and the manner of their organization will evoke added atoms, all of which must be interpreted in terms of culture, situation, and context. In short, although in discussing a putatively universal framework I must define constituent structure as an abstract system, in an actual decoding situation the specific constituent structure of the text will simply be part of the total form-meaning composite, which includes the lexical items in the text.

2.1.2 Although Halliday (Halliday and Hasan 1976:1-2) appears to doubt that constituent structure goes beyond the clause level, it seems to me that the work reported by Longacre (1968, 1972, 1976b, 1977), Hale (1973), and Trail (1973) shows convincingly that it is both possible and useful to carry constituent structure right up to the discourse level. Pike and Pike (1977, chap. 1 and appendix 1) take the story of the rich young man found in Matthew 19:16-22 and diagram the constituents at every level from morpheme up to the whole story. I see no way to deny that such a diagram has some validity. It is not the whole story, to be sure, but it is part of the story.

It is a commonplace in English composition that many letters have three constituents at the highest level: introduction, body, and conclusion. The same can be said of many sermons. In a three-point sermon the body has three constituents, and so on. However, it must be admitted that the size and nature of some of the putative constituents at each ascending level (or perhaps every other level, see 2.4) become increasingly disparate. Thus, in Paul's letter to the Colossians, the introduction consists of nominal clauses occupying but four lines of text; while the body consists mainly of verbal clauses occupying 168 lines (the conclusion reverts to nominal clauses and occupies two lines). The two volumes of Longacre (1977) contain numerous examples of particles and affixes in a variety of languages in Colombia and Panama that function at levels above the sentence; they may fairly be called paragraph-, section-, or discourse-level constituents.

Constituent structure seems to be the principal vehicle for expressing hierarchy at the clause level and below. Although it continues to be a factor at the sentence level and above, another vehicle or organizing factor begins to come to the fore at the sentence level—taxis.

2.2 **Taxis**. There are two kinds of taxis: 'hypotaxis' and 'parataxis', or subordination and coordination, respectively.[11] Taxis seems to be the principal vehicle for expressing hierarchy above the sentence level. It appears to be such a basic and crucial distinction that I would like to claim that for any language there will be two distinct sets of signals, one hypotactic the other paratactic, without overlap. I would like to maintain the claim even when the logical structure appears to contradict it; when there is such a skewing between discourse and logical structure, it will be the result of the author's strategy, deliberate and significant. For instance, in Romans 1:9 the conjunction γαρ is used to link verse 9 to verse 8. The two verses are logically parallel, but I claim that γαρ is always a hypotactic signal in the discourse system of

---

[11] There is also hypertaxis, or superordination, but it is mainly relevant to Prominence and will be discussed in detail in chapter 4. With reference to Hierarchy, its function is paratactic and will be discussed briefly at the end of this section as dequotation.

Koine Greek, and that the author uses it here to indicate that in the exegetical outline verse 9 is to be indented relative to verse 8.

2.2.1 Having mentioned the possibility of skew between discourse and logical structure, I will digress to consider the difference between them. I will begin with the question of how to distinguish between discourse system and logical or propositional system. I have already distinguished the discourse system of a language from the discourse structure of a text. Presumably we must also distinguish logical 'system' from the logical 'structure' of a text. But is logical system universal or language specific? If it is universal, it must be different from discourse system which is language specific, and in that event, it should be possible to distinguish between them. I have already characterized discourse system as the conventions in any given language for handling all the factors listed in my framework. The logical system I would equate with the semantic hierarchy. I like the way that Beekman and Callow describe it (1977).[12] It is clearly a hierarchy: 1) components (atoms, features), linked by attribution, compose concepts; 2) concepts, linked by roles, compose propositions; 3) propositions, linked by relations, compose paragraphs. Or, to put it more precisely:

concept equals a central component to which any other components are linked by attribution;
proposition equals a central concept to which any other concepts are linked by role;
paragraph equals a central proposition to which any other propositions are linked by relation.

---

[12] I believe Beekman and Callow have succeeded in specifying/describing the long-elusive third hierarchy in tagmemic theory, but since it says nothing about the lexicon of a given language, Pike and Longacre will probably not agree. This semantic hierarchy cannot be factored out of a given language in the way that is true for phonology and grammar; rather it is the culmination of many years of musing by many people on the nature of logical structure. For a somewhat different approach, see Schank (1975).

The above is a theoretical construct, independent of any language or surface structure. I agree with Beekman and Callow that this hierarchy is universal.

(The definition of paragraph given above may be sufficiently new that an illustration will not be out of place. Although skew may and does occur, a semantic paragraph will normally map directly onto a grammatical paragraph. The first paragraph in section 2.1.2 is such a paragraph and will serve our present purpose. The independent clause in the first sentence gives the central proposition to which all other propositions in the paragraph relate, directly or indirectly. The dependent concessive clause in the first sentence is directly related to the independent clause. The second sentence gives a specific illustration of the central proposition and is related directly to it. [Each sentence has embedded propositions, but to factor them out would only complicate the illustration.] Sentences 3 and 4 are comments upon sentence 2 and thus indirectly related to the central proposition.)

In contrast to the universal logical system, a proposed propositional (logical) structure of a particular text will be discourse specific. It is a specific and selective combination of the lexicon of the language involved and the semantic hierarchy, and it will be conditioned by the grammatical organization of the text. The discourse structure of a text, on the other hand, is the result of the interplay of all the factors in my framework. I would insist, in analyzing a text, that nothing may be claimed for either structure (discourse or propositional) that cannot be tied to a signal in the text.

2.2.2 Returning to taxis, it is commonly signaled by conjunctions but is only part of their function. The lexical items we call conjunctions are but one way of encoding what Beekman and Callow call 'interpropositional relations' (1974, chap. 18).[13] Longacre devotes a chapter to a

---

[13] On page 291, footnote 2, they list a number of articles representing earlier discussion of the subject.

similar treatment, using a calculus (1976a, chap. 3); Grimes calls them 'rhetorical predicates' in his treatment (1975, chap. 14); Frederiksen (1975) has a thorough discussion from a different perspective. I take it that all these authors are positing lists of such relations which are putatively universal. I would agree that we may assume a finite etic list of relations from which each language makes its selection. For instance, Copala Trique (Mexico) appears not to have a way of expressing a concession-contra-expectation relation like 'the more you explain, the less I understand' (Hollenbach 1975:10). As to the precise composition of such a list, we have the old problem of splitters versus joiners, but I would insist that any distinction contrastively signaled in any language must be included in the etic roster. However, it should be possible to organize the relations in a Hallidayan system which would enable us to choose the degree of delicacy required in a given situation. For an example of such a network diagram see Hollenbach (1975:4-5).

But is it possible to organize the relations in terms of taxis? Grimes attempts to do so, speaking of paratactic, hypotactic, and neutral predicates (1975, chap. 14). He gives only two, 'alternative' and 'response', which will invariably be paratactic on the surface; he gives a number which will invariably be hypotactic on the surface, and then goes on to say: "The third and most common rhetorical predicate in text is the neutral predicate, which can assume either form." That is, be either paratactic or hypotactic on the surface. What interests me here is the implied claim that on the surface these rhetorical predicates must be either paratactic or hypotactic, not neutral. This accords with my claim at the beginning of this section, so far as it goes. Since Grimes is referring to logical relations and my claim is limited to surface signals, his notion of 'neutral predicates' is not a challenge to my claim.[14]

---

[14] Grimes would agree (personal communication) that a given signal is always one or the other in intent, and I think we are agreed that any skewing between logical and discourse structure is due to strategic choice. "Relations of dominance and subordination have to do ultimately with the staging of parts of a discourse. The

Actually, what Grimes has done is to coin two generic predicates: 'collection' and 'covariance', and to group a number of relations under each. If the specific relations are taken individually, they tend to be either paratactic or hypotactic.

Pitkin (1977a and 1977b) argues for an operational (functional) rather than a structural analysis of hierarchy (much like tagmemics), but he wants it to be binary. He notes that, except for the 'series-coordination' relations, the relations are binary—they link only two propositions or entities. I gather that he regards all the binary relations to be hypotactic. He notes that the effect of their operation is clearly hierarchic. Similarly, Beekman and Callow (1974:284) place all relations in two categories: 'addition' and 'associative'. The former are all paratactic, while the latter are all hypotactic. I am inclined to agree with them.

2.2.3 Hollenbach suggests that any language will exhibit three subsets of relations (overlapping but not identical: intrasentential, intersentential, and interparagraph) and adds the following comment:

> The distinction between 'subordination' and 'coordination' should probably be limited to only intra-sentential relations. Whereas inter-sentential relations may be coordinate, as defined in this paper, there is no meaningful sense in which non-coordinate thematic propositions can be considered as subordinate to each other. They share equal thematicity. In descriptions of surface structure, for instance, I have not heard of anyone proposing that one independent clause in a discourse should be described as subordinate to another independent clause (1975:20).

I do in fact propose "that one independent clause in a discourse should be described as subordinate to another independent clause" in

---

speaker imposes a perspective on the purely cognitive aspects of meaning. This suggests that whether a neutral predicate is taken as paratactic or as hypotactic depends upon other decisions in the area of staging" (Grimes 1975:226).

descriptions of surface structure. Hollenbach's argument from 'equal thematicity' is based on the propositional structure, which is not the same as the surface structure. But I would like to pick up his notion of three subsets of relations. It may be that we have something of a relational continuum linking up with the peripheral roles at the lower end. The similarity of roles and relations is confirmed, I think, by the circumstance that a single preposition may be used to signal either role or relation. In the now well-worn example of someone eating his pie with his spoon, wife, or ice cream, 'with' signals different roles (assisted by the lexicon); in 'with the advent of the steam engine, transportation was revolutionized', 'with' signals an intrasentential relation. Which leads me to repeat a point made earlier: namely, that 'relation' is part of grammar in a way analogous to 'role'. The definition of a coordinate sentence will include the appropriate relation, for example.

2.2.4 Returning to the subject of taxis, even if the signals are unambiguously hypotactic or paratactic, there will still be a question as to the precise point where a signal applies. With hypotaxis the problem is less acute since the particular constituent which governs the hypotaxis will presumably be somewhere in the immediate context. Still, the choice of the governing constituent can be a puzzle. Appeal must be made to the context in cases of doubt. With parataxis the question of point of contact can be severe—to what point or level in the preceding outline is the signal (or signals) parallel? Again, the context will be the final board of appeal. I would suspect a signal which was both paratactic and anaphoric of being a fairly high level signal.

2.2.5 As promised in note 11, I here take up the phenomenon that Charles Hockett (1968:99-104) calls 'dequotation'. His discussion revolves around overt editing. Consider, for example, "I think he's a dirty sk..., er, that is to say, I have definite reservations about his character." What is the status of "er, that is to say"? It serves as a superordinate predicate, but in a marked position since it interrupts the normal or expected flow of constituents at a lower level. Although in a structure diagram it should presumably be raised above the base line (an instance of hypertaxis), it seems to me that its 'function' is paratactic: the intent is supposedly to correct a mistake, to replace one piece with another, but the first piece remains in the text with the result that there are two parallel pieces. (It should be noted that this sort of thing is often done deliberately, so that 'dequotation' must be given a place in the discourse system.) There are several other kinds of hypertaxis that are mainly relevant to Prominence, rather than to Hierarchy, so I will discuss them in chapter 4.

There is a third vehicle or organizing factor that may assist us in determining the hierarchical structure of a text—span.

2.3 **Span**. It was Grimes's discussion of 'span analysis' (1975:91ff) that focused my attention on span as an analytic tool. I am indebted to him and to Beekman[15] for many of my ideas on the subject. In Grimes' words, "spans represent stretches of text within which there is some kind of uniformity" (1975:91). Such stretches of text are usually at least of paragraph length, so that the usefulness of span as an aid to discerning the hierarchical organization of a discourse is chiefly at the paragraph level and above. It should be noted that span (like taxis and many specific signals) may function in more than one macrosystem, singly or simultaneously. In fact, the primary relevance of span is probably to Cohesion, although it does contribute to Hierarchy on occasion. I will discuss span under four headings: phonological, grammatical, lexical, and kinds of information.

2.3.1 Phonological. I include this heading in the interest of completeness, but I think it is the least important of the four. Occasionally one encounters an obvious multiple repetition of a certain

---

[15] For several summers Beekman has directed a course in discourse analysis of New Testament books, especially the epistles, in which I participated in 1975. Span is one element in his procedure.

sequence of sounds or symbols that seems to be deliberate and contributes to the organization of the text. Wise (1971:4) observes that in a Nomatsiguenga (Peru) myth about a buzzard, there are phonological clues when the buzzard speaks, i.e., is quoted. The extent of the buzzard's speech would be signaled by a phonological span. Sapir (1949:186) described something similar in Nootka mythology—an instance of a general phenomenon in northwestern Amerindian languages. In my own study of Apurinã (Brazil), I have noted the same sort of thing: not only animals but people are identified phonologically when they are quoted. At certain social functions two speakers engage in a rather lengthy ritualistic exchange. They speak in turns and each turn may last several minutes. Within each turn or monologue, there is a distinct phonological pattern: the speaker develops a theme for a sentence or two, and then goes back and restates it in slightly different terms; but the restatement is given in a much lower volume and fades off until it is scarcely audible. Each such cycle might be called a phonological span which signals a paragraph.

Some public speakers have characteristic phonological patterns that correspond to some extent with the hierarchical organization of their speech. A politician may switch in and out of a local dialect where he is campaigning, producing phonological spans (and perhaps grammatical and lexical spans as well). The telling of an ethnic joke or the mimicking of a drunkard may involve a phonological span. I can conceive of the possibility of a kinesic span. Certain declamatory styles might be said to have gesture spans. Even though much of this sort of thing may be idiosyncratic, if it correlates with the organization of the text, it furnishes a clue to that organization.

2.3.2 Grammatical. Such grammatical factors as person, tense, aspect, mood, or voice may characterize a span. Person spans can be used quite effectively as illustrated by Paul's letter to the Romans. After the usual extended nominal sentence which opens the letter, there is a clear 1st person singular and 2nd person plural span from verse 8 through the first sentence of verse 16. From there to the end of chapter 1 there is a 3rd person span. 2:1 abruptly opens a 2nd person singular span which extends through verse 5; 2:6-16 is a 3rd person span. 2:17 begins another 2nd person singular span which extends to the end of the chapter, but fades out. The first eight verses of chapter 3 are mixed, and then 3:9-4:25 is mostly 3rd person. 5:1-11 is a 1st person plural span, while 5:12-21 forms a 3rd person span. 6:1 starts a 1st person plural span which gives way to 2nd person plural from verse 11 to the end of the chapter. 7:7-25 forms a clear 1st person singular span, and so on. A study of the text reveals that a sudden shift from one person span to another almost always coincides with a high level cut in the discourse outline. Such a span may coincide with a section that has several paragraphs within it.

Tense and aspect spans may also help with outlining decisions, on occasion. Although not so obvious as the person spans, Romans has some tense spans that are probably related to its organization. 1:21-28 is an aorist span; 2:1-28 is a present tense span (and also an active voice span); 4:20-23 is an aorist span (and also passive); 5:15-21 is an aorist span; 7:4-13 is an aorist span; but 7:14-25 is a present span. In Xavante (Brazil) a span analysis revealed that events operate under one aspect system and nonevents under another (McLeod 1975). One may encounter passive spans, imperative spans, subjunctive spans, interrogative spans (Romans has several stretches characterized by a series of questions—3:3-9 has nine rhetorical questions and 8:31-35 has seven). There may be participial, infinitival, or nominal spans. Some such spans may be fortuitous, so it should not be automatically assumed that a given span is relevant to the hierarchical structure of the discourse, or it may be functioning in a different macrosystem, like Prominence or Style. A signal may function in several systems simultaneously. A given span is just one clue to be added to the other clues available. Where a number of spans are coterminous, there is a good probability that a significant break is being signaled.

2.3.3 Lexical. A lexical span may be signaled by extensive repetition of lexical items (same or related) or by relative discreteness of lexical field. I am not referring to propositional structure here, but to the general impression one receives immediately upon reading or hearing a text. For example, in Romans 2:12-27 the root meaning 'law' occurs twenty-two times. We are clearly in the presence of a lexical span (one might say a phonological one as well, because of the massive repetition of the three letter sequence νομ-). Also, Romans 7:1-8:7 is another span dominated by 'law', along with 'flesh' and 'death'. Chapter 4 is a span about Abraham. In short, where the subject matter of a stretch of text is obvious and unified, its boundaries will likely be fairly sharp and presumably coincide with a section in the outline. (That will not be quite the case when an author, like Paul, makes a habit of having the subject matter overlap the section boundaries—i.e., anticipates the next section while bringing the first to a close and referring back to the first while opening the second. In that case the lexical span will only give approximate boundaries.)

2.3.4 Kinds of Information. Grimes discusses seven 'kinds of information' with reference to span analysis: events, participants, setting, background, evaluations, collateral, and performatives (1975, chap. 6). Although just what an author does with these kinds of information is crucial to the macrosystem I call Strategy, and is of possible relevance to the other macrosystems as well, my concern here is with their contribution to Hierarchy. Just how they contribute may vary according to the discourse genre of the text being analyzed. In a narrative discourse, 'events' and 'participants' will presumably be central and the other 'kinds' peripheral. In an expository discourse, events and participants may come in only in anecdotes or illustrations and so their significance to the hierarchical structure may be quite different than in narrative. To the extent that different kinds of information occur predictably in different parts of a discourse, they may facilitate analysis (cf. Labov and Waletzky 1967). Of course they would have to be distinguishable, and it is a happy circumstance that different kinds of information tend to be typically encoded in distinct grammatical constructions.

The events in a discourse may be analyzed in terms of sequence, duration, and grouping. If any spans become evident, they may correspond to paragraphs or sections. It is the identification and orientation of participants in connection with the event line that sheds more light on the outline, at least in narrative.[16] A span would be a stretch of text where one participant has the initiative with respect to other participants and events, or is in focus; a switch of initiative or focus to another participant would signal a boundary at some level (cf. Becker 1965). Sometimes there is a regular sequencing of the orientation of participants to events throughout a narrative. Wise and Lowe give a good example of how it works out in Nomatsiguenga (1972). They applied a theorem based on the theory of finite permutation groups that Lowe had worked out previously in connection with English pronominal reference (Lowe 1969; Pike and Lowe 1969). I believe Lowe's theorem is a valuable tool; for a presentation of it see one of the above articles or Grimes' discussion of it (1975, chap. 18).

"Where, when, and under what circumstances actions take place constitute a separate kind of information called setting" (Grimes 1975:51). Whether a setting is spatial, temporal, or psychological, it can

---

[16] H.A. Gleason, Jr., with his students at Hartford led one of the first major assaults on the discourse bastion. Much of their work centered upon events and participants and became part of the foundation upon which subsequent work has built. Working within a stratificational framework, they did not focus upon hierarchy, although Brennan (1968) gave some attention to it, but their sort of a display lends itself to span analysis. In fact, the Thurman chart used by Grimes is confessedly a development of the diagrams used by Gleason and Cromack (Grimes 1975:82).

be a help in segmenting a text. The stretch of text dominated by, or lying within the scope of, a given setting may be viewed as a setting span. The likelihood is high that a change of setting will coincide with the beginning of a new paragraph or section. Again, a whole paragraph may be given to establishing a setting for a whole discourse, presumably at the beginning. Grimes cites the way setting works in a variety of languages (1975:52-5).

What Grimes calls "background" is explanatory information which tends to have a logical sounding structure. In nonsequential texts, it may be the central kind of information, so that its usefulness for span analysis will be mainly in narrative discourse. When a significant stretch of text is given over to explanation, we might speak of it as a background span. This might represent a paragraph, but sometimes it may be given in just a phrase or a word, and in such cases will make no contribution to the hierarchy via span. Just what an author explains and how he explains it is an important part of his strategy and will be discussed under that macrosystem. Some kinds of background information shade off into collateral information. Whereas 'background' intends to explain, 'collateral' "intends to lay out a range of possible actions so as to set off the main action by contrast with . . . alternatives to it" (Grimes 1975:60). Collateral focuses on what might have happened, but did not, or on what may yet happen. Questions, predictions, and commands, as well as negation and adversatives often express collateral information. Again, sometimes a big enough stretch is involved to form a span.

Although 'evaluations' may shade off into background or setting, it seems useful to designate them as a kind of information. Evaluative material may be brief and occur just about anywhere in a text (cf. Labov and Waletzky). Exhortations and stories with a moral may make such extensive use of evaluation that it may help in segmenting the text. A narrative may have an evaluation span.

With reference to 'performatives', I suppose it will be generally agreed that a performative of some kind is implied by or underlies every utterance. In that event, the fact or presence of some performative is 100 percent predictable. A stretch of text governed by one performative may be called a performative span. I assume that a change in performative will invariably be relevant to the hierarchical organization of a discourse. Grimes (1975) discusses performative information, basing his conclusions on phenomena from some fifteen languages.

In addition to Grimes' seven kinds of information, there may be yet other considerations that may profitably be analyzed in terms of span. For any such, as well as for the ones discussed above, it probably will be the case that their main contribution is to other macrosystems. The point that this section has tried to make is simply that they may, on occasion, contribute to the establishing of the outline of a discourse by way of span. Span joins with taxis and constituency to give the total picture.

2.4 Conclusion. I wish to emphasize, in closing the discussion of this macrosystem, that I have been discussing hierarchy as a component of, or factor in, the discourse system of a language, which system controls the options a speaker may exploit in organizing a discourse. (The hierarchical structure of a given discourse will be but an exponent of the macrosystem.) Much of that control is channeled through Hierarchy. Because the macrosystems all operate simultaneously (from a decoding perspective), making use of the same signals (partly), it may prove difficult to neatly factor out and distinguish the hierarchical structure of a text from its total discourse structure. My present view is that the hierarchical structure of a text may best be displayed by a specialized structural diagram.

From such a diagram we may extract the outline of a discourse. I wish to claim, however, that a discourse outline will differ in two respects from the type of outline in general use: 1) I was taught that an outline should never have a solitary subdivision, but I claim that a discourse outline may have them. 2) Every exegetical outline I recall seeing has contiguous descending steps beginning at the same point (e.g.,

I. 1:1-
    A. 1:1-
        1. 1:1-)

but I claim that in a discourse outline, no two beginning points may be precisely the same. To illustrate both contentions, I suggest the following outline for the fourth chapter of Romans:

    2. 4:1-25
        a. 3-21
            1) 6-8
            2) 9-21
                a) 13-21
                    (1) 17-21
        b. 22-25.

With respect to my first claim, in a conventional outline subdivisions a) and (1) above would not be allowed unless one could produce a b) and a (2) to match them. In decoding a text, one may encounter a single paragraph at the end of a section that is clearly delineated itself but is subordinate to something in the preceding paragraph. If such a paragraph is to be acknowledged in the outline, it must appear without a mate. In the example given, not only do verses 17-21 form such a paragraph, but verses 13-21 form such a subsection.

With respect to my second claim, in a conventional outline 2., a., and 1) above would begin with verse 1. But, there should be independent criteria for positing different levels. In the illustration, b. is parallel to a. but not to 2., so there must be some overt signal(s) to justify the separation of 2. and a. Such a signal may range from a whole paragraph to a single conjunction; in the illustration above it is verses 1-2.

When such a signal is less than a paragraph, what might its theoretical status be with reference to the grammatical hierarchy? I believe the answer may lie in Pike's notion of 'paired levels' (Pike and Pike 1977, chap. 2). Although Longacre takes exception to the idea of paired grammatical levels (1976a:284), he himself has recognized that every other level is typically a string structure while the levels in between are typically a nesting structure (1970a:188; 1976a:282). I agree with Hollenbach that there is a level above the paragraph, which he calls "section" (1975:3). Synthesizing selectively, I offer the chart in figure 2.[17]

Typically String	Typically Nested
discourse	situation
paragraph	section
clause	sentence
word	phrase
morpheme	stem

Figure 2

[17] I am aware that the proposed chart is completely inadequate above the paragraph level (but it will do for my immediate purpose). If Paul's letter to the Romans is defined as a discourse, then many intermediate levels will be required between discourse and paragraph. Also, I have said nothing about dialogue and conversation. In Fulani (Stennes 1969), a certain kind of story telling is controlled by a recognized format involving a standard opening and closing. Further, if more than one such story is to be told, there is a specified connector which must be used between them. If such a Fulani story is defined as a discourse, then the series of connected stories will require a higher level. And so on.

As Longacre observes, sentence, phrase, and stem invite recursion, whereas clause and word do not. Sentence and phrase typically have one dominant or 'Head' constituent which may occur alone. In that event, the filler for the constituent or slot will be clause and word, respectively. Clause and word typically have a plurality of constituents which are essentially of equal rank. To put it another way, all clause-level constituents/slots may be filled by a phrase, but all sentence-level constituents may not be filled by a clause, and an independent clause may occur only in the Head slot, and only an independent clause (or several) may occur there. The horizontal lines in figure 2 do seem to correspond to a real organizational barrier. A clause-level slot may be filled by either a phrase or a word, but a given sentence-level slot may not be filled by either a clause or a phrase.

With reference to the status of a high-level signal that is less than a paragraph, I will draw a comparison between section and sentence. The constituents of a sentence may be quite disparate. In the sentence 'Perhaps he went to New York yesterday', one constituent is an independent clause and the other is a single word. Similarly, the Head constituent of a section will be one paragraph (or several), but there may also be an opening constituent filled by just a sentence or two, or even a phrase or word. Assuming that Romans chapter 4 is a 'section', it should be possible to imagine a sentence with a similar outline:

Furthermore,
    his answer is wrong
        because . . .
        and . . .
            in that . . .,
    while yours is right.

Returning to my two claims, I wish to emphasize the difference between them. The first one I consider to be of minor importance; it is just something that happens now and then. Sometimes the encoder has only one subpoint and lets it go at that. The second one I consider to be of considerable importance, a basic principle. If separate identifying criteria do not exist, how is the positing of two levels to be justified? If separate identifying criteria do exist, a failure to recognize them overtly in the outline will give a distorted view of the discourse structure. The outline of this treatise affords an example of the problem. At the beginning of the second chapter I have both Part I and chapter 2. However, the content germane to chapter 2 follows figure 2. The previous pages are germane to Part I which includes chapters 2 to 7. They are the signal that separates the 'Part' level from the 'Chapter' level. But our accepted outlining conventions do not accommodate this sort of thing very well. To make a separate chapter out of the closing paragraphs of chapter I and the opening of chapter 2 would give a distorted picture of the structure of the discussion, but to have a page or so of text between two chapters but not a part of either would go contrary to traditional practice. The expedient I adopted is an effort to make the best of an unsatisfactory situation.[18]

---

[18]If convention did not dictate that the Introduction be chapter 1, a simple solution would be available. The outline would be as follows:

```
Introduction
Part I:  The Framework
    Chapter 1:  Hierarchy
    Chapter 2
    etc.
Part II:  The Application
    Chapter 7
    etc.
Conclusion
```

3 Cohesion

Cohesion reflects a second basic human limitation: we can speak and hear only in a linear sequence. Further, there seems to be a limit to how much information one signal can carry, and how much new information the mind can accommodate, and how fast. Every language seems to have a good bit of redundancy built into it, and also a sort of shorthand ('pro' forms) to make that redundancy more economical. In the discussion of cohesion, we are concerned with anything that signals redundancy as well as anything that serves to tie a discourse together in a linear way. This will include the sorts of things that are discussed under the headings of 'unity' and 'coherence' in textbooks on English composition. The perspective is linear and to some extent cumulative. The term 'cohesion' is borrowed from Halliday, although I am using it in a somewhat wider sense than he does.[19] He defines it as a semantic relation between an element in a text and some other element (in the same text) crucial to its interpretation. The ways wherein my use of the term differs from his should become evident from the following discussion. I suggest that cohesion is signaled by five organizing factors: grammatical agreement, phoric reference, conjunction, lexical association, and given information—which will be treated in that order.

3.1 **Grammatical Agreement.** This includes what has traditionally been called 'government' and 'concord' (cf. Gleason 1961:159-66). The first term is usually applied when an inflection signals the syntactic function of its host. The most common example is probably the case endings on nouns in many languages; thus a nominative case ending often indicates that the noun to which it is joined is the subject of its

---

[19] Halliday taught a course on Cohesion in English at the L.S.A. Linguistic Institute in the summer of 1973. Our text was a prepublication draft of the book by Halliday and Hasan (1976).

sentence. It has a cohesive function to the extent that it may be redundant in a given instance. In the case of a noun in the nominative case, redundancy could result if the subject of a sentence predictably occurs in a certain relative linear position, or if the noun in question is the only one that could he the subject (for lexical reasons, or if it were the only noun). But it is in connection with concord that government is mainly relevant to cohesion. Concord refers to the obligatory agreement or correspondence between two or more words with reference to signals or markers for categories like person, case, gender, or number. Thus in Latin an adjective must agree with the noun it modifies with respect to the three categories of case, gender, and number. If case is an example of government, then a discussion of concord in Latin must evidently mention government, but it is mainly the concord that is cohesive. Where an instance of concord applies only within a phrase, the cohesive effect will be minimal, but it will be there.

Concord is the most obvious form of grammatical agreement. Adjective-noun concord may range from the meager 'this dog' versus 'these dogs' of English to the number, gender, case concord of Latin or the number, gender, definiteness of Hebrew, to the complex concord of the Bantu languages. Concord may attach to other categories: animate/inanimate in Cheyenne; possessed/abstract or positive /negative in Apurinã; shape in some Arawakan languages; texture in some Philippine languages, and so on. Subject/verb concord frequently reflects number and gender. Coordinate verbs or predicates will agree or be compatible in tense and mood. The tense of a verb will agree with an overt temporal constituent in the same clause. Some languages have signals in one clause that govern or agree with some feature of the succeeding clause. Thus, Cashibo (Peru) has dependent verb suffixes that signal whether the following independent clause will be transitive or intransitive and whether the subject will be the same or different (Shell 1957). All such forms of grammatical agreement introduce some degree of redundancy into a text and contribute to its linear cohesion.

For the most part, however, grammatical agreement operates on a low level and will not be as important as the other organizing factors in signaling the cohesion of a discourse.

This is the place to mention what Gleason calls 'enation' and 'agnation'. As he defines enation, "two sentences can be said to be enate if they have identical structure, that is, if the elements (say, words) at equivalent places in the sentences are of the same classes, and if constructions in which they occur are the same" (1965:199). Agnation is defined as follows:

> Pairs of sentences with the same major vocabulary items, but with different structures (generally shown by differences in arrangement, in accompanying function words, or other structure markers) are agnate if the relation in structure is regular and systematic, that is, if it can be stated in terms of general rules (Gleason 1965:202).

I take it that enation and agnation have some cohesive value and are a sort of grammatical agreement, although agnation also partakes something of what I call given information (see section 3.5).

3.2 **Phoric Reference.** I use 'phoric' as a cover term for anaphoric, cataphoric, and exophoric reference.

3.2.1 **Anaphora**, a coreferential link between some element in a text and a prior element (in the same text), carries a large share of the cohesive load in a discourse. Any sort of pro-form—pronoun, pro-verb, pro-adverb, pro-adjective, pro-clause—will have phoric reference, usually anaphoric. I include here the forms Halliday discusses under "substitution" (Halliday and Hasan 1976). Pronouns in a narrative discourse have a cohesive function as well as contributing to participant orientation. The English words 'so', 'thus', and 'therefore' may stand for the preceding sentence or sometimes even a paragraph or more. Pro-forms are a shorthand for repeating information.

Ellipsis is an even shorter hand, the ultimate in economy. Ellipsis occurs when a specific structural slot (or slots) is left vacant in the second of two coordinate structures. In that event, the missing information must be supplied from the equivalent slot(s) in the preceding structure. When ellipsis is used properly, the missing information can infallibly be supplied, so there is redundancy and cohesion. Ellipsis is strictly a grammatical matter and is not to be confused with implied or implicit information. Although ellipsis most often occurs between two clauses or sentences, it may extend over a string of them. In Apurinã an independent clause may be followed by a series of uninflected verb stems with the participants and inflection of the clause holding constant throughout. In Bahinemo (Papua New Guinea) real time in relation to the real world is signaled only at the beginning of a narrative paragraph, but that orientation holds for the whole paragraph (Longacre 1972:47). Perhaps some setting and performative spans (discussed under hierarchy) could be seen in this light. When spatial or temporal orientation remains constant for a stretch, there is probably some cohesive effect.

The phenomenon that Longacre (1968) and Grimes (1972 and 1975) call "linkage" probably belongs here (rather than under 'lexical cohesion') because it is grammatical. Linkage involves the verbatim repetition or the paraphrasing of a clause (or more, or less) in going from one sentence to another or from one paragraph to another.[20] It is anaphoric. Any form of repetition is cohesive, but this type is especially strong. Longacre discusses linkage in several languages of the Philippines: Atta, Bontoc, Manobo, Negrito, Sambal, and Tagabili

---

[20] In languages where linkage occurs only between sentences within paragraphs, the absence of linkage would be a strong signal of paragraph boundary, as in Sanio-Hiowe of Papua New Guinea (Lewis 1972). In such an event, linkage contributes to Hierarchy as well as Cohesion. The same will be true of languages where linkage occurs only between paragraphs (but not between sentences within a paragraph), as in Saramaccan of Surinam (Grimes and Glock 1970).

(among others). Grimes cites Bororo and Kayapó (Brazil), Chuave, Oksapmin, and Sanio-Hiowe (Papua New Guinea), and Saramaccan (Surinam) as languages that have linkage. Gleason (1968:47) cites an example from Tonga narrative which reveals it to be a linking language. Kayapó is worthy of special mention in that linkage in narratives involves the repetition of whole paragraphs, virtually verbatim (Stout and Thomson 1971). The term 'linkage' is here used of an obligatory feature of the grammar of a language—there will be at least some situations where it must be employed. One can produce a similar pattern of repetition in English (or any other language?), of course, but since it is optional it is just an instance of repetition, which I would class as lexical cohesion.

3.2.2 **Cataphora**, a coreferential link between some element in a text and a subsequent element (in the same text), is comparatively less frequent than anaphora and probably less cohesive. Since its effect is precisely to keep the decoder in suspense until the requisite referent is supplied, it places an added burden upon the short-term memory. But to the extent that there is redundancy there will be cohesive effect. The suspense created by a cataphoric form usually starts to be relieved within the same sentence or else the immediately following one, as in "This is how you make pancakes. Take . . . sift . . . add . . . mix . . . etc." It may extend over the entire discourse.

The phenomenon that McCarthy (1965), Longacre (1972), and Grimes (1975) call "chaining" is cataphoric. Typically, there is a string of clauses whose verbs have limited inflection followed by a clause whose verb is fully inflected for person, number, mode, tense, and aspect (Longacre 1972). The fully inflected verb signals the end of that string, and the scope of its inflection (at least some of it) extends backward over all the clauses in its string or chain. Another feature of chaining is that each nonfinal clause in a chain will signal whether the subject of the following clause will be the same or different. Thus, both characteristics of a chain are cataphoric. It is clear that they both have some cohesive value also.[21] Longacre's discussion is based on some fifteen languages of Papua New Guinea—the only area where chaining has so far been reported.

3.2.3 **Exophora** is defined as a coreferential link between some element in a text and an element outside of the text. Although some linguists may object that exophora is not a legitimate part of linguistics, I submit that any thorough effort at discourse analysis must take account of it. In "I want <u>this one</u>", 'one' substitutes for and points to a referent which lies outside the text. In such a case, or in "Put it <u>there</u>", there probably will be some gesture to help the hearer identify the referent. Although Halliday denies cohesive effect to exophora as used in the examples above, I believe they satisfy his definition of cohesion: a semantic link between an element in a text and some other element crucial to its interpretation.

When an epic tale is told within its source culture, less is overtly stated than is necessary to understand the story. The narrator assumes that his audience knows the details of the story and can fill in what he does not mention, and so leaves out what does not suit his immediate purpose. Twaddell expresses it well in his discussion of *The Hildebrandlied*.

> *It was the singer's task to retell a well-known story worthily. Accordingly, the narrative technique was one of allusion, implication. The singer had no need to introduce the characters or describe their adventures and their fates; the audience knew already. So the singer had to hint skillfully at the related antecedent actions, to present the hero as doing or saying something that must have resulted from a psychological state which, therefore, the audience had to infer from the deeds and the speeches. The singer had to present overt behavior*

---

[21] Although there may be some question as to the level at which a chain functions, chaining contributes to Hierarchy as well as Cohesion.

and words, not for their own sake, but as clues to the motivations of the behavior and words, and he must not clumsily specify that motivation (1976:6).

In such a discourse, exophoric signals would be just as cohesive as anaphoric ones, at least to hearers 'in the know'.

If my wife and I were discussing preparations for Thanksgiving Day, it would be entirely appropriate for me to ask, "Have you bought the turkey yet?", without there having been any prior mention of 'turkey' in our conversation. My use of 'the' is exophoric and indicates that I expect my wife to know what I am talking about. I claim that 'the turkey' is given information; that it contributes to the unity of our discussion of preparations for Thanksgiving Day; that it has cohesive effect therefore. But the point of reference is in our culture, wherein we always have turkey for Thanksgiving, not in the linguistic context.

In Mundurukú (Brazil) some verbs have ideophones which may be uttered in a series when the sequence is predictable, as in describing an attack on an enemy village (Marjorie Crofts, personal communication). For initiated hearers just the sequence of ideophones enables them to visualize the scene. Might we not posit exophoric ellipsis in such a case and grant that it has cohesive value?

The epic tale is not the only genre that depends on cultural cohesion (exophoric reference to the culture). The reporting of political and sports events in newspapers makes use of cultural cohesion. So do comic strips and cartoons. Similarly, some plays on words and literary reference would fall flat without it. Any obvious reference to ongoing cultural tradition may have some cohesive value.

3.3 **Conjunction**. Like grammatical agreement and phoric reference, conjunction is a form of grammatical cohesion. Although conjunctions contribute to hierarchy by signaling taxis, it is clear that they also have a cohesive function. They help to tie a discourse together. Each language will have its own roster of ways to signal conjunction. In their analysis of conjunctive relations in English, based on lexical forms, Halliday and Hasan come out with ten "additive" relations, ten "adversative" relations, fifteen "causal" relations, and twenty-two "temporal" relations (1976). Their list is based strictly on English and reflects a rather delicate grid—for instance, they make more than twice as many distinctions as do Beekman and Callow (1974). The latter are concerned to develop a universal list of semantic relations, and while conceding that it is possible to make finer distinctions, they feel that their list is adequate for their purposes. To the extent that the Halliday and Hasan distinctions are really logically or semantically distinct, they may be incorporated in a universal roster of relations viewed as an etic list from which each language draws. For the purposes of the framework that I am proposing; 'conjunction' stands for the particular way that a given language encodes semantic relations. From a decoding perspective it becomes a form of grammatical cohesion.

Although general agreement as to the composition of a putative universal roster of semantic relations is probably still over the horizon— for one thing, most of the languages of the world have yet to be analyzed, and I would insist that any relation contrastively signaled by any language belongs in the roster[22]—I will include a list here just for illustrative purposes. It is taken from Hollenbach (1975:4-5).

> Temporal relations: cooccurrence, simultaneous, circumstance /included event, antecedent/subsequent, beginning/ postspan, prespan/end.
> Causal relations: means/purpose, means/result, reason/result, cause/effect, stimulus/response.
> Logical relations: grounds/implication, condition/consequence, contrary-to-fact condition/contrary-to-fact consequence, concession/contraexpectation.

---

[22] I do not mean that we must study all languages before saying anything about universals, but we should do so before attempting a definitive statement.

Equivalence relations: greater/lesser, comparison, generic/specific, restatement, positive/negative, contrast.

N-ary relations: coordination, inclusive alternation, exclusive alternation.

3.4 **Lexical Association**. The factors discussed under grammatical agreement, phoric reference, and conjunction may be said to signal grammatical cohesion. In this section I discuss lexical cohesion (Halliday's designation), namely, the cohesive effect achieved by choice of vocabulary. The options Halliday and Hasan (1976) suggest for categorizing lexical cohesion may be represented by the matrix in figure 3.

		Reference			
		Identical	Inclusive	Exclusive	Unrelated
Lexical item	Same item				
	Synonym				
	Superordinate				
	General word				

Figure 3

I suggest an alternate matrix in figure 4 to serve as a guide for the following discussion.

		Reference		
		Same	Related	Unrelated
Lexical item	Same item			
	Synonym			
	Superordinate			
	General word			
	Hyponym			
	Hyperonym			
	Metonym			

Figure 4

I will use figure 4 as a point of reference only; I am not concerned to defend it.

In "Let me tell you about dogs. Dogs are . . .", the second 'dogs' illustrates the use of the same lexical item with the same reference. In "Jim Smith was an unusual fellow. On one occasion the chap . . .", 'chap' is a synonym of 'fellow' and both are lexically superordinate to the referent 'Jim Smith'. In "Let's not talk about what happened at the party; I want to forget the whole affair", 'the whole affair' is a general phrase having the same referent as 'what happened at the party'. The two rows labelled 'Hyponym' and 'Hyperonym' represent the two halves of synecdoche, its part for whole and whole for part dichotomy (and by extension, specific for generic and generic for specific). Perhaps they could be combined under a single label such as 'Synecdonym'. The intersection of Hyponym with Same reference would represent a proper instance of synecdoche, as in "All the inhabitants of the village were massacred, a total of 237 souls" where 'soul' stands for the whole person. By 'metonym' I mean a close association of some sort. The intersection of Metonym with Same reference would represent an instance of metonymy. Consider the following example (taken from *Alice in Wonderland* via Halliday and Hasan).

> The last word ended in a long bleat, so like a sheep that Alice quite started (1). She looked at the Queen, who seemed to have suddenly wrapped herself up in wool (2). Alice rubbed her eyes, and looked again (3). She couldn't make out what had happened at all (4). Was she in a shop (5)? And was that really—was it really a sheep that was sitting on the other side of the counter (6)?

I take it that 'sheep' in sentence (6) is a case of metonymy since the referent is the Queen wrapped in wool. Where two items have the same referent, the presence of cohesion seems obvious enough. The sort of cohesion represented by the Same column is quite similar to anaphoric reference.

Turning to the Related column, the text about Alice may furnish an instance or two. I would say that 'the counter' in sentence (6) is a hyponym (or else a metonym) of 'shop' in sentence (5), with a related reference. I think the same relationship obtains between 'wool' in (2) and 'sheep' in (1). I take 'sheep' in (1) to be a metonym of 'bleat' in (1) but am in doubt as to whether the reference is related or unrelated. Part of the problem is that related and unrelated are relative terms. By related I mean that the cohesive item is closely related to the referent, though different in some obvious way. By unrelated I mean a looser or more general relation between cohesive item and referent. The term cannot be taken in an absolute sense, for then there would be no cohesion. With reference to 'sheep' and 'bleat', I am inclined to assign the relationship to the Unrelated column.

Now for another example (also from Halliday and Hasan):

A. Why does this child wriggle so? My children don't wriggle.

B. Children always wriggle.

'Children' in A is virtually the same lexical item as 'child', but the reference is unrelated, while in the case of 'children' in B it is related. In this example both instances of 'children' seem to be equally cohesive.

I use Matthew 27:20-25 as a final example.

The chief priests and elders persuaded the crowd that they should ask for Barabbas, and destroy Jesus. (1) The governor answered, "Which of the two do you want me to release to you?" (2) They said, "Barabbas". (3) Pilate said to them, "What shall I do then with Jesus, the one who is called 'Messiah'?" (4) All of them said, "Let him be crucified!" (5) So the governor said, "Why? What evil has he done?" (6) But they just yelled all the louder, "Let him be crucified!" (7) When Pilate saw that he was getting nowhere, but rather that an uproar was developing, he took some water and washed his hands in front of the crowd saying, "I am innocent of the blood of this righteous person. You see to it!" (8) And all the people answered, "His blood be on us and on our children!" (9)

I take it that there is cohesion between 'crucified' in (5) and 'destroy' in (1), but is the reference same, related, or unrelated? In an interesting way, 'I am innocent of the blood of this righteous person' (8) seems to be almost a synonym for 'washed his hands' (8). It is a linguistic explanation of a symbolic act. Wherever one may plot this instance on the matrix there evidently is cohesion; to the watching crowd it was probably unusually strong. I think there is clearly a metonymic relationship between 'blood' (8 and 9) and 'crucified' (5 and 7), but is the reference related or unrelated?

I have used the matrix in figure 4 as a point of reference to illustrate something of the variety of forms that lexical association may take. That variety falls on a continuum ranging from strong cohesion and identical reference to weak cohesion and remote lexical association. The relative discreteness of lexical field characteristic of a lexical span will have some cohesive effect. The predictability of occurrence and colocation of lexical items enters in here—the more predictable, the more the cohesive effect. (Grammatical spans and phonological spans will have some cohesive effect.) Although my discussion of lexical association is based solely on English examples, I believe every language will have something analogous (chapter 9 contains many examples in Koine Greek). Like anaphora, lexical association carries a large share of the cohesive load in a discourse.

3.5 **Given Information**. The term comes from Halliday's "given/new" dichotomy (1967 and 1968). I take it that by 'given' is meant information that the encoder treats as being already available to the decoder. The encoder's choices in this regard are part of Strategy since they can be quite manipulative—he can put the decoder at a psychological disadvantage by acting as if the decoder knows something which in fact he does not. With reference to Cohesion, however, I restrict the meaning of the term to information that is genuinely available in, or recoverable from, the prior context. The part of a sentence in a given text that we would designate as given information will presumably be largely made up of the sorts of elements already discussed under phoric reference and lexical association—they are the trees making up the given information forest. The sum of the parts does not equal the whole, so that it is valid and useful to introduce given information as a separate organizing factor. The individual elements having phoric reference or lexical association may refer back to different places in the prior context so that a given-information block may represent a new construct or combination of those old elements. In that way it has a separate identity and has its own cohesive effect. It contributes to the unity of the text. Presumably there is a correlation between repetition of information and unity of the text. I consider that whatever contributes to unity contributes to cohesion, so I have not discussed unity as a separate entity.

What Grimes calls "overlays" (1972 and 1975) represent a special use of given information which has considerable cohesive force. For a description of this technique and a fuller account of its function, see section 4.1.1.

I spoke above of information that is 'genuinely recoverable' from the prior context. I recognize that such a concept is partly hypothetical and quite relative. The amount of recoverable information will vary from decoder to decoder. The intellectual capacity, alertness, familiarity with the subject matter, and presuppositions of the decoder will all influence what he recovers. In short, cohesion varies with the decoder (which is partly why some students understand a lecture and others do not). Still, it should be possible for us (a number of people) to discuss a given discourse and reach general agreement as to what information has received previous mention in the text. But what about information recoverable from situation and culture? Are they not part of the prior context?

We all know from experience how boring, often exasperating, even insulting, it is to listen to someone who insists on going over in detail what we already know, what we consider to be obvious. We expect the speaker to make an intelligent guess as to what is common knowledge and get on with telling us something new. In other words, the encoder's strategy must include what he does with information available from the culture and the situation as well as what has already been encoded (cf. Dahl 1976). This means that such information must be considered as given, and when reference is made to it there is a cohesive effect. Twaddell's comments on *The Hildebrandlied* noted above are relevant here as well.[23]

There are doubtless other factors that have some cohesive effect. Things like meter, rhyme and syntactic parallelism will probably make some contribution to Cohesion. Similarly a characteristic, and therefore predictable, form that belongs to a certain genre may have such an effect. In short, anything that helps bind a text together in a linear way is to that extent contributing to Cohesion.

---

[23] While I insist that situation and culture are part of the prior context upon which given information may be based, I freely confess that I do not know how to handle it. In my experience with trying to translate the New Testament into indigenous languages of Brazil, I have seen the question of what to do with implicit or implied information (as we called it) to be a serious problem. In decoding a piece of ancient literature, how do we distinguish between fact and fancy while trying to reconstruct the contribution of situation and culture to the text? But we must try—ignoring the problem is not a valid option; it will not go away. In Matthew 3:7 (well into the document, therefore), "the Pharisees and Sadducees" are just plopped into the narrative without any semblance of introduction, and John the Baptist proceeds to call them a "brood of vipers" and to tell them not to say, "We have Abraham as our father". Evidently the author assumed that everyone in his day needed no introduction to Pharisees or Sadducees, or Abraham. But if we are to understand the narrative, we have to find out something about them. And if we want others to understand it, we must supply some such information. But how much?

In short, I am entering a plea that more linguists recognize both the legitimacy and necessity of grappling with the role of situation and culture in discourse analysis. Only by grappling with the problem will solutions be forthcoming.

4 Prominence

Prominence reflects a third basic human limitation: we can only perceive something if it stands out from its background. Whether in music, art, or discourse, we look for 'the point', a theme, a plot—if we fail to find any, our reaction will predictably be negative; our legitimate expectations will not have been met.

> A story in which every character was equally important and every event equally significant can hardly be imagined. Even the simplest story has at least a central character and a plot, and this means one character is more important than the others, and certain events likewise. Human beings cannot observe events simply as happenings; they observe them as related and significant happenings, and they report them as such (K. Callow 1974:49).

Although some public speakers seem to be able to avoid prominence so successfully that at the end of their effort no one is able to recall what they said, that very circumstance illustrates the function of Prominence and its necessity for normal communication.

> A discourse must not only have cohesion but prominence. If all parts of a discourse are equally prominent, total uninteligibility results. The result is like being presented with a piece of black paper and being told, "This is a picture of black camels crossing black sands at midnight" (Longacre 1976b:10).

The problem of terminology which seems to confront us everywhere in linguistics is probably more acute here than usual. In Grimes' words, "we have the words 'topic', 'focus', 'theme' and 'emphasis' appearing freely in the linguistic literature, but with such broad ranges of overlap and confusion that they are nearly useless" (1975:323). In consequence Grimes entitles his chapter "Staging", by which he means thematic prominence. Rather than coin new terms, I will employ familiar ones, defining them as I go. My discussion of

Prominence is heavily influenced by Kathleen Callow's excellent chapter on the subject, and I use her terminology and definitions. Her definition of prominence follows:

> The term _prominence_, throughout this chapter, refers to any device whatever which gives certain events, participants, or objects more significance than others in the same context.
>
> . . . It here covers the entire area for which investigators have used such terms as theme, attention, focus, foreground, figure, topic, and emphasis (1974:50).

Although she traces her use of the term to Halliday (1973:113), it seems to me that his use and discussion are more limited than hers. Like Callow, I am using prominence in a very wide sense.

I believe there are three organizing factors that combine to produce the macrosystem Prominence, and find it hard to improve on Callow's statement.

> It will be maintained here that, in spite of the many terms now current for different kinds of prominence, and in spite of the innumerable overt forms taken by prominence features, there are nevertheless only three main values of prominence in discourse, and that all the different varieties and subvarieties of prominence in different languages occur with one or the other of these three values. Those values will here be called _theme_, _focus_, and _emphasis_, and each will be defined and described in turn. Notice that prominence values imply no particular correlation with any particular type of signal or combination of signals. It is not the nature of the signal, but the value that is signaled, that concerns us . . . .
>
> In distinguishing the different values of prominence it is perhaps helpful to consider the total discourse as analogous to a theatrical production. The theme is the unfolding plot, always seen against its background of minor characters and stage properties. Focus is the spotlight, which may be playing continuously, or switched on and off as appropriate. Emphasis is the clash of cymbals or some similar climax in the accompanying music. Unfortunately, in real languages the three

are not always so easy to distinguish, owing to the complex nature of the signals involved and their relationship with the grammar. Nevertheless, the analogy provides a useful guide in trying to assess the value of prominence in any given case (1974:52-53).

Grimes also uses the analogy of a theatrical production (1975:327). So then, I suggest that prominence is signaled by three organizing factors: theme, focus, and emphasis. They will be defined and discussed in order.

4.1 **Theme**. With reference to prominence that occurs with thematic significance, Callow says:

Such information is prominent in the discourse because it carries the discourse forward, it contributes to the progression of the narrative or argument. It contrasts with non-thematic material, which rather serves as a commentary on the thematic, but does not in itself contribute directly to the progression of the theme. The theme-line or time-line (which are variant forms of thematic material) extend throughout the body of the discourse (1974:52).

'Theme' is here considered to be the most basic form of prominence. Its scope or domain is a whole discourse or a stretch of text that is directed toward a single objective. Hollenbach uses the term in the same way: "I use the term 'theme' to refer to the essential development of a discourse or part of a discourse" (1975:2). (Note that this use of 'theme' is very different from Halliday's.) In comparison, 'focus' and 'emphasis' represent variations within the larger domain of theme—they have a lesser domain. Not only do the organizing factors have distinct domains, varying in size, but individual signals also have their domains, also varying in size.

If theme extends over a whole discourse, it must have some organization or we could not keep track of it. But how is that organization signaled or what form does it take? It is difficult to make a generalized statement for several reasons. Different languages seem to use different combinations of signals and to use similar signals in different ways. The studies that have been done within the area of Prominence are so disparate as to orientation and terminology that apart from checking a language personally one cannot be sure whether the signals discussed are reflecting theme, focus, or emphasis (in terms of my framework), or some combination of them simultaneously (or something else, in the event that my framework is inadequate). And we simply do not know enough yet. Speaking of discourse structure in general, Grimes opines that "what we do not know is more important at this stage than what we have found" and that "the biggest gap in our understanding is in the area of staging" (1975:359). Still, we must try.

4.1.1 Temporal Sequence. It may be that the way 'theme' is organized varies according to discourse genre; in fact, it may help to define genre. The genre class (discourse type) that has received the most attention so far is narrative. Following the lead of the Hartford school, it has become customary to speak of an event line or time line when referring to those parts of a narrative which carry the plot forward, because they are usually in temporal sequence. Where there is a title or stated topic for a narrative, such as "The Tortoise and the Hare", it will presumably indicate the central participant(s) and/or event. In some cases it will be the most prominent element in the whole discourse. But a title will only be the starting point for what is here called theme, which refers to the essential development of a narrative. Perhaps 'theme line' is a better term for it. Taber (1966) called it "figure", as opposed to "ground", in his discussion of Sango narrative: figure is constituted by participants "whose actions move the story along" and events which "constitute the progression of the story". Sheffler (1978), in her discussion of Mundurukú (Brazil) discourse, calls it "primary content", as opposed to "secondary content".

> Primary content reports the progress of specific agents toward stated targets or goals, and the impeding or promoting of that progress by other participants . . . . Secondary content consists of descriptions,

explanations, conclusions, and summaries of primary events and the included participants. It provides the background against which the narrative is told.

The most thorough and helpful discussion that I have seen with reference to distinguishing theme (or event line) from background is in Grimes (1975, chaps. 4 and 6). By factoring out of a narrative the kinds of information that Grimes calls "setting, background, evaluation, and collateral" (see sect. 2.3), one may reasonably assume that most, if not all, of what is left will be thematic. As a rule of thumb, we may say that if a piece may be removed or transferred without disrupting the development of the discourse, then it is not thematic.

Although different languages have different conventions, the findings of those who have already written on the subject suggest that thematic and nonthematic material may characteristically be encoded in different ways; each will find distinctive grammatical expression. Thus, in Angaataha (Papua New Guinea) there is a difference between primary and secondary verbal inflections in narrative: primary verbs signal events that are important to the story, while secondary verbs signal background material (Roberta Huisman 1973). In Canela (Brazil) one particle is used to signal important material, and a different particle to signal unimportant material. In Kayapó (Brazil) there is contrast between thematic paragraphs and nonthematic paragraphs.

Mention was made in chapter 3 of the rhetorical pattern that Grimes calls "overlay". He describes it as follows.

> *The overlay technique involves putting together two or more PLANES, each of which constitutes a narration of the same sequence of events. The first plane consists largely of new information. The second plane, and others that follow it, begin the sequence over again. Furthermore, they consist partly of new information that is being given for the first time in that plane, partly of given information such as that which is referred to anaphorically, and partly of information that is being repeated piecemeal from an earlier plane (1975:292-93).*

Each 'plane' repeats part (not all) of the preceding one while presenting some new information of its own. Grimes says of this repetition, "This repeated information has a special status; it is the highlighted information that ties the whole overlay together. Informationally it is the backbone of the whole structure" (1975:293). In discussing a Borôro (Brazil) text reported by Crowell (1973), the events are listed in presumed actual sequence and designated by letters, A through H. The text consists of four planes, each containing its own selection of events, as follows:

plane　1, B D G
　　　　2, D F G
　　　　3, C D F G H
　　　　4, A E H
(Grimes 1975:294).

If repetition is taken as the criterion for inclusion in the theme line, then only events D, F, G, and H qualify. In such an event, the thematic material is clearly identified.

The notion of 'plot' *à la* Propp (1958), with its mounting tension leading to a climax and resolution, is evidently valid for some narratives and is distinct from the event line. It seems to be an extra, high-level organization that is diagnostic of a specific type or genre of narrative, although Longacre feels that "something like plot characterizes other forms of discourse than narrative. If we grant that any discourse is going somewhere, it follows that it does not simply start and stop but that it often has some sort of peak between" (1976a:212). He goes on to discuss the following devices as markers of peak (climax) in narrative: rhetorical underlining (parallelism, paraphrase, tautologies), concentration of participants (crowding the stage), heightened vividness (shift of tense, person, genre), change of pace, change of vantage point or orientation (1976a:217-28). He feels that it is principally rhetorical underlining that marks peak in non-narrative discourse. At this writing I do not consider climax or plot to be part of the Prominence system. I am inclined to assign plot to genre (chap. 6) or to constituent structure.[24]

Nor may we exclude plot from the *discourse* system. Several languages provide overt evidence that plot is part of the organizing system. As noted by Labov and Waletzky (1976) the consistency with which speakers of English insert evaluations at transition points in a plot (the preferred place is between complication and resolution) argues for an intuition about plot structure.[25] Ömie (Papua New Guinea) seems to have a particle that signals transition points between segments defined

---

[24] In the case of the plot that is characteristic of folktales, I am inclined to view it as part of that genre structure. As I argue in chapter 7, the choice of genre precedes the selections from the first four macrosystems, so that the choice of folktale will include plot among the constraints that the choice of that genre imposes upon the other systems. In that event, although the climax of a folktale would presumably coincide with the theme line at the appropriate spot, it would be distinct from the theme line.

Another possibility is to assign plot to constituent structure, analogous to my treatment of role and relation (cf. Longacre 1976a:213 for a similar idea). Beekman and Callow (1977 course notes) suggest that paragraphs may have a plot role, like climax or resolution. Following that suggestion, my discussion of grammatical hierarchy as a form/meaning composite (sect. 2.1.1) could be extended as follows: *discourse* equals a combination of sound plus meaning plus attribution plus role plus attitude plus relation plus plot. Similarly, my discussion of semantic hierarchy (sect. 2.2.1) could be extended as follows: paragraphs, linked by plot roles, compose discourses. Here again, the climax of a discourse would be distinct from the theme line, even though coinciding with it.

[25] Labov and Waletzky state that narrative normally has an evaluative function; without evaluation it is "empty or pointless". Evaluative comments are usually asides and external to the plot; they would also be external to the narrative and lie outside the "event line" (theme line). But if Labov and Waletzky are right, then giving evaluations will often be an important part of a speaker's purpose in telling a narrative. Should not something that important be in the theme line? Something similar occurs in logical discourse. Asides and digressions may be said to be nonthematic by definition, and yet there are times when the main point a speaker wishes to make is given in an aside or digression. The solution I suggest is that theme, like other features of language, may be used manipulatively. It is a timehonored military strategy to attack from an unexpected direction.

as elements of a plot (June Austing, MS). I believe Kayapó has a particle with a similar function.

> *Fore of New Guinea uses tense to signal not chronological progression but dramatic progression within a narrative. The main body of a story is in the far past tense, but when approaching the peak, it shifts to past tense, and at the denouement changes to present tense, returning finally to far past tense for the end of the narrative (Callow 1974:27).*

Longacre's discussion of peak-marking devices mentioned above includes examples from several languages. Once we are alert to the possibility, we may find overt plot-marking devices in all languages.

4.1.2 Logical Sequence. In nonnarrative discourse, especially exposition and exhortation, logical sequence is central, rather than temporal sequence. Here we may still speak of a 'theme line' but not of 'event line' or 'time line'. How is the theme line organized? On the assumption that logical connectors are either paratactic or hypotactic, I will argue that theme in nonnarrative discourse is organized hierarchically, at least partly. The only frankly hierarchical treatment of theme I have seen is that of Beekman and Callow (1976), so I will compare my view with theirs.

Beekman and Callow consider prominence to be part of semantic structure (I assign it to the discourse system). Their lowest hierarchical level with reference to both semantics and prominence is the 'concept'. A 'concept' is defined in terms of components (atoms, features) of meaning, much as a phoneme is defined in terms of phonetic features. More precisely, a concept is defined in terms of components (one of them central) and the relationship between them, which they term "attribution". Where prominence comes in is in their notion of two contrasting centers, one static and the other dynamic. In their words, "The *static center* is the center which is determined by structural considerations; i.e., it can be determined apart from context. The *dynamic center*, on the other hand, can only be determined by the context; both are aspects of the feature of prominence" (Beekman and Callow 1976:11).[26] They apply this distinction at every level of the hierarchy: concept, proposition, paragraph, and section.

I fail to see how both types of center could be part of Prominence. Certainly from a decoding perspective only the dynamic center seems to be a viable candidate since any concept (or proposition, etc.) will of necessity be in a context. I will digress here to discuss the notion of static center since I believe it is relevant in a tangential way. Beekman and Callow consider that the static center of a concept like 'boy' is the generic concept 'being', rather than 'human', 'male', or 'nonadult', because the last three are related to the first rather than to each other. I believe there is general agreement among semanticists about such an analysis, just as with the view that the center of a proposition is a predicate. What is of interest here is the notion of a central element with associated noncentral elements. Is this an evidence at the deepest or most abstract level that the human mind cannot process information apart from such a distinction? I believe so. I would say that the only contribution of the notion 'static center' to Prominence is to prove that it is necessary, even at the abstract level. But when it comes to evaluating the prominence structure of a given discourse, everything has a context, and 'dynamic center' takes over. Thus, in 'A boy could not do that', the dynamic center of 'boy' would be 'nonadult', 'male', or 'human', depending on whether the referent of 'that' is a task appropriate to a man, a girl, or a monkey; but in no case is any special attention given to 'being' (the static center).

---

[26] In their 1977 revision of the course notes, they have changed the terminology, but their essential thinking seems to be the same. "The nucleus is the center which is determined by comparing concepts which are members of a generic set, which means it can be determined apart from context. The focal center, on the other hand, can only be determined in context; both are aspects of the feature of prominence" (sect. 2.1.1). What in 1976 was "static center" is now "nucleus", and what was "dynamic center" is now "focal center".

Returning to the hierarchical organization of theme, I will begin with the phrase level (a concept may be encoded in anything from a morpheme to a phrase). I confess that the relevance of even the dynamic center of a concept to theme escapes me. In the example used above it is the whole concept 'boy' that enters into the thematic structure, not just 'male' or 'human'. Nor will one component have priority. At this level 'boy' is functioning as a chunk, regardless of internal structure. I suggest that it is the grammatical properties of a phrase rather than the semantic properties of a concept that are relevant to thematic structure. Because a phrase may be composed of a Head plus modifiers, all of which become one concept; and because a modifier may be an embedded clause, a phrase constitutes an efficient vehicle for getting any desired combination of information into the theme line. I do not see one part of a phrase as being more thematic than the rest of it. What is important about a phrase, in the present context, is its potential to become the thematic constituent in a clause, which amounts to saying that theme starts at the clause level, not below. That is, only a clause-level constituent may be thematic—a phrase is all or nothing.

Beekman and Callow (1976) move from concept to proposition (recall that they relate prominence to the semantic hierarchy). The static center of a proposition is the predicate, regardless of context. The dynamic center of a proposition is determined by the context and is called "topic". They go on to say that "each proposition may be analyzed as a topic/comment combination" (1976:21). So far as I can see, their topic/comment distinction is identical to Halliday's theme/rheme, except that in their use they seem not to distinguish between semantic structure and surface structure. Grimes uses "topic" for the surface and "theme" for the semantic equivalent (1975:324). From a decoding point of view, only one set of terms is necessary. Since theme is signaled by grammar, I will discuss it in grammatical, or surface, terms.

I would say that a clause (not a proposition) may be analyzed as a topic/comment combination. 'Topic' is what is being talked about, and 'comment' is what is being said about it. If I have understood Halliday correctly, my use of topic/comment is equivalent to his theme/rheme, at the clause level. Halliday's concept was developed specifically for English, and my own thinking has, inescapably, an English bias. I do not claim that every language will have a topic/comment distinction at the clause level, but I suspect that many so-called free-word-order languages will have—the point being that the word order is not free at all but tied to thematic structure—e.g., English, Greek, Bacairí, Borôro, and Apurinã, for a start. (I doubt that the word order in any language is genuinely free; any change will signal a nuance of some sort.) As Halliday pointed out (1967 and 1968), degree of transitivity is related to theme, at least in English, as is voice. Use of the passive voice is one way to make the direct object be the topic of the clause; it is the unmarked way. I assume that any marked construction will signal Prominence of some sort, probably emphasis.

Related to the difference between marked and unmarked constructions is the difference between obligatory and optional ones. In English a clause must have a topic; it is obligatory since the first constituent is thematic. It is the norm that theme be indicated this way at the clause level (in English) just as it is the norm for the Subject to be the first constituent. But there may be extra, optional signals. In English, clefting, tagging, and reprise (e.g., 'Mary, she likes poodles') are optional devices. However, I think they relate to emphasis rather than theme, or perhaps in addition to it. But other languages may very well have optional devices that do signal theme—Bacairí (Brazil) and Inga (Colombia), for instance.

My remarks concerning clause will apply also to simple sentences, but I believe it is necessary to consider sentences separately (from clauses) because they evidently carry a different range of thematic options. In a complex sentence (in English) such as "If he lied to me, I won't let him go to the party", I take it that the whole protasis is what is being talked about and is therefore the topic of the sentence, as distinct from the topics of the included clauses. Kalinga (Philippines) evidently can have a sentence topic which is distinct from the topic of its principal clause (Richard Gieser, MS). I believe Beekman and Callow run into difficulty here because they jump from proposition to paragraph, since their treatment is tied to the semantic hierarchy. Figure 5 is taken from their course notes and shows up the problem nicely.

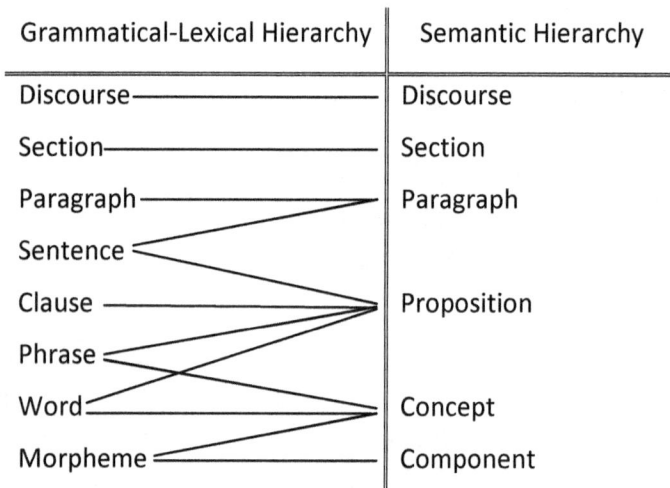

Grammatical-Lexical Hierarchy	Semantic Hierarchy
Discourse	Discourse
Section	Section
Paragraph	Paragraph
Sentence	
Clause	Proposition
Phrase	
Word	Concept
Morpheme	Component

Figure 5

There is no semantic level in figure 5 to match sentence—a simple sentence would represent a proposition, and a complex/compound sentence would represent a semantic paragraph. In practice they do press into service a "propositional string", which seems to match sentence, while denying theoretical status to it. "While the propositional string is not a semantic unit, it is of considerable usefulness in describing the main thrust and import of a paragraph" (Beekman and Callow 1976:35). I agree with the composition of their semantic hierarchy, but feel that it is a mistake to treat Prominence in terms of that hierarchy. It seems clear to me that languages have distinct sets of prominence signals attaching to clause, sentence, and paragraph respectively and that prominence is part of the grammar.

At the paragraph level Beekman and Callow again distinguish between "static center" and "dynamic center", but I would not know how to separate them in a decoding situation. Only at the paragraph level (and above) does the notion of dynamic center (or any center) come into its own with reference to theme. It is probably safe to say that the central (topic) clause of a paragraph (unless parenthetic) will certainly be in the theme line. At this level they speak of a theme/development distinction parallel to the topic/comment distinction for propositions, wherein "theme" is the main proposition ("topic" plus "comment") of the paragraph and "development" is all the remaining propositions, which support the theme. Their use of theme here is different from mine. By 'theme' I mean the theme line that presumably pervades the paragraph, rather than just a topic sentence.

From paragraph on up the hierarchy I feel unable to say anything definite. The statements and discussions of prominence signals at the paragraph level and above that I have seen sound more like focus to me than theme, but I am not in a position to demonstrate either one. It is clear, however, that there are prominence signals whose domain is a paragraph, while there are others whose domain is a section or episode. I feel more comfortable discussing paragraph and section-level prominence in terms of focus.

At the outset of this discussion I said that theme in non-narrative discourse "is organized hierarchically, at least partly". Upon reflection it is clear that theme must also have a linear quality, which is reflected in the term 'theme line'. My basic rule of thumb is that if a piece may be removed without disrupting the flow of the argument, then it is not thematic. On the assumption that the topic clauses of all paragraphs (with the possible exception of embedded and parenthetical ones) will necessarily be in the theme line, I would argue that any stepping-stones (usually a clause) logically necessary to get from one topic clause to the next must also be in the theme line. The theme line will conform to the structural diagram and be hierarchical in that sense. They will not be identical since the diagram includes everything, whereas the theme line does not.[27]

---

[27] As I have described theme, it is not hierarchical in a constituent structure sense; the topic of a paragraph does not derive from the topics of all the included clauses, etc. In fact, some (or many) clause and sentence topics will not be in the theme line at all. Nor will all of them contribute to focus or emphasis. I have left them out in the cold, and yet I feel that they do belong under Prominence. Although in following K. Callow and Hollenbach (by speaking of "theme" in terms of theme line) I have criticized Beekman and Callow with their notion of "centers" at all levels, that criticism may be premature. Perhaps we need both approaches and should view "theme" as being expressed in two distinct ways: in a theme line (temporal or logical), and in a taxonomy of topics coinciding with the grammatical levels of clause, sentence, paragraph, and section. It should be noted that there will be some overlap between the two expressions of theme, that the taxonomy of topics relates to the grammatical hierarchy, and that the taxonomy is not a constituent structure—clause topics do not compose sentence topics do not compose paragraph topics, etc.

Evidently Grimes also has come to view Prominence (he calls it Staging) as hierarchical. One of his students, Paul Clements, has based his thesis on that view. As Clements explains the procedure for establishing the hierarchy of a text, there are three basic rules: 1) "Identify the topic of each clause and simple sentence." 2) "Decide whether the topic is new (never previously mentioned) or old (mentioned in an earlier topic or comment). If new—assign it one level below the previous topic. If old—assign it the same level as its first mention." 3) "If a topic is coordinated with an earlier topic or comment, assign it the same level as that earlier topic or comment." Then there are five secondary rules that also come into play: 4) "Topics of embedded sentences or subordinate clauses are assigned one level below the topic of the sentence in which they are embedded or to which they are subordinated." 5) "New topics which follow an embedded sentence or subordinate clause are assigned one level below the last unembedded or unsubordinated topic (unless otherwise coordinated)." 6) "An old topic is never placed lower in the hierarchy than it would be placed if it were a new topic." 7) "Explicit signals always take precedence over implied signals." 8) "In cases of conflict, the higher numbered rule always takes precedence over the lower numbered rule." (Clements 1976:26-29) It seems to me that Grimes and Clements are using elements from three of my macrosystems—Hierarchy, Cohesion, Prominence—in coming up with their "staging structure". (As illustrated in Part II, I prefer to check out each system individually before trying to bring them together.) The result of their procedure is clearly hierarchical, although not in a constituent structure sense. However, it is not a hierarchy of theme, as I use the term, unless one equates hierarchical structure with thematic structure. Since I

4.2 **Focus**

Prominence that occurs with 'focus' significance is saying to the hearer, "This is important, listen." It picks out items of thematic material as being of particular interest or significance. Different items may be picked out for focus at different points along the theme-line: the domain of focus varies from language to language, but is rarely longer than two or three paragraphs, sometimes much shorter (Callow 1974:52).

I view focus a little differently. To me it says, "This is the central element in this stretch of text", or some such thing. The domain of focus will normally be a paragraph or a section. It differs from theme in that it only attaches to a particular participant, event, or place, etc., or perhaps to a whole clause or sentence, whereas thematic material will be deployed throughout the paragraph or section. I see focus as cooperating with or contributing to theme, but believe it is both valid and useful to distinguish between them.

Focus may be obligatory or optional. In Cashinawa (Peru) it is obligatory and signaled by position. "The first word in the text body is highlighted as the topic in primary focus for a paragraph or series of paragraphs until another focused item . . . is picked up in the narration" (Cromack 1968:309). Note that the domain extends over at least a paragraph. In Bacairí (Brazil) focus is obligatory and signaled by the pronominal system: only one participant may be in focus in a given paragraph or episode (Wheatley 1973:106-7). In Otomí (Mexico) focus is optional and may be signaled by a variety of devices, including repeated reference (Wallis 1971). There may be both primary and secondary focus, as illustrated in chapter 10.

In Longuda (Nigeria) episodes, one participant is designated as the thematic (in-focus) character, and his status affects the use of all

---

have motivated and characterized Hierarchy and Prominence as clearly distinct systems, I am not able to go along with the procedure outlined above.

pronouns throughout the episode (John Newman, MS). I believe something similar happens in Shipibo (Peru) and other languages. I will use these languages and a statement by K. Callow to try to pinpoint the difference between 'theme' and 'focus', at least in one situation.

> Where . . . the topic which the rest of the clause is talking about is exactly what would have been expected from the preceding discourse, then of course it carries no prominence at all. This would occur, for instance, where a subject pronoun occurred first in thematic position, but referred to exactly the same participant who had been repeatedly referred to as subject throughout the paragraph. It may still be true that that participant is highly prominent in said paragraph or series of paragraphs, but the word which refers to him is not the prominent word in that particular clause (1974:58).

In languages where a certain pronoun is reserved for the focal participant and is obligatorily used when referring to that participant, once he has been introduced, the occurrence of that pronoun will certainly be predictable. But I cannot agree with Callow that it would carry "no prominence at all" in such an event. Whenever such a pronoun is in the theme line, as clause topic or whatever, it must have some thematic prominence. I would agree that it has neither focal nor emphatic prominence, unless it be that by virtue of referring to the focal participant there is some focal prominence. I suppose that a pronoun that is used exclusively for focal participants is continuing the function of the device(s) that established the focal participant in the first place. Still, I prefer to define focus in terms of the device(s) used to establish the identity of a focal element. Any subsequent reference to that element throughout the paragraph or section I prefer to handle as being part of theme. One might reasonably insist that both theme and focus are being served in such a case, but it seems to me that once past the identifying device(s), focus melts or shades off into theme. Perhaps an analogy will help: I liken 'theme' to a large wave and 'focus' to a small wave on the face of the large wave. The small wave is part of the big wave and yet has a separate identity. The device(s) that signals focus I liken to the crest of the small wave; the continuing reference to a focal element I liken to the body of the small wave which soon fades into the big wave—the big wave predominates.

4.3 **Emphasis**

Prominence that occurs with emphatic significance normally involves the speaker-hearer relationship in some way. It says to the hearer either "You didn't expect that, did you?", or "Now, I feel strongly about this." In other words, emphasis has two different functions: it highlights an item of information which the narrator considers will be surprising to the hearer, or else it warns the hearer that the emotions of the speaker are quite strongly involved. Both functions tend to operate over a relatively short domain, to have typical intonation patterns as part of the signal, and to be extra-systemic in structure; hence they are treated here as variant forms of the same basic value (Callow 1974:52).

I would use 'emphasis' to refer to any localized highlighting, whatever the author's purpose might be. Emphasis will usually attach to a single word or phrase, by which I mean that that will be the extent of its domain. Emphasis will seldom attach to more than a sentence since in the nature of the case there must be contrast—if everything is emphasized there is no emphasis. Emphasis will not necessarily be connected to either focus or theme, though it may be. A given device may serve more than one organizing factor simultaneously. Thus I would say that a marked clause topic in English may have both thematic and emphatic prominence.

Grimes has some lists of sentences (the same basic sentence) showing something of the range of possible combinations and variations of marked topic and emphasis in English (1975:329-31). There may be degrees of emphasis, and more than one element in a sentence may be emphasized—again, if too many things are emphasized the effect is diluted. Grimes gives the following range of devices for distinguishing "topic" (most of his examples I would classify as 'emphasis'): fronting, inflection, pronouns, agreement, partitioning (pseudoclefting), extra-position (clefting), tagging, and reprise. He then has a table showing possible combinations of these devices (Grimes 1975:343).

Quite a variety of devices may be used for signaling emphasis. Special stress or intonation (spoken) or italics and punctuation (written) are common devices. English also has reprise, tagging, clefting, pseudo-clefting, and front-shifting. Vagla (Ghana) has tone perturbation, vowel lengthening, and emphatic pronouns and particles. Hindi and Panjabi use emphatic particles. In Halăng (Vietnam) one may use rhetorical questions. Ayoré (Bolivia) uses repetition. Oksapmin (Papua New Guinea) and Inga (Colombia) have back-shifting. Otomí has front-shifting. Each language will have its own possibilities, and those possibilities may vary with discourse genre.

4.3.1 Dequotation. So far as I know, Hockett (1968) was the first to call attention to dequotation. It deserves more attention than it has received. Although the germinal idea comes from Hockett, I owe much of the understanding of the subject reflected in the following discussion to Gleason. At the end of my discussion of taxis I characterized dequotation as overt editing and treated it as a low-level paratactic device. I think overt editing is a paratactic device, but it is only one kind of dequotation.

I would characterize dequotation as the shifting and infixing of some constituent into a constituent at the same or a lower level, but without changing its rank. It creates a discontinuous constituent. Its genius may be appreciated by comparing it to embedding and fore-grounding (fronting). In embedding a construction is demoted, it becomes a constituent at a lower level (e.g., a clause becoming part of a phrase). In foregrounding, the constituents at a given level are reordered, but without splitting up any of those constituents.

In English, dequotation usually involves the back-shifting of a sentence-level constituent. In that connection I find it useful to distinguish between sentence adverbs on the one hand and performatives or superordinate predicates on the other. With reference to sentence adverbs, a sentence-level constituent is back-shifted and 'infixed' in another constituent, but without becoming a part of that other constituent. It becomes as it were a cyst within the second constituent, and since it retains its rank, a sort of hypertaxis results. For example, in "As inflation worsens, making ends meet becomes increasingly difficult", we have a sentence with two constituents: a sentence adverb and an independent clause in unmarked order. If we change it to "Making ends meet, as inflation worsens, becomes increasingly difficult", "as inflation worsens" now lies within the clause but is not a constituent of that clause; it remains a sentence-level constituent and is thus higher in rank than the clause-level constituents on either side of it. We now have a marked order.

With reference to superordinate predicates, the hypertaxis is more pronounced because the construction that is infixed is semantically higher in rank than the construction in which it is placed, even though grammatically they may be constituents at the same level. But even grammatically I believe there is a clear difference between sentence adverbs and superordinate predicates. For example, I will compare "I think it is snowing" and "It is, I think, snowing". I believe it may reasonably be diagrammed as follows:

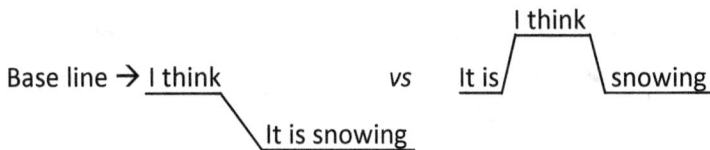

Base line → I think   vs   It is / I think \ snowing
                 \ It is snowing

Looking at the first utterance grammatically, I analyze it as a clause with three constituents: 'I', 'think' and 'it is snowing'. In the second utterance both the Subject and the Predicate (verb) have been infixed in the third constituent (a dependent clause), which gives quite a different feel than the infixing of a sentence adverb in an independent clause. Similarly I think there is a difference in 'feel' between "It is snowing, I think" and "Making ends meet becomes increasingly difficult, as inflation worsens"; I would claim dequotation for the former but not the latter. In the latter there has been reordering of constituents, but no infixing and hence no hypertaxis (unless we wish to say that the sentence adverb has been infixed in the independent clause, albeit without splitting any constituent. I must admit that putting the sentence adverb at the end of the clause has much the same effect as putting it in the middle). In the first case there is no infixing either, but the dependent clause has been chosen as the base line, as it were, so that hypertaxis does result.

Some things that look like adverbs may actually be elliptical performatives and should be handled as superordinate predicates. Thus, "Frankly, he talks too much" I consider to be short for "I tell you frankly, he talks too much", so I would call "He talks too much, frankly" an instance of dequotation.

Direct quotation offers perhaps the most unambiguous examples. Contrasting "Joe said, 'Go away before I lose my temper'" with "'Go away', Joe said, 'before I lose my temper'" and "'Go away before I lose my temper', Joe said", it seems clear that in the second two cases the direct quote forms the base line, whereas in the first case, the performative does.

As to the significance of dequotation, it seems to relate to both emphasis and theme. With reference to emphasis, dequotation emphasizes the item isolated by that process, not the 'dequoted' item itself. For example, in "grace to you and peace" (Colossians 1:2), the clause-level constituent "to you" has been infixed in another clause-level constituent, "grace and peace", with the result that "grace" receives some emphasis. It seems to me that there are degrees of hypertaxis, and in that event I would claim that the strength of the emphasis conveyed corresponds to the number of degrees of hypertaxis. I suggest that an infixed adverb or a suffixed performative rate one degree, an infixed performative (or superordinate predicate) rate two degrees, and if a level is skipped the value be doubled. An illustration will not be out of place. The following sentence from a sermon preached by J.W. Burgon at Oxford on May 19, 1861, came to my attention as I was mulling over the subject of dequotation; it is made to order. "The Bible in truth, as one grows older—to me at least it seems so—becomes almost the only thing in the world really deserving of a man's attention." Before evaluating degrees of dequotation it is necessary to postulate an unmarked order. I suggest the following analysis:

at least it seems to me that

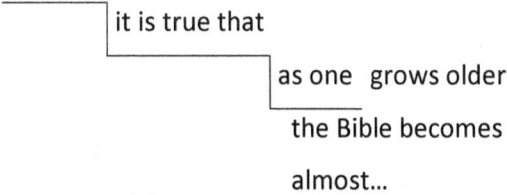

it is true that

as one grows older

the Bible becomes

almost...

By way of preliminary comment, I take "at least" and "as one grows older" to be sentence adverbs; I take "in truth" to represent a superordinate predicate which I have given as "it is true that"; "to me" is forefronted in its clause and receives emphasis thereby, but it is further emphasized by the dequotation of "at least" (which would not be dequoted if it were not for the forefronting of "to me"). Now I plot the dequotation in figure 6, retaining the exact words and order of the quoted sentence. (It will be noted that level 3 is vacant. This is a consequence of awarding double value to a skipped level. If "it is true that" had a dequoted sentence adverb, that adverb would occupy level 3.)[28]

5			at least	
4			to me	it seems so
3				
2	in truth			
1		as one grows older		
The Bible				becomes . . .

Figure 6

Well, having done it I am not sure what it proves. There is so much dequotation in this example that it seems almost selfdefeating. Still, a few observations may be made. The clause of which "the Bible" is the subject is the base line. Its topic, "the Bible", is emphasized with a vengeance; however, the infixing of "at least" combined with the forefronting of "to me" results in considerable emphasis upon "me" as well. The placing of "to me it seems so" at level 4 illustrates what I mean by double value for skipping a level—that clause skipped over an intervening clause to be infixed in a clause two levels down. On the

---

[28] Peter Reich has raised the question (personal communication) of how to accomodate the possibility of open-ended recursion of dequotation in my scheme of levels. E.g., the sentence adverb "as one grows older", which I have assigned to level one, could itself harbor a dequoted item, like "as one grows, you know, older". In order to retain a fixed value or definition for the levels, I propose to handle the recursion as follows:

```
        b.
    2. a.
        c.
        b.
    1. a. and so on.
```

That is, I would add as many letters as necessary at the appropriate level in order to accommodate the example before me. In this case, "you know" would be at level 1.b., while "as one grows . . . older" would be at level 1.a.

possibility that the extra emphasis on "to me" is skewing the effect of the dequotation, I will put that clause in unmarked order. I proceed to list various arrangements of the sentence in ascending order of degrees of hypertaxis, according to my scheme, with "at least it seems so to me" remaining constant at level 4.

4   "In truth, as one grows older the Bible—at least it seems so to me—becomes almost . . . ."

5   "In truth the Bible, as one grows older—at least it seems . . . ."

6   "As one grows older the Bible, in truth—at least it seems . . . ."

7   "The Bible in truth, as one grows older—at least it seems . . . ."

Is my intuition rigged by now, or is there really a progression there?

Returning to the significance of dequotation, with reference to theme it results in a marked sentence or clause topic, as the case may be. In English, at least, dequotation seems to be a device to get an item that would otherwise be 'topic' out of that position. In the case of superordinate predicates, dequotation results in a change of base line. All in all, dequotation emerges as an important prominence-signaling device.

4.3.2 Promotion. I came across the phenomenon that I will call 'promotion' while analyzing the Greek text of Colossians (see Part II). I characterize promotion as the shifting of some constituent to a spot appropriate to a higher-level constituent—sort of the opposite of dequotation. Something like 'NOT-hopping' does not qualify since the negative moves from one phrase-level slot to another analogous phrase-level slot. If necessary, function can be added to the definition; promotion is a very marked procedure and results in strong emphasis upon the promoted item.

The first instance of promotion that I recognized is in Colossians 1:9: "in him all the fullness was pleased to dwell". "In him" is part of the infinitival phrase, "to dwell in him", and yet it occurs in a spot appropriate to a sentence-level constituent. The only instances I have seen so far involve a shift forward, but promotion is distinct from foregrounding in that the latter does not involve a seeming change in rank. The difference can be illustrated with the example above: in English, the unmarked order is "all the fulness was pleased to dwell in him"; to foreground "in him", it would be "all the fulness was pleased in him to dwell", as opposed to the promotion illustrated above.

Whereas a dequoted item is not emphasized (quite the contrary), a promoted item is strongly emphasized—significantly more so than a foregrounded item. It is clear that promotion is a device for signaling emphasis. I take it that in the example above "in him" becomes the marked topic of the sentence, so that we may say that promotion contributes to theme in a way similar to dequotation; they both result in a marked topic.

In sum, I have proposed that the macrosystem Prominence is signaled by three organizing factors: theme, focus, and emphasis. While they may cooperate, they are distinct. Although there may be further factors that contribute to Prominence, I insist that we need at least these three.

5 Style

Style reflects if not a basic human limitation, at least a basic human characteristic: we are social beings. (I am using 'style' as a cover term for anything that reflects or serves a social perspective.) As soon as two human beings attempt to communicate with each other, some sort of relationship must be posited, a relationship inescapably defined in terms of social factors. Something so basic to the human condition must inevitably be reflected in language. Dell Hymes is only one of many who so affirm.[29] He suggests that we should think of a community, or a person, in terms of a repertoire of "ways of speaking" and proceeds:

> *Ways of speaking, in turn, comprise speech styles, on the one hand, and contexts of discourse, on the other, together with the relations of appropriateness obtaining between styles and contexts. Membership in a speech community consists in sharing one or more of its ways of speaking—that is, not in knowledge of a speech style (or any other purely linguistic entity, such as a language) alone, but in terms of knowledge of appropriate use as well. There are rules of use without which rules of syntax are useless. Moreover, the linguistic features that*

---

[29] Halliday is another. He posits "social structure" as one of five elements in the sociolinguistic universe and says concerning it: "The social structure refers specifically to the organization of society. This permeates all forms of interaction and exchange of meanings by the members; but it enters into the picture that we are building up here in two significant ways. In the first place it is a part of the environment; hence it is a part of what is being transmitted to the child through language. In the second place it is a determinant of the transmission process, since it determines the types of role relationship in the "primary socializing agencies," the social groups through which a child takes out his membership of the culture—the family, the young children's peer group, and the school—and so creates the conditions in which the child lives and learns. Our understanding of how this happens is very largely due to Bernstein. Bernstein's work demonstrates that the social structure is not just a kind of incidental appendage to linguistic interaction, as linguists have tended to think of it, but is an integral element in the deeper processes that such interaction involves" (1975:128-29).

enter into speech styles are not only the "referentially-based" features usually dealt with in linguistics today, but also the "stylistic" features that are complementary to them, and inseparable from them in communication. Just as social meaning is an integral part of the definition and demarcation of speech communities, so it is an integral part of the organization of linguistic features within them (Hymes 1974:53).

Hymes goes on to state that the organization of linguistic features in social interaction discloses orientations toward persons, roles, statuses, rights and duties, deference and demeanor (1974:61). Perhaps the best-known overt and systematic type of social orientation is the honorific systems found in some languages. Some are quite complex, but even where the choice is between only two forms, the range and interaction of factors impinging upon the choice can be formidable. Paul Friedrich (1966) cites ten factors as determining the appropriateness of one or another of the pronominal usage patterns in nineteenth century Russian novels. They are: the topic of conversation, the age or sex or generation of the conversation partners, the kinship relationship between the partners, shared membership in a dialect or social group, the possession of relative jural or political authority on the part of one of the participants, and the degree of emotional solidarity between the two. He also discusses some of the problems involved in deciding which pattern to use, and in changing patterns. Anyone who speaks such a language knows that the dilemma can be painful. The point I wish to make here is that the choice of one pattern or another (in such languages) is obligatory—a social orientation is built right into the grammar. We have a clear Whorfian situation: the members of such a culture are forced to speak and think in such terms.

I am using Style as a cover term for anything that reflects or serves a social perspective, and not in the sense of a certain author's style (which

I would take to be the pattern of his use of all the macrosystems).[30] Here again there is confusion in the use of terms, so I will please myself, defining as I go. By way of introduction to the several organizing factors that contribute to Style, I will discuss the scheme presented by Martin Joos in *The Five Clocks* (1962)—still the most helpful treatment of style that I have seen.

> Here are, in order of importance, four of the usage scales of native central English:

AGE	STYLE	BREADTH	RESPONSIBILITY
senile	frozen	genteel	best
mature	formal	puristic	better
teenage	consultative	standard	good
child	casual	provincial	fair
baby	intimate	popular	bad

> These four scales are essentially independent; relations among them are not identities (1962:13).

When Joos says "four of the usage-scales", he is evidently allowing for the possible existence of others. I think there are certainly other factors that must be considered, whether or not they lend themselves to such neat usage scales. But taking the ones he offers, I will evaluate them in terms of my framework and decoding perspective.

I see no way to include his "responsibility" scale in a framework for discourse analysis, even though I think there is some merit in his discussion of it. I agree that there are persons in any speech community who, by virtue of their social position or language skills, have a

---

[30] Gleason has defined style as "the patterning of choices made within the options presented by the conventions of the language and the literary form" (1965:428). I think I am saying the same thing in different words.

disproportionate influence in determining the norms or standards for language use. If norms are not maintained, the organizing system of language will fall apart and communication will break down. Most native speakers can and do make value judgments about variant forms of a given expression, and may even employ such adjectives as "good", "fair", or "bad" in so doing. But aside from forms that most members of a community would declare to be clearly pathological, the variants will be appropriate to different levels in Joos' style scale. In analyzing a discourse, we will not ask whether a certain form is good or fair but whether it signals a formal style, a casual style, or whatever.

As for "breadth", Joos' total discussion of it is as follows:

> This scale measures breadth of experience and of self-limitation. From popular English up to standard English, your experiences broaden your usages; and from there up to genteel you narrow them again to suit your personality. Nothing further (1962:13).

I have doubts about the validity of this scale. I believe its constituents join "age" and a variety of other factors in constituting what I will call 'code'. What Joos calls "style" I call 'register', and will discuss his treatment of it under that heading.

To proceed with the presentation of my framework, I suggest that the macrosystem Style is signaled by the following organizing factors: register, code, dialect, and idiolect—which I discuss in that order.

5.1 **Register**. Halliday has defined register in terms of *field*, *tenor*, and *mode*. I have not found that division to be helpful, so I will not make use of it; perhaps his distinctions are more delicate than my framework requires. When he links register to the context of situation, however, I believe Halliday is getting at the essence of the concept:

> A register can be defined as a particular configuration of meanings that is associated with a particular situation type. In any social context, certain semantic resources are characteristically employed; certain sets of options are as it were 'at risk' in the given semiotic

environment. These define the register. Considered in terms of the notion of meaning potential, the register is the range of meaning potential that is activated by the semiotic properties of the situation (Halliday 1975:126).

Register is controlled by context of situation (and culture); any average speaker of a language changes register as needed.

For a practical exposition of the subject, I prefer Joos' treatment to Halliday's. Substituting 'register' for Joos' "style", Joos presents five registers: frozen, formal, consultative, casual, and intimate. His characterization of the different registers is so well done that it deserves to be quoted.

Joos starts out with the consultative register, which he considers to be the basic or central one, and says concerning it:

It supplies background information currently, and the listener participates fully. His participation insures that there shall be neither too little nor too much background given. If too little, he will break in to ask for elucidation; if too much, he may say 'yes I know.' The diction is kept in accurate balance with the requirements: the pronunciation is clear but does not clatter, the grammar is complete but for an occasional anacoluthon, the semantics is adequate without fussiness. All is adjusted by instantaneous homeostasis, and the speaker does not compose text more than two or three seconds in advance. He could not in any case, since he must expect the hearer to insert a word or two every six seconds. Being thus entirely automatic, it is the most strictly organized type of language. Its grammar is central to all the possibilities of grammar, and the grammars of all other styles are formed by adding archaisms and other complications to the consultative grammar; the pronunciations of all other styles are most simply described as departures from consultative pronunciation; the meanings of any word which occurs at all in consultative style are basically its consultative meanings, to which each other style adds specific meanings as necessitated by its own function: private

> meanings in intimate style, slang meanings in casual style, technical meanings in formal style, allusive meanings in frozen style (1962:24).
>
> The two defining features of consultative style are: (1) The speaker supplies background information—he does not assume that he will be understood without it . . . . (2) The addressee participates continuously (1962:19).

The defining features of Joos' "casual" register are also two: ellipsis and slang. The term 'slang' is not intended in a derogatory sense here but refers to any expression used in an esoteric way. The point of both features is that one must be an insider to understand.

> Besides these two pattern devices—ellipsis and slang—casual style is marked by an arbitrary list of formulas, all very stable, which are learned individually and used to identify the style for the hearer's convenience. 'Come on!' has been one of these identifiers since before the time of Shakespeare (see _The Tempest_, line 308); and all this while, every adult native speaker of English to whom it was addressed has unconsciously known that the speaker was using casual style and has reacted accordingly—and the speaker, without knowing why he did it, has used it to procure that reaction (1962:21).

Now comes a final comparison of the consultative and casual registers which leads into the discussion of a third register, "intimate".

> Both colloquial styles—consultative and casual—routinely deal in a public sort of information, though differently: casual style takes it for granted and at most alludes to it, consultative style states it as fast as it is needed. Where there happens to be no public information for a while, a casual conversation (among men) lapses into silence and kidding, a consultative one is broken off or adjourned. These adjustments help to show what sort of role public information plays in the two colloquial styles; it is essential to them both.
>
> Now in intimate style, this role is not merely weakened; rather, it is positively abolished. Intimate speech excludes public information (Joos 1962:22).

By excluding public information he means the pointed avoidance of any information "from outside of the speaker's skin". Evidently the assumption is that partners in an intimate relationship will understand each other so well as to be able to guess each other's thoughts and feelings. Again Joos offers two features to characterize the intimate register: extraction and jargon. Extraction may be defined by comparing it with ellipsis. "An elliptical sentence still has wording, grammar, and intonation. Intimate extraction employs only part of this triplet." He further characterizes this register as follows:

> *Intimate style tolerates nothing of the system of any other style: no slang, no background information, and so on. . . . The imputations of all other styles are similarly corrosive. Accordingly, intimate codes, or jargons, are severely limited in their use of public vocabulary. Each intimate group must invent its own code (1962:23).*

It seems to me that Joos is being extreme here. Surely the partners in an intimate conversation will mix some ordinary language with the extraction and jargon, and do so without corroding their relationship. Or conversely, a 'phatic' element—that which is primarily directed at building and maintaining personal bonds—probably pervades all registers, even though it is especially appropriate to intimacy. I suspect that the notion of register is better treated as a continuum than as a row of pigeonholes: more will be said about that presently.

Moving on to the "formal" register, the crucial difference between it and the consultative register is that participation drops out. Once again Joos offers two characteristic (or 'defining') features: detachment and cohesion.

> *Formal style is designed to inform . . . . The formal code-labels inform each hearer that he is in a formal frame, is not to make insertions but must wait until authorized to speak, and is being given time to plan reactions . . . .*
> *Lacking all personal support, the text must fight its own battles. Form becomes its dominant character . . . . The pronunciation is explicit*

> *to the point of clattering; the grammar tolerates no ellipsis and cultivates elaborateness; the semantics is fussy. Background information is woven into the text in complex sentences. Exempt from interruption, the text organizes itself into paragraphs; the paragraphs are linked explicitly . . . (Joos 1962:25).*

It may be that audio feedback disappears in a situation requiring a formal register, but visual feedback is still there. Any alert speaker will observe whether or not his audience is following the exposition and presumably will make adjustments as indicated.

As for the "frozen" register, Joos has this to say:

> *Frozen style—a style for print and for declamation—is defined by the absence of authoritative intonation in the text, as also by the fact that the reader or hearer is not permitted to cross-question the author. Relative to the other styles, these peculiarities clearly are defects in the frozen style, preventing it from functioning as they do. Freed from those other functions, frozen style develops its own functions, by common consent surpassing the others. From the surpassing excellence of good frozen style, our folklore has derived the mistaken theory that it is the ideal of all language (1962:27).*

It seems to me that Joos was not able to characterize this register as well as he did the others. He seems to limit it essentially to written discourse, while the other registers have their origin in oral discourse. In this view, the essence of good writing is an author's ability and success in 'packing' several layers of meaning into his text, which a good reader may recover by successive rereadings (a good imagination helps). I take the view that the difference between oral and written discourse is a question of medium (not style), which I will discuss later as a separate macrosystem.

I doubt that the frozen register should be limited to written discourse. Toda (India) songs qualify as oral poetry. They must obey certain highly stylized conventions (Emmeneau 1964). Similarly, Hopi secular chants are formal announcements, characterized by unique features of vocal inflection, pitch, and melodic form (also syntax and lexicon) (Black 1967). If something like Homer's *Iliad* was first in oral form, it might qualify as oral frozen register.

Joos summarizes the difference between the several registers as follows:

Good intimate style fuses two personalities. Good casual style integrates disparate personalities into a social group which is greater than the sum of its parts, for now the personalities complement each other instead of clashing. Good consultative style produces cooperation without the integration, profiting from the lack of it. Good formal style informs the individual separately, so that his future planning may be the more discriminate. Good frozen style, finally, lures him into educating himself, so that he may the more confidently act what role he chooses (1962:27).

I believe he has made a clear case for positing at least four registers for English. His characterizations are tied to English and will not necessarily hold for other languages, but I claim that every language will have some system of register. The identifying signals or conventions will vary from language to language, and they may vary widely.

I wish to comment upon two further observations by Joos. First, he recognizes that a speaker (writer) may shift from one register to another, even within the bounds of a single sentence, and goes on to say, "normally only two neighbouring styles are used alternately, and it is anti-social to shift two or more steps in a single jump, for instance from casual to formal" (1962:17). Whether or not it is antisocial, I think such a shift is certainly a marked procedure and calls attention to itself; its precise impact will depend on context and situation.

Second, it seems clear that he views the registers as distinct levels. Speaking of a "normal citizen" he affirms:

What he does know is that his usage varies, as he thinks. The fact is that his several usages do not vary enough to matter, any one of them.

> *They alternate with each other, like his pajamas and overalls and*
> *committee-meeting suit, each tailored so as not to bind and so that he*
> *finds the pockets without looking (1962:10-11).*

I suspect that the boundaries are not that neat. Rather, I would say there is a continuum from intimate to formal.[31] It is possible to characterize stretches along the continuum, as Joos has done, but they shade into each other. Still, there must be an emic difference between registers, or else how can we account for the violent reactions that may follow when an unacceptable register is employed—as when a subordinate fails to use a deferential register in addressing his superior. But the edges are fuzzy. It may be that some kinds of variation come into play here. The work of Labov (1969; but see Bickerton 1971), Sankoff (1971) and others, treating variation in terms of percentages, may prove to be useful in analyzing register: if a certain construction, say, is chosen 70 percent of the time, the effect tends toward the formal; if it is chosen only 30 percent of the time, the effect tends toward the casual. The total effect will depend upon the whole bundle of choices that impinge on register. There will be trade-off and interplay between/among the signals.

Although there are differences in register that are clearly emic, I am not prepared to draw any precise lines. Rather than speak of discrete registers, like formal or casual, I am presently inclined to characterize the register of a given discourse as being more or less formal, or more or less casual, or as varying from formal to casual and back again. Further, a continuum from "intimate" to "frozen" is inadequate; room must be made for characterizations that do not fit there. The difference between the way a military officer addresses a soldier and how the soldier replies is a matter of register. A difference in register may exist between master and servant, between professor and pupil, between parent and child, between old person and young person, etc. A

---

[31] Gill and Gleason seem to hold a similar view for Panjabi (1963:283).

profession or academic discipline may have its own register. We are reacting to register when we say that someone is 'talking up' or 'writing down' to his audience. The difference between literature prepared for children, teenagers, or adults is one of register. So-called baby talk (spoken by adults, not babies) is a register. I would speak of the possible variations in register as forming a field, rather than a continuum; it requires at least two dimensions to plot them.

Register may be specialized, and may vary from area to area or group to group. In Tagalog a type of pig latin is popular. Although not restricted to any age, sex, or social group, its use is especially popular among adolescents and unmarried teenagers. The actual forms used vary in time and from ingroup to ingroup, since the pig latin is supposed to be esoteric (Conklin 1956). This is a specialized type of register. (Its use is linked to purposes like amusement—test of skill, teasing, joking— and concealing meaning from the uninitiated.) Haas (1957) observes that elaborate gradations of politeness and vulgarity of speech are particularly characteristic of the Bankok area in Thailand, as compared to outlying areas of the country where the gradations are less elaborate.

What Charles Ferguson calls "diglossia" probably belongs here. His discussion is based on Arabic, Modern Greek, Swiss German, and Haitian Creole (with brief reference to Tamil, Chinese, and the emergent Romance languages). In many speech communities two distinct varieties of the same language are used in rather clearly defined sets of situations. Calling one variety "high" (H) and the other "low" (L), he feels able to make a generalized statement as to the sorts of situations where one or the other will be used in all four of the defining languages: H will be used in sermons, political speeches, university lectures, news broadcasts, and newspaper editorials; L will be used in giving instructions to workmen, in conversation with family and friends, and in folk literature (Ferguson 1959). Since the H and L varieties differ noticeably in phonology, grammar, and lexicon (more so in some cases than in others), they would seem to qualify as dialects, except that the H variety is not the mother tongue of anyone in the speech community in question (no one learns H in the home). Since the choice is dictated by situational context, H and L seem clearly to be related to register. H will evidently be at the formal end of the continuum, while L will presumably operate from intimate up to (and including) consultative (on Joos' scale).[32] In sum, I conceive register to be the effect produced by the totality of such choices as are dictated by appropriateness to a given social situation.

5.2 **Code**. Whereas register is largely deliberate (though also sub-conscious) and a reflection of the social situation in which a discourse takes place, 'code' is largely automatic and a reflection of the social condition of the speaker without respect to the immediate situation. I am using 'social condition' loosely to cover factors like age, sex, caste, or class.

I suspect that in most, if not all, languages there will be some characterizable difference between male speech and female speech. In some cases the difference is considerable and obvious, while in others it is slight and subtle. Among the languages with a pronounced difference are Chukchee (Siberia) (Bogoras 1921) and Koasati (Louisiana) (Haas 1944). Others are Black Carib (Guatemala), Carajá (Brazil), Chiquitano (Bolivia), Gros Ventre (Montana), Yana (California) and Zulu (South Africa). Mazateco (Mexico) whistle speech is codelike in that only males whistle (Cowan 1948). A man uses the male code automatically; the relevant choices are not conscious ones (by and large). Of course he is aware of the female code and can use it if occasion demands (e.g., in quoting a woman). This last observation will be especially true where

---

[32] Some writers have extended the use of the term 'diglossia' or 'triglossia' to cases where bilingual or trilingual speakers switch languages more or less predictably, according to subject matter, for instance. This sort of thing probably belongs under Strategy. A language switch, or spelling out words in the presence of small children, with a view to privacy, clearly relates to Strategy.

the differences are obvious. In a language like English where the differences are slight and subtle, the average male may not be able to characterize the female code (although he may recognize some individual signals).

Many languages will have a characterizable difference between adult and teenage or child speech, and some languages may have a number of age codes. In some languages there is a formal shift in age grade (with the corresponding code) after an initiation ceremony or marriage. An interesting instance of age-related code occurs in Hanunóo (Philippines). There are at least eleven pig-latin-like ways of modifying 'normal' speech, some of them quite complicated (it is even possible to combine some of them). The pig latin is used predominantly by marriageable but unmarried youth, and primarily in courting. Although adolescents can be heard using some of the simpler types (practicing, presumably), married adults revert to it only at feasts where everyone pretends to be marriageable (Conklin 1959). Unlike Tagalog, the different kinds of pig latin follow specific rules which are stable. Pig latin in Hanunóo is codelike in that it attaches to age group and social status, and yet is registerlike in that it occurs in a specified context of situation. (Its use is linked to purposes like concealing identity and showing off skill.)

The prominence of speech as an indicator of social status in foreign lands seems to be well accepted, but its prominence in America has not been recognized to the same extent. Ellis (1967) presents research findings to show that Americans' speech does reveal social status. Just by listening to recorded one minute samples of speech of persons from different educational and social backgrounds, the listeners, themselves from different backgrounds, were able to determine with a high degree of agreement and accuracy the speaker's social status. Differences of regional dialect did not inhibit the listeners from recognizing a speaker as being upper, middle, or lower class in social status. Even when speakers were given a role to play and told to try to 'fake' their voices to make them sound upper class, the listeners were still able to determine a speaker's social class, although the 'batting average' dropped somewhat. Choice of vocabulary, sentence length, sentence structure, and fluency appeared to be factors involved in the evaluation process. But an experiment wherein the speakers simply counted from one to twenty at a set rate of speed and wherein the listeners were able to identify the social status of a speaker with considerable accuracy, suggests that pronunciation of words, consonant articulation, vowel quality, and perhaps tonal qualities are also factors in the listener's reaction. In other experiments, the listeners were asked to make a value judgment about the type of work each speaker would be best suited for, and again there was a correlation between suggested level of employment and perceived social status. Ellis concludes that the implications of speech are recognized by all Americans, and they label the speaker as belonging to a certain social class. In short, we recognize and react to class code. The results of Ellis' experiments also suggest that the social acceptability of one's speech is a source of discrimination.

The difference between rural and urban speech is often noticeable but not of such an extent that we would want to call them dialects. However, we are on a continuum in this case, and the dividing line between "code" and "dialect" is an arbitrary one. This would not be so if we could say that one defining feature of code is that it be derivable by rules, that is, one code from another. Since a dialect shift involves a number of new elements, it would be possible to distinguish between code and dialect. However, in some languages the difference in sex codes involves sets of vocabulary items that are unrelated; one set is not derivable from the other by rules. Although most code changes can be characterized by rules, I hesitate to define code in this way.

Similarly, the diagnostic speech traits of a subculture may be viewed as either code or dialect depending on the extent of divergence from a declared norm. If that norm is the common ground shared by a number of subcultures, it is equivalent to what Bernstein (1966) has called a "restricted code" (as I understand it). The full code of a subculture Bernstein has called an "expanded code", which I am calling simply 'code'. (Perhaps the stereotypes used when quoting a drunk or telling an ethnic joke belong here as well.)[33]

Any language/culture will have a number of codes, and any individual will function in several codes simultaneously, inescapably. The codes overlap and yet retain their identity. Although most speakers of a language react to a use of code that is out of character, they may never have consciously focused on the signals that are diagnostic of any code, and so they tend to stay faithfully within their own. But skillful manipulators of a language often do figure out what is happening, at least to some extent, and are able to function in more than one code of a set (like the age set). Any exploitation of this ability will be based on the social value of the codes.

Register and code are powerful organizing factors because social values seem to be closely connected to our emotions. Carelessness in the use of Hierarchy, Cohesion, or Prominence may slow down the communication process, but carelessness in the use of register (especially) and code may result in anger and a fight. Any discourse will have both register and code. Their signals may be phonological, grammatical, or lexical; or any combination of them.

5.3 **Dialect.** For most purposes 'dialect' belongs in macrosystem G, "Language and Culture", such as when a whole discourse reflects a

---

[33] There are two further considerations that may assist us in distinguishing 'code' from 'dialect'. In general everyone in a speech community understands the codes, but not a different dialect. Receptive ability may exceed productive ability to a greater extent with respect to dialect than to code.

single dialect. But when more than one dialect occurs in a discourse there are social implications. A politician may use some of the local dialect in his speech in arder to gain rapport. When a speaker switches from one dialect to another within a discourse (or conversation), it is a deliberate choice and its significance is social. It is only in such a case that dialect contributes to Style.

5.4 **Idiolect**. By 'idiolect' I mean idiosyncratic elements in the speech of an individual that are not part of the organizing system of the language. They might be dismissed as background noise or excess baggage except that they often do serve to identify a speaker or writer. Things like idiosyncratic pronunciation, intonation, affectation, rate of delivery, characteristic vocabulary, etc., help us recognize a voice on the phone, in the dark, or around a corner. (Those aspects of voice quality that are beyond a speaker's control are not included in idiolect.) That on occasion people will try to imitate or disguise a voice indicates that it has significance, and I take it to be basically social. But the main reason I include idiolect is because it is necessary to isolate and factor out any truly idiosyncratic elements in a discourse or they will skew our inter-pretation of the rest. I feel it is wise to place this category overtly in the framework to remind the analyst to check for this sort of thing. By idiolect I do not mean personal style in the sense of an author's characteristic pattern of selection within the organizing system and lexicon of a language. In general, any element that other native speakers reject, denying that it is part of the language, should be scrutinized but not automatically deleted. Some signals, notably of register and code, may not be recognized in isolation.

5.5 There may be other factors that belong in this macrosystem. I will briefly comment upon two treatments of style not yet mentioned by way of showing how my scheme compares with theirs as well as suggesting possible further factors. In his essay on style, Nils Enkvist has the following statement:

We must also distinguish between the definition of style in general and the description of specific style categories. At first sight, the latter seem to yield readily to norm-bound definition, and every literate person is prepared to distinguish a host of norm-defining features in a number of styles. Such features may be stated in terms of metre ('heroic couplets'), time ('Elizabethan style'), place ('Yankee humour'), language, dialect, writer ('Byronic style'), or literary work ('Euphuism'), school of writers ('romantic style'), genre ('poetic style, journalese'), social situation ('Sergeant-Major of the Guards addressing recruit'), and so forth (1964:25).

His "metre" and "genre" I would consider as genre. Although I will discuss genre in connection with the next macrosystem, Strategy, I wonder if it belongs here instead. It may be that progressive subdivisions of genre shade off into register. Enkvist's "writer" and "literary work" I would handle as a characteristic pattern of selection from all the macrosystems. His "romantic style" is a combination of genre and characteristic pattern of selection, I think. His "language" and "dialect" I handle together under the macrosystem "Language and Culture". My guess is that his "Yankee humour" is a combination of genre and dialect or code. I would class his "Elizabethan style" as a combination of dialect and register. His "social situation" is a case of register. In short, my present reaction is that my framework accomodates the sorts of features that Enkvist advances here.

In her discussion of register, Ruqaiya Hasan writes:

The total set of factors correlating with the varieties of register can be listed briefly as follows:

(1) Subject-matter of discourse
(2) Situation-type for discourse
(3) Participant roles within discourse
(4) Mode of discourse
(5) Medium of discourse   (1973:272)

I judge that subject matter belongs neither to register nor to Style; I will discuss it under "content" in the next chapter. Her "situation-type" relates to the nature and purpose of a transaction. It seems to be essentially what I call 'register', although it may partake something of genre and what Halliday has called "uses of speech". They are:

Instrumental	"I want"
Regulatory	"do as I tell you"
Interactional	"me and you"
Personal	"here I come"
Heuristic	"tell me why"
Imaginative	"let's pretend"
Informative	"I've got something to tell you" (1975:37)

The choice of a given 'use' has social implications, so this may be the macrosystem where "uses of speech" should be discussed. However, I regard the uses to be a reflection of purpose, which is intimately related to Strategy. Hasan discusses "participant roles" in terms of who is communicating with whom, where there is a difference in age, sex, or some other social variable. I agree that that correlates with register. Persuasive, explanatory, and imperative are given as examples of her "mode of discourse". I see them as a combination of genre and modality (see chap. 6). As for medium (spoken versus written), I consider it to be a separate macrosystem (see chap. 7). Here again I think my framework is adequate.

6 Strategy

Strategy reflects a basic characteristic of communication and of most human behavior; it has a purpose. Conscious speech is inescapably intentional. "The speaker or writer selects the content of his communication, and also the function of that content, so as to achieve the purpose of his communication" (Beekman and Callow 1974:288). Even though the precise workings of the mind which result in a given stream of speech may be largely subconscious, they are governed by a purpose, a purpose which may itself be partly subconscious. Whether conscious or subconscious, there must be a purpose, and that purpose will determine the choices to be made. I understand Halliday to have made essentially the same point.

> *Not only does any system of linguistic features derive from some function of language, perhaps more than one, through which it can be related to situations of use, but in addition, this fact may also determine, at least in part, the form taken by that system and its exponents in the grammar (1970:361).*

What Halliday calls "uses of speech" or "models of language" (1973:9-20) seems to me to be a specification of purpose. He suggests that a child first learns to "mean" in seven ways: instrumental, regulatory, interactional, personal, heuristic, imaginative, and informative. If a person uses speech to find something out (heuristic), it is a reflection of his purpose. The total purpose that a speaker has may be a combination from among the above and/or other elements. As elements of purpose, they influence the choice of genre as well as other organizing factors yet to be discussed.

At the beginning of Part I, I stated that the macrosystems overlap and occur simultaneously while retaining a distinct identity. This is especially true of the four already discussed. Although there may be cooperation among them at various points, they are independent. One macrosystem cannot be said to control or 'use' another (on occasion they may get in each other's way so that certain combinations are impossible). The macrosystem presently under discussion, Strategy, is different from the others in that it does control or 'use' them. For any discourse, Strategy goes into the organization of its Hierarchy, Cohesion, Preminence, and Style, but I would not call them 'organizing factors'. There are several factors, not yet discussed, which seem to be more intimately or obviously related to Strategy, and I will call them the organizing factors for this macrosystem. If they seem to be a little disparate, it may be because I am using this macrosystem as something of a catchall (and yet each factor belongs here). So then, for Strategy I propose the following organizing factors: content, genre, information rate, modality, and sincerity.

6.1 **Content**. In some ways 'content' seems to be the most basic factor in Strategy. Content involves the choice of what to say and what to leave unsaid, whereas all the other factors are involved in the choice of how to say it. The specific selection of information to be encoded will be influenced by the speaker's judgment as to what knowledge his audience shares with him, the subject matter (which may involve cultural conventions) and, perhaps, by the register he decides to use, while being guided by his purpose. From a decoding perspective we are confronted with a text (spoken or written) which gives us not only the author's choice of what to say but also of how to say it, all intertwined. If we call his choice of what to say (i.e., the result of that choice) the referential meaning, we must still distinguish and factor out the nuances supplied by other factors, notably Prominence and Style. Just how referential meaning works is an important question, one which I am not prepared to answer. I think, however, that the validity and usefulness of the framework I am proposing does not depend upon an answer to that question.

What does concern me, though, is the relationship of implied or understood information to content. Where the speaker refrains from overtly stating something because he is sure that his audience is aware of it and will supply it in the decoding process, should we not say that such information is part of the content? The speaker is counting on his hearers to supply that information, and if they fail to do so, their understanding of his communication will be impaired. I would like to define content as that which the encoder expects the decoder to reconstruct, stimulated by the text. And yet, since Strategy comes in precisely in deciding how much to state overtly, content, as an expression of Strategy, must be limited to that which is overtly stated. But the abstraction (or 'total meaning') evoked by a discourse will be considerably more than content as just defined; it will include implied or understood information.

Still, what is not said may be more important to a speaker's purpose than what is. Several years ago I heard Richard Elkins tell of an experience while living among the Manobo (Philippines). He was sitting conversing with the chief of the village when a man arrived from a distant area. The chief asked how things were going, and they talked back and forth for a while. Suddenly the chief became agitated and cried out, "My son is dead, my son is dead!" Elkins was quite taken aback; he speaks the language fairly well and thought he had understood what was said, and had caught no mention either of the chief's son or of death. At an opportune moment he asked what had happened and learned that the man had come specifically to bring the chief the bad news. He did so using euphemisms and hints. Evidently in that culture bad news is not stated overtly. (In our own culture politicians seem to have a similar skill.) In the illustration above should we not say that the essential content of the man's communication was the death of the chief's son? But it was not overtly stated.

I think Andrew Ortony may be pointing us toward a solution in his article, "Why Metaphors are Necessary and Not Just Nice" (1975). Presumably it will be generally agreed that content must not be limited to the denotation of the several words or lexemes in a text. The whole is greater than the sum of its parts. Once in a context, a lexeme has a referential meaning which will not be identical with its denotation. Ortony reminds us that what we experience as conscious perceivers is continuous, not in discrete packets. He notes further:

> The continuity of experience is not purely a question of temporal flow. It has ramifications for memory. Memory for what has been perceived incorporates some of this continuity. It has long been acknowledged by philosophers and more recently by psychologists and linguists that words do not have distinct, sharply delineated meanings. Wittgenstein in the "Investigations" expounds at length on this problem with respect to the single word "game." A recent study by the linguist Labov (1973) demonstrates the fuzziness of the word "cup" and a few enlightened cognitive psychologists are currently investigating what they call "semantic flexibility." A moment's thought about a paradigmatic example of reference reveals that the range of applicability of a word is fuzzy. While there is fairly universal agreement as to what is a prototypical red, it is obvious that its limits are indeterminate . . . .
>
> The purpose of considering this kind of continuity for word meanings is to suggest that words have to be sufficiently flexible to cover the range of possible applications. It is the objects, events and experiences that continuously vary: words have to follow suit <u>when they are used</u>. Words partition experiences but the experiences they partition are not identical: consequently words have to be sufficiently flexible to enable the most varied members of the set partitioned to be referenced by them. If there is any sense in maintaining that words have fixed meanings it can only be that independent of context they relate to their prototypical non-linguistic counterparts. The continuity of experience, therefore, is not just a temporal continuity: it is, as it were, a continuity in "referential" space and it is the total continuity of

*experience which at once underlies and necessitates the use of
metaphor in linguistic communication. Language and logic are discrete
symbol systems. Thus, the task we have to perform in communication
is to convey what is usually some kind of continuum by using discrete
symbols. It would not be surprising if a discrete symbol system were
incapable of literally capturing every conceivable aspect of an object,
event or experience that one might wish to describe. A thesis of this
paper is that this deficiency is filled by metaphor (Ortony 1975:46).*

I take it that content and reference must account for metaphor (as
well as other figures of speech). The discreteness of reference may fall
anywhere on a continuum from strictly literal to wildly metaphorical.
Once we grant that reference must be discussed in terms of such a
continuum, it follows that content must follow suit.

Ortony presents his view of metaphor in terms of three theses: the
compactness thesis, the inexpressibility thesis, and the vividness thesis.
He discusses "compactness" in terms of particularization by which he
means the process of filling out the mental picture evoked by a
statement; the picture is filled out on the basis of the decoder's own
knowledge and experience.

*The point and virtue of particularization is that it enables language
comprehension to take place without the need for the message to
explicitly spell out all the details. Even if this were possible it would be
too boring and time consuming for either or both the speaker or hearer
in the normal course of events. But, particularization serves an even
more important function—it is the language comprehender's digital-
to-analog converter; it takes him nearer to the continuous mode of
perceived experience by taking him further away from the discrete
mode of linguistic symbols. What metaphor does is to allow large
"chunks" to be converted or transferred; metaphor constrains and
directs particularization (Ortony 1975:47).*

By way of illustration he discusses the example, "He dived into the
icy water like a <u>fearless warrior</u>", and sums it up like this:

> *. . . what has been said in a word is something like "He dived into the icy water bravely, strongly, fearlessly, aggressively, in a determined manner, etc., being muscular, large and so on." This "chunk" of unspecified features or characteristics is what is transferred, all parceled up in the two words "fearless warrior" (1975:48).*

The metaphor is more concise and effective than a detailed list of characteristics would be, but it leaves the characteristics unspecified. It helps the decoder fill out the mental picture, but no two decoders will fill it out in quite the same way.

I believe Ortony's treatment of metaphor furnishes an analogy for handling any form of communication that is not overtly stated. Particularization is the mechanism involved in allusions (cultural, historical, experiential), literary reference (high or low, like TV commercials), implied and 'understood' information. In each case the encoder banks on a reservoir of knowledge and experience shared by the decoder. Still, there must be some overt signal to activate the particularization process. Although I feel that reference must allow for allusions, implications, and metaphors, I would insist that nothing may be affirmed about the discourse structure of a given text which cannot be tied to some signal in that text. I would also say that no two surface forms that are deliberately different in any way can represent identical abstractions. Gleason seems to be of a similar opinion (1977:492); as is Grimes: "Every distinction in the system corresponds to a surface distinction somewhere, though not necessarily in all its possible combinations" (1975:352).

Since I have just included allusions, implications, and metaphors in 'reference', I can not equate content (as an expression of Strategy) with it. But by dividing reference into overt and covert, I believe content may be equated with overt reference.

6.2 **Genre**. Along with deciding what to say, a speaker must decide how to say it. Perhaps the first choice to be made in that connection is that of genre, unless it be that of Medium (see sect. 7.1). Before discussing genre I wish to distinguish it from discourse type. 'Type' designates an etic distinction, one of a roster that we would expect to be reflected in any language—a putative universal. 'Genre' designates an emic distinction, one that is language specific. A given genre may include a mixture of discourse types.[34] The genre rosters of two languages may very well contain several that are very similar (or even identical?), but presumably the two rosters will not be identical. For purposes of discussion, type logically precedes genre, so it will be considered first.

6.2.1 Discourse Type. As a result of two workshops in the Philippines (Sept. 1967 to May 1968) involving twenty-five languages and dialects, Longacre posited a taxonomy of four basic prose types: narrative, procedural, expository, and hortatory. They were defined by two parameters: ±sequence in time and ±projected time (Longacre 1968). (He also mentioned three other types—dramatic, activity, and epistolary—that did not fit the scheme.)

More recently Longacre has attempted to distinguish between "deep structure genre" and "surface structure genre", using different parameters and characterizations for the two schemes (1976a:200-02). At that point he defined his terms as follows: "I will use *genre* to indicate a broad and rough grained taxonomy of discourse, whether in the deep or in the surface structure. *Type* when used will correspond to specific surface structure classification in a finer grained taxonomy" (Longacre 1976a:198). I am not convinced of the validity of his distinction between deep and surface genre, unless his deep genre is to be viewed as an etic roster from which each language makes its own

---

[34] Gleason (personal communication) has defined genre as a conventional mixture of discourse types. He would say, for instance, that folktale and short story are distinct genres; a folktale is a combination of narrative plus dialogue, while a short story is a combination of narrative plus dialogue plus description (narrative, dialogue, and description are here taken to be types).

selection. From a decoding perspective we need only one roster of types with their characterizations.

Longacre is presently suggesting a system having two primary parameters (±chronological linkage and ±agent-orientation) and two secondary parameters (±projected time and ±tension) thereby allowing for sixteen discourse types (see Forster 1977). The idea of primary and secondary parameters may be viewed as the beginning of a "system" *à la* Halliday. I would suggest that such a system is the right device for organizing both discourse type and genre. Rather than proliferating binary parameters, the genres of each language might better be plotted on a system according to the relationships that they exhibit and to the degree of delicacy that seems warranted. There would be no pressure to create a symmetry. Deibler's analysis of Gahuku genre (see fig. 7) would fit very nicely on such a system.

Different discourse types will predictably have different confi-gurations or patterns of selection from the several macrosystems. Different selections will be central versus peripheral. In narrative we may expect temporal relationships to be central and others peripheral; in description it will be special relationships; while in exposition it will be logical relationships. What Grimes calls "kinds of information" (see sect. 2.3) will be used differently according to type. As he states it,

> *Different kinds of discourse seem to select different kinds of information around which to organize the rest. Narratives and procedures, as Longacre has pointed out (1968), take the time oriented parts of the material as their backbone and hang identifications and explanations on as peripheral elements. Explanations and exhortations, on the other hand, put the covariance relationship in the center of things and subordinate events to it. Complex combinations of these and other relationships can make the organizing principle vary from one part of a text to another (Grimes 1975:257).*

A given discourse may contain a mixture of types, as when a hortatory discourse contains a narrative (usually to illustrate a point) or a poem. (One result of such a mixture will be spans of discourse type which will be relevant to Hierarchy.) Although, as already suggested, a given genre may be characterized as a specified mixture of discourse types, the analysis of a text in a given genre must include a distinguishing of the components and any variation in type that they represent.

6.2.2 Discourse Genre. Each 'genre' will have a diagnostic set of characteristics which distinguish it from the others. By way of specific illustration I give a chart showing genre characteristics in Gahuku (Papua New Guinea) discourse (Fig. 7). The chart is based on Longacre's discussion (1972:150-51) which is based on an unpublished description done by Ellis Deibler ("Discourse structure in Gahuku"). I have entered on the chart only the values that Longacre specifically stated; the blank squares mean that nothing was said, but it may be assumed that the incidence there is significantly lower than "very high". I have used an asterisk to mark the characteristics that Longacre considers to be diagnostic. Except for rows 1 and 3, "incidence of" should be read with each of the features. (For our present purpose a precise understanding of the features is not necessary.)

I take it that we can posit distinct diagnostic sets for the last five genres at least. The two narrative genres are distinct from all the others but are distinguished from each other only by "topical clause". Incidentally, the list of features on the chart is suggestive of the sorts of things that one should consider in attempting to characterize different genres. Longacre mentions a number of further features relevant to other languages (1972:152-54). Different languages may not necessarily have identical rosters of genre, nor will the diagnostic set of characteristics attaching to a given genre, say procedural, necessarily be the same in different languages.

A glance at figure 7 makes clear that the choice of a genre has a controlling or restricting effect upon the speaker's use of grammatical (and probably lexical and phonological) features. Thus, in Gahuku the choice of the "story" genre means that the speaker may not use conditional and contrast sentences, future tense, nor imperative mode. In Longacre's words,

> It is obvious that choice of discourse types is legislative as to many features of the discourse itself. The varied taxonomic features used to distinguish one discourse type from another may be considered to be features of the discourse dictated by choice of that type. It is of interest to note here, however, how differing parts of a discourse influence in a delicate way the choice of surface structure features (1972:155).

	NARRATIVE		PROCE-DURAL	DISCRIP-TIVE	EXPOSITORY		
	general	story			general	prayer	hortatory
Number of clauses per sentence	very high	very high	med	low	low	med	low
temporal clauses and sentences	very high	very high	high				
overall variety of final and medial clauses					*very high		
conditional and contrast sentences	very low	nil				nil	*very high
existential clause	very low	very low	nil	*very high	very low	nil	very low
phrasal sentence	very low	very low	nil	*very high	very low	nil	very low

topical clause		very high					
past tense	very high	very high					nil
habituative aspect			*very high				
future tense		nil	*very high			nil	
imperative	nil	nil	nil	nil	nil	very high	very high
equivalent action clauses and purpose	low	low	low	low	low	*high	low

Figure 7. Genre characteristics in Gahuku discourse

6.2.3 Except where a speaker/writer departs from the norm for some reason, there will be a predictable correlation between purpose and genre, so that from the genre of a text it should be possible to guess at the author's general purpose: to inform, to exhort, to entertain, etc. (Actually, the remark above is just as appropriate to discourse type as it is to genre, but the choice of genre is clearly a reflection of author purpose as is the particular mixture and arrangement of types that a discourse embodies, so I cannot limit this discussion to either genre or type.) Problems in analysis may well result, however, when the speaker departs from the normal correlation of purpose with genre.

Longacre discusses possible reasons for such a departure.

The deep structure motive may be somewhat disguised by resort to a surface structure of radically different form. Apparently the disguising of the underlying motive can make the presentation all the more effective. Thus, in that people do not like to be urged to change their conduct, presenting this hortatory material as a narrative or a drama may make it easier for them to accept it. Likewise, expository material

*may be livened up by being cast into a narrative or dramatic form.
And, as we have seen, narrative material may achieve poignancy by
being cast into procedural form and procedural material may attain a
certain concreteness and authority by casting it into narrative form
(1976a:208-09).*

I suspect that this sort of thing may itself be quite predictable when
the normal correlation conflicts with a social factor, such as difference
in age or rank. Someone of inferior age or rank finding it necessary to
exhort a superior will almost certainly take refuge in some other genre
than hortatory. In a more general way, the blurring of genre distinctives
may have something to do with rapport. For instance, the avoidance of
second person forms in hortatory discourse will tend to soften the
impact on the hearer. In such a case the genre will presumably still be
recognizable from its other diagnostic features. Or, a speaker/writer
may depart from the norm just for variety's sake, or to disguise (or seem
to disguise) his real motive.

The point I am trying to make in this section is simply that the
correlation between genre and author purpose will not always be
straightforward. When it is not it will be marked. As with marked
procedures at other levels and in other systems, to the extent that
decoders recognize the markedness and can discern the encoder's
purpose, the signals to which they are reacting will be part of the
discourse system.

6.3 **Information Rate**. "The speaker, in addition to having to decide
on the content of what he is talking about and how it is to be organized,
decides also how much of it he thinks his hearer can take in at one time"
(Grimes 1975:274). Two factors enter into 'information rate': the actual
speed of delivery (words per minute) and the ratio of 'given' (and 'zero')
to new information. The first factor is so obvious as to require little
discussion. Decoding takes time, and a sensitive speaker will monitor
the feedback from his audience to make sure he is not talking too fast
for them, unless he is being manipulative. A speaker wishing to

stampede others into some course of action or to stifle opposition may attempt to confuse them by talking so fast that they are unable to evaluate what is being said.

The more crucial factor is the ratio of given information to new. Much of my thinking on this subject I owe to Halliday (1967:199ff.) and Grimes (1975, chap. 19). The ratio may range from nearly zero given in telegraphic style to nearly zero new in ritualistic utterances. Happily, telegrams are usually short and the recipient has leisure to decode it. A ritualistic utterance may be long and rattled off at a great rate without taxing the decoder. More normal types of communication will fall somewhere in the middle.

Nida and Taber suggest that most languages seem to average 50 percent redundancy rate at the lexical level; that is, the average ratio of given to new would be around fifty/fifty. They go on to state, "From all the evidence we have, it is also assumed that most languages have approximately the same rate of flow of information for corresponding types of style and levels of usage" (Nida and Taber 1969:163). I would agree that in any given language there will be a correlation of some sort between register (their "levels of usage"?) and information rate, and so also for genre (their "types of style"?). I seriously doubt, however, that "approximately the same rate of flow" will necessarily obtain between languages.

Zapotec (Mexico) evidently has a penchant for doublets, parallelisms, and reduplication that pervade the language, so that any English text rendered in good Zapotec will come out appreciably longer on that account (Ruegsegger 1966).[35] Mention has already been made of some

---

[35] I was with Ruegsegger in Mexico during the summer of 1966 and gained the clear impression that the converse would not be true. That is, a Zapotec text rendered in good English will not come out longer (of course, a literal translation of all the doublets would result in a version as long as or longer than the original, but it would not be "good English"). I have also had personal contact with Stout and Thomson in

languages that use what Grimes calls "overlays" and "linkage". The use of these devices tends to slow down the information rate. Kayapó (Brazil) has a linkage pattern that involves whole paragraphs—a narrative paragraph will be followed by a linking paragraph that is almost an exact repetition of it. An English narrative rendered in Kayapó would come out appreciably longer than the original.

Mamaindé (Brazil) is extreme with reference to the normal rate of information introduction; it is by far the slowest that has come to my attention. As Peter Kingston explains it, "On average, it takes between one and two clauses to convey every single item of information. For example on average, it would take about three clauses to convey the information, *the man beat the dog*, since there are three items of information: the man, beat, the dog" (1973:13). The extreme degree of repetition may be clearly seen in the following extract from a recorded Mamaindé discourse.

> *I am not going to see the Nagarottu.*
> *As they are wicked, I am not going.*
> *As they are wicked, I am not going.*
> *The Nagarottu are wicked.*
> *As they are wicked, I am not going.*
> *I am staying here.*
> *I am staying here, in my village.*
> *They are wicked.*
> *The Nagarottu are wicked.*
> *As they are wicked, I am angry.*
> *As they are wicked, I am angry.*
> *I am not wicked.*
> *Just the Nagarottu are wicked (Kingston 1973:15).*

I take it that the normal rate of flow of information in Mamaindé is significantly slower (less) than it is in English.

Brazil and gained the impression that the converse would not be true for Kayapó either.

Two other factors impinge on information rate. One is the use of 'fillers', words that are empty, that convey zero information. The use of fillers evidently gives the decoder more time to process the information he is receiving. Another is the density or specific semantic gravity of the new information. In "John napped" versus "John took a nap", "napped" and "took a nap" are synonymous, but "napped" has a greater density—the same semantic content is conveyed by a shorter signal. The choice of synonyms with greater density will tend to speed up the information rate, and vice versa.[36]

The way in which new (or conversely, given) information is signaled will vary from language to language and quite possibly between genres within one language. In English new information is partly signaled by intonation and stress. In Oksapmin (Papua New Guinea) verb inflection is also used. In languages that use overlays, like Saramaccan (Surinam) and Borôro (Brazil), material that is not in an overlay will presumably be new. In Tucano (Colombia), new information may be primary or secondary, and these two kinds of new information are characteristically encoded in different sentence types, while given information is characteristically encoded in yet others (Welch 1977).

In some languages (if not all) information is packaged into "units" (Halliday) or "blocks" (Grimes), which have a "focus" (Halliday) or "center" (Grimes). Such blocks are important for the manipulation of

---

[36] It can be argued that the example I used to illustrate density is more appropriate to register. It does illustrate register, but I believe it also serves for density; it is normal for a given signal to function in more than one macrosystem simultaneously. If it could be shown that density is controlled by register, that it has no independent existence, then it would not belong under Strategy.

For a helpful discussion of how to go about discovering the conventions for signaling given and new information in some language, I refer the reader to K. Callow (1974, chap. 5). Her treatment of "patterns of expected information" and the differences between languages as to what kinds of information are obligatory suggests an avenue of investigation that merits more attention. Such considerations will almost certainly prove to be relevant to information rate.

information rate. In English the normal or unmarked correlation is one information block to a clause, but a clause may be divided into two or more blocks, producing a different effect. Furthermore, in English short information blocks usually correlate with a high rate of information injection and long blocks with a low ratio of new information. Grimes has an entertaining discussion of two ways in which this correlation can be manipulated. "The first is the practice of some radio and television newscasters to speak in rather large, well organized information blocks even when they are communicating new information at a high rate" (1975:275). He suggests that the audience gratefully receives the implied fiction that they are already well informed about the news items. "The other exception is in the opposite direction. As is well known, politicians tend to speak in very short information blocks" (Grimes 1975:276). Here he suggests that the opposite fiction operates, the implication that a great deal of new and important information is being imparted.

So then, the way an encoder blocks off information and the rate at which he injects new information are clearly reflections of the strategy he adopts to achieve his purpose.[37]

6.4 **Modality**. I follow Grimes (1975, chap. 15) in using 'modality' as a cover term for "mood" and some other things. My understanding of the term is similar to Halliday's. "Modality is a form of participation by the speaker in the speech event. Through modality, the speaker associates with the thesis an indication of its status and validity in his own judgment; he intrudes, and takes up a position" (Halliday 1970:335). He also speaks of modality in terms of "the speaker's

---

[37] Before taking leave of information rate, perhaps mention should be made of Chafe's suggestion that something "given" can lose that status if it is not mentioned for a while (1974). As an expression of Strategy an encoder may treat given information as though it were new, but it will be a marked procedure and the real status of the given information will remain unchanged. I do not agree with Chafe's suggestion.

assessment of probability and predictability" (1970:349). In short, modality has to do with the attitude adopted by the encoder.

The classical distinction between indicative, subjunctive, and optative may be interpreted in terms of degree of certainty which the speaker/writer is claiming for what is said. In some languages one is obliged to specify whether his statement is based on experience, hearsay, or guesswork. Inga (Colombia) has a series of clitics that signal "action witnessed-affirmative", "action witnessed-negative", "action reported to the speaker", "action deduced by the speaker as having probably occurred", and "action speculated as possible by the speaker" respectively (Levinsohn 1975:14). An unmarked Inga sentence need not have any such clitic, which gives an honest encoder the option of not specifying degree of certainty; a dishonest encoder has the further option of employing a clitic falsely. Cogui (Colombia) is reported to offer a narrator some twenty ways of evaluating the material he is presenting, and he must use one of them (Forster 1977:13).

The choice between "I want . . ." and "I would like . . ." is a strategic one. The decision to be polite or rude, pleasant or belligerent, complimentary or derogatory, positive or negative, conciliatory or arrogant is a question of Strategy. I would include here some of the things Hymes designates as "key" (1972), such as mock versus serious, irony, and sarcasm.

Closely related to the considerations in the previous paragraph is the matter of the encoder's emotional involvement in his discourse. Evidently a twin set of paradigms exists for Kham (Nepal) clauses such that one function of one of the sets is to signal that the speaker is personally involved (Watters 1978). In 3rd person narrative discourse in Salt-Yui (Papua New Guinea), the degree of emotional involvement of the narrator dictates the choice of mode: indicative, declarative, or assertive (Longacre 1972:156). The phenomenon that literary critics refer to as the "author's voice" would appear to be an indication of the emotional involvement of the encoder. The relative degree of affective usage probably belongs here as well.

Another factor is the assignment of communication roles, the decision to state, question, or command. In a normal or unmarked case, the decision will be reflected in the use of a declarative, interrogative, or imperative form, respectively. But it is possible (in English anyway) to make a statement while using an interrogative or imperative form, and so on. Pike and Pike offer a chart and examples of the possibilities (1977:49-50). Such choices are also a reflection of Strategy.

Degree of "transitivity" (cf. Halliday 1967:34ff.) is also a factor. If a child drops a glass of milk on a cement floor, his first response to a parental "What happened?" may well be "The glass broke". If pressed for more detail, the response will likely be "It slipped from my fingers and broke". On the third try he might get around to saying "I dropped it". The child's choices are clearly strategic.

Another factor is "viewpoint". "The rules for proper management of the speaker's picture of what is inside the heads of the persons, real or fictitious, about whom he is talking, are collectively known as viewpoint" (Grimes 1975:319). Grimes speaks of an "omniscient" viewpoint, wherein the speaker has access to the mental processes of all the participants in the discourse; a "first person" viewpoint, wherein the speaker is one of the participants and has access to his own mental processes; a "third person subjective" viewpoint, wherein the speaker is not a participant but has access to the mental processes of one participant; and a "third person objective" viewpoint, wherein the speaker has access to no one's mental processes. The choice of viewpoint is an element of Strategy.

Very closely related to viewpoint is the assigning of attitudes to speaker, audience, and culture. By virtue of the thoughts, words, and actions ascribed to participants, clear attitude portraits can be drawn. In this way the encoder may seek to propogate his own interpretation or evaluation of the subject matter in hand.[38]

6.5 **Sincerity**. By 'sincerity' I simply mean whether the encoder is being straightforward, or misleading. By 'straightforward' I mean using the several resources of the language according to their accepted value in the speech community. By 'misleading' I mean a departure from such accepted value (it is possible to mislead inadvertently, of course, but I am focusing on deliberate choice). I do not mean the difference between marked and unmarked forms—marked forms have an accepted value. Nor do I consider misleading to be equivalent to the term manipulative as I have used it above; any misleading usage will be manipulative, but not necessarily vice versa. The decision to mislead is clearly a matter of Strategy.

6.6 The First Four Macrosystems. As noted at the beginning of the discussion of Strategy, the use made of the factors that make up the first four macrosystems must reflect, in some sense, the global strategy of the encoder. Still, I feel that there is a difference in degree between them and the five organizing factors just discussed. But among the first four macrosystems, some factors seem more obviously related to strategy than others, and they deserve mention here. The whole Prominence macrosystem seems to me to be more ovbiously related to Strategy than the other three macrosystems. The decision of what to place on the theme line, what to place in focus, and what to emphasize is an important expression of the encoder's strategy. The choice of register and the manipulative use of code and dialect are also obvious

---

[38] In Subanon (Philippines) there is a fairly complicated taxonomy of terms for various kinds of skin disease, and the terms form a system reflecting several levels on a generic-specific continuum (Frake 1961). Such disease is an important factor in a number of social contexts so that an encoder needs to know just what level of generality to use when making a reference to it. In such a culture, level of generality could be used manipulatively and thus be a reflection of Strategy. I am not sure how to classify it unless it be under modality, which is already something of a catchall.

expressions of an encoder's strategy. Such a relationship does not vitiate the separate identity of the Style and Prominence macrosystems.

6.7 This concludes my discussion of Strategy, and therefore of the five macrosystems that combine to define the discourse system of a language, and to dictate the discourse structure of a text. As stated at the outset, I regard the systems as being simultaneous and overlapping. They interact but are distinct. From a decoding point of view the several systems are simultaneously present (that is, the results of their operation), but from an encoding point of view Strategy is logically prior to the other four. Among the organizing factors that signal Strategy, content (the choice of what to say) is primary and genre is probably next (it imposes some constraints on the signaling of other factors). There are several other considerations that while not contributing to discourse system as such, represent prior constraints upon the factors that contribute to that system. For that reason they must be included in a framework for discourse analysis. I now turn to a discussion of these considerations.

7 Medium, Language, and Culture

7.1 **Medium**. I am here primarily concerned with only two media—spoken and written. To the extent that there is a sign language that can be said to be really English, as opposed to American Sign (Amislan), sign is a third medium for English. Mazatec (Mexico) whistle speech is another example of medium. Apparently it has no known lexical limitations. It is usually used in situations where the subject matter is highly predictable, but not necessarily so (Cowan 1948). I gather from Carrington (1969) and Herzog (1945) that in a number of African languages drum talk is yet another example of medium.

As already hinted, the choice of medium is really an expression of one's strategy, but I have separated "Medium" from "Strategy" because it is prior to the other choices. It seems to me that up to a point there is a progression of control or a logical order in which factors apply. It begins at the bottom of my framework outline and works up. Thus, the choice of language limits or controls all the other choices. Then the choice of medium limits the remainder, and then Strategy. I draw the line between Strategy and Medium because when a decoder sets out to analyze a discourse, the language and medium are already known, but the rest of the encoder's strategy is not.

It is generally agreed, I suppose, that languages possessing many years of written tradition have recognized conventions that distinguish oral medium from written medium. But is such a situation the result of necessity, or of chance? I would agree with Gleason (1965:36) that the difference is necessary. There will be a difference in distribution and kind of redundancy between media. A written medium must compensate for the loss of gestures, facial expressions, intonation, change in tempo, force, and voice quality.

Once while attempting to transcribe a recorded Apurinã (Brazil) text, I had a continuing hassle with the native speaker who was helping me. Accepting the primacy of the spoken medium and having been taught that "the informant is always right", I wanted an exact transcription, but time and again the one helping me would simply refuse to allow it; although still illiterate, he insisted on editing the text (even though it was someone else's—his father-in-law's, in fact).

Field workers of the Summer Institute of Linguistics, because they start with an unwritten language, reduce it to writing and teach the people to read it, have been able to observe directly the birth of a written medium. Martha Duff describes contrastive features of written and oral texts in Amuesha (Peru), a recently literate tribe.

> *A characteristic feature of the written text is that it shows clearer organization than the oral text. This is because the author has had time to plan the development of the story which results in the lack of stutters, hesitation words, anacoluthons, and abnormal ordering of words and sentences due to afterthoughts (1973:2).*

The improved organization extends to the whole text—a written story will have an ample setting (introduction), whereas an oral story tends to have little or none. "In the written text, paragraph breaks are consistently, overtly marked with some temporal word . . ." (1973:3)—their use is not consistent in oral text (where intonation and pause signal the break). "On the sentence level, one of the outstanding differences between the oral text and the written text is the use of relationals between clauses; in the written and edited texts, some overt means is used to show the particular relationship between the two clauses" (1973:4)—juxtaposition and intonation serve in oral texts. In written dialogue each change of speaker must be overtly stated, whereas in an oral recounting of a dialogue, a change in voice quality to impersonate the several speakers is sufficient. There is a general tendency to greater explicitness in written text in contrast with oral. In the "Build Up" paragraph in an Amuesha story, the oral form "is characterized by sentences in which the main verb of one sentence is repeated as a dependent verb in the following sentence, . . . But in the written text the main verb is never repeated" (1973:6). I take it that the last feature mentioned bespeaks an advantage that a written medium offers: the possibility of review. I should mention that the literary style described above was not invented or imposed by Duff; it was developed by the newly literate Amueshas themselves.

The point of this discussion is to affirm the probability that there will be a describable difference between the spoken and the written media in any language. For purposes of discourse analysis, any features that are simply a consequence of the medium in which the discourse is presented should be factored out first before attempting to set out the discourse structure.

7.2 **Language.** Anyone who has attempted to translate a piece of literature of any complexity from one language to another will know what this section is about. No two languages are identical in phonology, morphology, or lexicon, and each of these elements will impose some constraints upon a discourse. Account should be taken of such constraints before proceeding to the analysis of a discourse.

I characterize a language in terms of phonology, morphology, and lexicon. I offer the chart in figure 8 as a basis for my discussion of this characterization.[39]

---

[39] As best I can sort it out, the essential ingredients of the chart come from three sources. My basic trimodal and hierarchical orientation I owe to Pike. Gleason's insistence upon a distinction between system and structure is reflected in my *language specific* versus *discourse specific*. It was Beekman and Callow who convinced me that the semantic hierarchy is universal.

	Phonology	Morphology	Semology
Universal	(none)	(none)	semantic hierarchy
Language specific	phonological hierarchy (phonology)	grammatical hierarchy (morphology)	lexicon (no semology)
Discourse specific	phonological structure	grammatical (constituent) structure	propositional (logical) structure

Figure 8

While I say that there is no universal phonology or morphology, I do not deny the existence of certain principles that underlie the phonologies or morphologies of all languages; but I do not see them as comprising characterizable systems.[40] The semantic hierarchy was described in section 2.2.1—it is completely abstract, a theoretical construct. So far as I can see, it is the only characterizable system that is universal, underlying all languages equally.

Coming now to the "language specific" row, I suppose all theoretical camps will agree that each language has a characterizable phonology and morphology (however they may be labeled). I discussed them in section 2.1.1.1. By 'lexicon' I mean the roster of lexemes (including idioms) at the disposal of the speakers of a given language. The lexemes are not hierarchically arranged. There will be varying degrees of semantic relationship between/among lexemes, and some will fall on a generic-specific continuum, but there is no organization analogous to phonology and morphology. It will be observed that at this point I part

---

[40] I mean something more than just to allow formal universals (principles of organization) but disallow substantive universals (specific features)—the crucial concept here is *characterizable system*, irrespective of the status of formal or substantive universals.

company with those tagmemicists who are still looking for a third language-specific hierarchy, with those (like Halliday, Beekman, and Callow) who fuse lexicon with grammar, and with those who feel there is language specific semology. So then, for the purposes of section 7.2, I will say that a specific language is characterized by its phonology, grammar, and lexicon.

Much confusion can be avoided by maintaining a clear distinction between that which is language specific and that which is discourse or text specific—I reserve the term 'structure' for the latter. It is possible to extract and set out the phonological structure of a discourse, should one wish to, and also its constituent structure. (I believe the present approach offers a better way.) Similarly it is possible to extract the propositional structure of a text or discourse. It may be displayed by means of an appropriate calculus or by restating the text in kernel sentences, making all roles and relations explicit.[41] The propositional structure of a text is a specific and selective combination of the lexicon of the language involved and the semantic hierarchy. The propositional structure of a text will be just a part of its discourse structure. The discourse structure is the result of the interplay among all the factors included in my framework.

7.3 **Dialect.** Except where it is used manipulatively, as discussed in section 5.3, 'dialect' will be indistinguishable from 'language' for the purpose of analyzing a single given monologue discourse, since any expression of a language must inescapably be in one of its dialects. In a dialogue between speakers representing different dialects there will be dialect-specific features, distinct from the language-specific features, to be taken into account. Similarly, in going from one discourse to another,

---

[41] It should be noted that any such display is merely an attempt to approximate the abstraction represented by the text. It is impossible to actually achieve the abstraction by that means since any form used to express an abstraction imposes certain limitations upon it.

an analyst should be alert to distinguish and factor out any dialect-specific features. Dialect may be synchronic or diachronic—in switching from Chaucer to Shakespeare, for example, an analyst should make allowance for the diachronic dialect shift.

7.4 **Culture**. Although 'culture' impinges directly upon the discourse system, as discussed in sections 5.1 and 5.2 primarily, there are also cultural constraints that will not be a part of the discourse structure of a text, but which nonetheless limit the form such a text may take. The taboo systems in many African languages come readily to mind. In such languages certain circumlocutions are not really a reflection of strategic choice on the part of the encoder; they are imposed by the culture. (Well, one could violate the taboo and take the consequences, I suppose, but that would not be a normal option.) An attempt to discuss anything that lies outside the range of experience of a culture encounters special constraints. The struggle to convey a basic content takes precedence over the embellishments that might otherwise be present: the heavy load of foreign (as distinct from new) information will heavily restrict the viable encoding options. In brief, there may be restraints imposed by culture which should be recognized before proceeding to the analysis of a discourse.

7.5 **Situation**. I have already wrestled with the implications of 'situation' with reference to discourse analysis and discourse system (sects. 3.2.3, 3.5, and 6.1). I have no illustrations to offer in support of a claim that situation imposes prior constraints upon a discourse in a manner analogous to culture, language, and medium, but it seems to me to be a reasonable supposition, and the advent of an illustration would not surprise me. For the moment I will content myself with suggesting the possibility.

7.6 This concludes the presentation and discussion of my framework for discourse analysis. In the process I have offered a definition of discourse system, a characterization of language, and a clear distinction between discourse structure and propositional structure. I now proceed to apply my framework to a linguistic corpus by way of illustrating how and to what extent it may work. I will use the Greek text of Paul's letter to the Colossians.

PART II:
THE APPLICATION

INTRODUCTION TO PART II

The corpus I have chosen for the application is the Greek text of Paul's letter to the Colossians. My choice is based on the following considerations. As stated in the Introduction, a basic aim of this treatise is to devise a framework adequate for the analysis of expository discourse. Colossians is an expository discourse of sufficient length and complexity to provide a good test for my framework. My concern on this occasion is exclusively with discourse analysis, and what follows is in the nature of a linguistic exercise only. In consequence, I will not address any nondiscourse types of problems that may be thought to attach to the corpus I have chosen. Colossians falls within the area of my interest and expertise. Further, I hope that this discussion will be read by many of my colleagues in the Summer Institute of Linguistics, and its relevance and usefulness to them will be enhanced by the use of such a corpus.

For the purposes of the following exercise, I am assuming the integrity of the epistle. I follow the text in referring to the author as Paul. I am using my own edition of the Greek Text of the New Testament.

My procedure will be to take the macrosystems one at a time, plus the organizing factors within them, and try to trace their presence in the text and describe their contribution to its discourse structure.

ΠΡΟΣ ΚΟΛΟΣΣΑΕΙΣ

1 Παῦλος, ἀπόστολος Ἰησοῦ Χριστοῦ διὰ θελήματος Θεοῦ, καὶ Τιμόθεος ὁ ἀδελφός, **2** τοῖς ἐν Κολοσσαῖς ἁγίοις καὶ πιστοῖς ἀδελφοῖς ἐν Χριστῷ: χάρις ὑμῖν καὶ εἰρήνη ἀπὸ Θεοῦ Πατρὸς ἡμῶν καὶ Κυρίου Ἰησοῦ Χριστοῦ.

3 Εὐχαριστοῦμεν τῷ Θεῷ καὶ Πατρὶ τοῦ Κυρίου ἡμῶν Ἰησοῦ Χριστοῦ πάντοτε περὶ ὑμῶν προσευχόμενοι **4** (ἀκούσαντες τὴν πίστιν ὑμῶν ἐν Χριστῷ Ἰησοῦ καὶ τὴν ἀγάπην τὴν εἰς πάντας τοὺς ἁγίους), **5** διὰ τὴν ἐλπίδα τὴν ἀποκειμένην ὑμῖν ἐν τοῖς οὐρανοῖς, ἣν προηκούσατε ἐν τῷ λόγῳ τῆς ἀληθείας **6** (τοῦ εὐαγγελίου τοῦ παρόντος εἰς ὑμᾶς καθὼς καὶ ἐν παντὶ τῷ κόσμῳ, καὶ ἔστιν καρποφορούμενον καὶ αὐξανόμενον καθὼς καὶ ἐν ὑμῖν, ἀφ᾽ ἧς ἡμέρας ἠκούσατε καὶ ἐπέγνωτε τὴν χάριν τοῦ Θεοῦ ἐν ἀληθείᾳ), **7** καθὼς καὶ ἐμάθετε ἀπὸ Ἐπαφρᾶ, τοῦ ἀγαπητοῦ συνδούλου ἡμῶν, ὅς ἐστιν πιστὸς ὑπὲρ ὑμῶν διάκονος τοῦ Χριστοῦ, **8** ὁ καὶ δηλώσας ἡμῖν τὴν ὑμῶν ἀγάπην ἐν Πνεύματι.

9 Διὰ τοῦτο καὶ ἡμεῖς, ἀφ᾽ ἧς ἡμέρας ἠκούσαμεν, οὐ παυόμεθα ὑπὲρ ὑμῶν προσευχόμενοι καὶ αἰτούμενοι ἵνα πληρωθῆτε τὴν ἐπίγνωσιν τοῦ θελήματος αὐτοῦ ἐν πάσῃ σοφίᾳ καὶ συνέσει πνευματικῇ, **10** περιπατῆσαι ὑμᾶς ἀξίως τοῦ Κυρίου εἰς πᾶσαν ἀρέσκειαν, ἐν παντὶ ἔργῳ ἀγαθῷ καρποφοροῦντες καὶ αὐξανόμενοι εἰς τὴν ἐπίγνωσιν τοῦ Θεοῦ· **11** ἐν πάσῃ δυνάμει δυναμούμενοι κατὰ τὸ κράτος τῆς δόξης αὐτοῦ, εἰς πᾶσαν ὑπομονὴν καὶ μακροθυμίαν.

12 Μετὰ χαρᾶς εὐχαριστοῦντες τῷ Πατρὶ τῷ ἱκανώσαντι ἡμᾶς εἰς τὴν μερίδα τοῦ κλήρου τῶν ἁγίων ἐν τῷ φωτί· **13** ὃς ἐρρύσατο ἡμᾶς ἐκ τῆς ἐξουσίας τοῦ σκότους καὶ μετέστησεν εἰς τὴν βασιλείαν τοῦ Υἱοῦ τῆς ἀγάπης αὐτοῦ, **14** ἐν ᾧ ἔχομεν τὴν ἀπολύτρωσιν διὰ τοῦ αἵματος αὐτοῦ, τὴν ἄφεσιν τῶν ἁμαρτιῶν·

15 ὅς ἐστιν εἰκὼν τοῦ Θεοῦ τοῦ ἀοράτου, πρωτότοκος πάσης κτίσεως, 16 ὅτι ἐν αὐτῷ ἐκτίσθη τὰ πάντα—τὰ ἐν τοῖς οὐρανοῖς καὶ τὰ ἐπὶ τῆς γῆς, τὰ ὁρατὰ καὶ τὰ ἀόρατα, εἴτε θρόνοι εἴτε κυριότητες εἴτε ἀρχαὶ εἴτε ἐξουσίαι—τὰ πάντα δι᾽ αὐτοῦ καὶ εἰς αὐτὸν ἔκτισται· 17 καὶ αὐτός ἐστιν πρὸ πάντων, καὶ τὰ πάντα ἐν αὐτῷ συνέστηκεν. 18 Καὶ, αὐτός ἐστιν ἡ κεφαλὴ τοῦ σώματος, τῆς ἐκκλησίας·

ὅς ἐστιν ἀρχή, πρωτότοκος ἐκ τῶν νεκρῶν, ἵνα γένηται ἐν πᾶσιν αὐτὸς πρωτεύων, 19 ὅτι ἐν αὐτῷ εὐδόκησεν πᾶν τὸ πλήρωμα κατοικῆσαι 20 καὶ δι᾽ αὐτοῦ ἀποκαταλλάξαι τὰ πάντα εἰς αὐτόν, εἰρηνοποιήσας διὰ τοῦ αἵματος τοῦ σταυροῦ αὐτοῦ—δι᾽ αὐτοῦ, εἴτε τὰ ἐπὶ τῆς γῆς εἴτε τὰ ἐπὶ τοῖς οὐρανοῖς.

21 Καὶ ὑμᾶς (ποτε ὄντας ἀπηλλοτριωμένους καὶ ἐχθροὺς τῇ διανοίᾳ ἐν τοῖς ἔργοις τοῖς πονηροῖς) 22 νυνὶ δὲ ἀποκατήλλαξεν 22 ἐν τῷ σώματι τῆς σαρκὸς αὐτοῦ διὰ τοῦ θανάτου αὐτοῦ, παραστῆσαι ὑμᾶς ἁγίους καὶ ἀμώμους καὶ ἀνεγκλήτους κατενώπιον αὐτοῦ—23 εἴ γε ἐπιμένετε τῇ πίστει τεθεμελιωμένοι καὶ ἑδραῖοι, καὶ μὴ μετακινούμενοι ἀπὸ τῆς ἐλπίδος τοῦ εὐαγγελίου, οὗ ἠκούσατε τοῦ κηρυχθέντος ἐν πάσῃ τῇ κτίσει τῇ ὑπὸ τὸν οὐρανόν, οὗ ἐγενόμην ἐγώ, Παῦλος, διάκονος.

24 Νῦν χαίρω ἐν τοῖς παθήμασί μου ὑπὲρ ὑμῶν καὶ ἀνταναπληρῶ τὰ ὑστερήματα τῶν θλίψεων τοῦ Χριστοῦ ἐν τῇ σαρκί μου, ὑπὲρ τοῦ σώματος αὐτοῦ, ὅ ἐστιν ἡ ἐκκλησία, 25 ἧς ἐγενόμην ἐγὼ διάκονος κατὰ τὴν οἰκονομίαν τοῦ Θεοῦ τὴν δοθεῖσάν μοι εἰς ὑμᾶς, πληρῶσαι τὸν λόγον τοῦ Θεοῦ, 26 τὸ μυστήριον τὸ ἀποκεκρυμμένον ἀπὸ τῶν αἰώνων καὶ ἀπὸ τῶν γενεῶν, νυνὶ δὲ ἐφανερώθη τοῖς ἁγίοις αὐτοῦ· 27 οἷς ἠθέλησεν ὁ Θεὸς γνωρίσαι τίς ὁ πλοῦτος τῆς δόξης τοῦ μυστηρίου τούτου ἐν τοῖς ἔθνεσιν, ὅς ἐστιν Χριστὸς ἐν ὑμῖν, ἡ ἐλπὶς τῆς δόξης· 28 ὃν ἡμεῖς καταγγέλλομεν, νουθετοῦντες πάντα ἄνθρωπον καὶ διδάσκοντες πάντα ἄνθρωπον ἐν πάσῃ σοφίᾳ, ἵνα παραστήσωμεν πάντα ἄνθρωπον τέλειον ἐν Χριστῷ· 29 εἰς ὃ καὶ κοπιῶ, ἀγωνιζόμενος κατὰ τὴν ἐνέργειαν αὐτοῦ τὴν ἐνεργουμένην ἐν ἐμοὶ ἐν δυνάμει.

2 Θέλω γὰρ ὑμᾶς εἰδέναι ἡλίκον ἀγῶνα ἔχω περὶ ὑμῶν καὶ τῶν ἐν Λαοδικείᾳ, καὶ ὅσοι οὐχ ἑωράκασιν τὸ πρόσωπόν μου ἐν σαρκί, 2 ἵνα παρακληθῶσιν αἱ καρδίαι αὐτῶν, συμβιβασθέντων ἐν ἀγάπῃ καὶ εἰς πάντα πλοῦτον τῆς πληροφορίας τῆς συνέσεως, εἰς ἐπίγνωσιν τοῦ μυστηρίου τοῦ Θεοῦ καὶ Πατρὸς καὶ τοῦ Χριστοῦ, 3 ἐν ᾧ εἰσιν πάντες οἱ θησαυροὶ τῆς σοφίας καὶ τῆς γνώσεως ἀπόκρυφοι.

4 Τοῦτο δὲ λέγω ἵνα μή τις ὑμᾶς παραλογίζηται ἐν πιθανολογίᾳ. 5 Εἰ γὰρ καὶ τῇ σαρκὶ ἄπειμι, ἀλλὰ τῷ πνεύματι σὺν ὑμῖν εἰμι, χαίρων καὶ βλέπων ὑμῶν τὴν τάξιν καὶ τὸ στερέωμα τῆς εἰς Χριστὸν πίστεως ὑμῶν.

6 Ὡς οὖν παρελάβετε τὸν Χριστὸν, Ἰησοῦν τὸν Κύριον, ἐν αὐτῷ περιπατεῖτε, 7 ἐρριζωμένοι καὶ ἐποικοδομούμενοι ἐν αὐτῷ καὶ βεβαιούμενοι ἐν τῇ πίστει, καθὼς ἐδιδάχθητε, περισσεύοντες ἐν αὐτῇ ἐν εὐχαριστίᾳ.

8 Βλέπετε μή τις ὑμᾶς ἔσται ὁ συλαγωγῶν διὰ τῆς φιλοσοφίας καὶ κενῆς ἀπάτης, κατὰ τὴν παράδοσιν τῶν ἀνθρώπων, κατὰ τὰ στοιχεῖα τοῦ κόσμου καὶ οὐ κατὰ Χριστόν. 9 Ὅτι ἐν αὐτῷ κατοικεῖ πᾶν τὸ Πλήρωμα τῆς Θεότητος σωματικῶς, 10 καὶ ἐστὲ ἐν αὐτῷ πεπληρωμένοι ὅς ἐστιν ἡ κεφαλὴ πάσης ἀρχῆς καὶ ἐξουσίας· 11 ἐν ᾧ καὶ περιετμήθητε, περιτομῇ ἀχειροποιήτῳ, ἐν τῇ ἀπεκδύσει τοῦ σώματος τῶν ἁμαρτιῶν τῆς σαρκός, ἐν τῇ περιτομῇ τοῦ Χριστοῦ, 12 συνταφέντες αὐτῷ ἐν τῷ βαπτίσματι· ἐν ᾧ καὶ συνηγέρθητε διὰ τῆς πίστεως τῆς ἐνεργείας τοῦ Θεοῦ τοῦ ἐγείραντος αὐτὸν ἐκ τῶν νεκρῶν.

13 Καὶ ὑμᾶς, νεκροὺς ὄντας τοῖς παραπτώμασιν καὶ τῇ ἀκροβυστίᾳ τῆς σαρκὸς ὑμῶν—συνεζωοποίησεν ὑμᾶς σὺν αὐτῷ· χαρισάμενος ἡμῖν πάντα τὰ παραπτώματα· 14 ἐξαλείψας τὸ καθ᾽ ἡμῶν χειρόγραφον (τοῖς δόγμασιν) ὃ ἦν ὑπεναντίον ἡμῖν, καὶ αὐτὸ ἦρκεν ἐκ τοῦ μέσου, προσηλώσας αὐτὸ τῷ σταυρῷ· 15 ἀπεκδυσάμενος τὰς ἀρχὰς καὶ τὰς ἐξουσίας, ἐδειγμάτισεν ἐν παρρησίᾳ, θριαμβεύσας αὐτοὺς ἐν αὐτῷ.

16 Μὴ οὖν τις ὑμᾶς κρινέτω ἐν βρώσει ἢ ἐν πόσει, ἢ ἐν μέρει ἑορτῆς ἢ νουμηνίας ἢ σαββάτων, 17 ἅ ἐστιν σκιὰ τῶν μελλόντων, τὸ δὲ σῶμα Χριστοῦ. 18 Μηδεὶς ὑμᾶς καταβραβευέτω, θέλων ἐν ταπεινοφροσύνῃ καὶ θρησκείᾳ τῶν ἀγγέλων, ἃ μὴ ἑώρακεν ἐμβατεύων, εἰκῇ φυσιούμενος ὑπὸ τοῦ νοὸς τῆς σαρκὸς αὐτοῦ, 19 καὶ οὐ κρατῶν τὴν κεφαλήν, ἐξ οὗ πᾶν τὸ σῶμα, διὰ τῶν ἁφῶν καὶ συνδέσμων ἐπιχορηγούμενον καὶ συμβιβαζόμενον, αὔξει τὴν αὔξησιν τοῦ Θεοῦ.

20 Εἰ οὖν ἀπεθάνετε σὺν Χριστῷ ἀπὸ τῶν στοιχείων τοῦ κόσμου, τί, ὡς ζῶντες ἐν κόσμῳ, δογματίζεσθε 21—"Μὴ ἅψῃ, μηδὲ γεύσῃ, μηδὲ θίγῃς!" 22 (ἅ ἐστιν πάντα εἰς φθορὰν τῇ ἀποχρήσει) κατὰ τὰ ἐντάλματα καὶ διδασκαλίας τῶν ἀνθρώπων? 23 Ἅτινά ἐστιν λόγον μὲν ἔχοντα σοφίας ἐν ἐθελοθρησκείᾳ καὶ ταπεινοφροσύνῃ καὶ ἀφειδίᾳ σώματος, οὐκ ἐν τιμῇ τινὶ πρὸς πλησμονὴν τῆς σαρκός.

3 Εἰ οὖν συνηγέρθητε τῷ Χριστῷ, τὰ ἄνω ζητεῖτε, οὗ ὁ Χριστός ἐστιν, ἐν δεξιᾷ τοῦ Θεοῦ καθήμενος· 2 τὰ ἄνω φρονεῖτε, μὴ τὰ ἐπὶ τῆς γῆς, 3 ἀπεθάνετε γάρ καὶ ἡ ζωὴ ὑμῶν κέκρυπται σὺν τῷ Χριστῷ ἐν τῷ Θεῷ. 4 Ὅταν ὁ Χριστὸς φανερωθῇ, ἡ ζωὴ ἡμῶν, τότε καὶ ὑμεῖς σὺν αὐτῷ φανερωθήσεσθε ἐν δόξῃ.

5 Νεκρώσατε οὖν τὰ μέλη ὑμῶν τὰ ἐπὶ τῆς γῆς: πορνείαν, ἀκαθαρσίαν, πάθος, ἐπιθυμίαν κακήν, καὶ τὴν πλεονεξίαν ἥτις ἐστὶν εἰδωλολατρία· 6 δι' ἃ ἔρχεται ἡ ὀργὴ τοῦ Θεοῦ ἐπὶ τοὺς υἱοὺς τῆς ἀπειθείας, 7 ἐν οἷς καὶ ὑμεῖς περιεπατήσατέ ποτε ὅτε ἐζῆτε ἐν αὐτοῖς. 8 Νυνὶ δὲ ἀπόθεσθε καὶ ὑμεῖς τὰ πάντα—ὀργήν, θυμόν, κακίαν, βλασφημίαν, αἰσχρολογίαν—ἐκ τοῦ στόματος ὑμῶν. 9 Μὴ ψεύδεσθε εἰς ἀλλήλους, ἀπεκδυσάμενοι τὸν παλαιὸν ἄνθρωπον σὺν ταῖς πράξεσιν αὐτοῦ 10 καὶ ἐνδυσάμενοι τὸν νέον, τὸν ἀνακαινούμενον εἰς ἐπίγνωσιν κατ' εἰκόνα τοῦ κτίσαντος αὐτόν, 11 ὅπου οὐκ ἔνι Ἕλλην καὶ Ἰουδαῖος, περιτομὴ καὶ ἀκροβυστία, βάρβαρος, Σκύθης, δοῦλος, ἐλεύθερος· ἀλλὰ τὰ πάντα καὶ ἐν πᾶσι Χριστός.

12 Ἐνδύσασθε οὖν, ὡς ἐκλεκτοὶ τοῦ Θεοῦ, ἅγιοι καὶ ἠγαπημένοι, σπλάγχνα οἰκτιρμοῦ, χρηστότητα, ταπεινοφροσύνην, πραότητα, μακροθυμίαν· 13 ἀνεχόμενοι ἀλλήλων καὶ χαριζόμενοι ἑαυτοῖς, ἐάν τις πρός τινα ἔχῃ μομφήν—καθὼς καὶ ὁ Χριστὸς ἐχαρίσατο ὑμῖν, οὕτως καὶ ὑμεῖς· 14 ἐπὶ πᾶσιν δὲ τούτοις τὴν ἀγάπην, ἥτις ἐστὶν σύνδεσμος τῆς τελειότητος.

15 Καὶ ἡ εἰρήνη τοῦ Θεοῦ βραβευέτω ἐν ταῖς καρδίαις ὑμῶν, εἰς ἣν καὶ ἐκλήθητε ἐν ἑνὶ σώματι· καὶ εὐχάριστοι γίνεσθε.

16 Ὁ λόγος τοῦ Χριστοῦ ἐνοικείτω ἐν ὑμῖν πλουσίως ἐν πάσῃ σοφίᾳ διδάσκοντες καὶ νουθετοῦντες ἑαυτούς, ψαλμοῖς καὶ ὕμνοις καὶ ᾠδαῖς πνευματικαῖς ἐν χάριτι ᾄδοντες ἐν τῇ καρδίᾳ ὑμῶν τῷ Κυρίῳ.

17 Καὶ πᾶν ὅ τι ἂν ποιῆτε ἐν λόγῳ ἢ ἐν ἔργῳ, πάντα ἐν ὀνόματι Κυρίου Ἰησοῦ, εὐχαριστοῦντες τῷ Θεῷ καὶ Πατρὶ δι᾽ αὐτοῦ.

18 Αἱ γυναῖκες, ὑποτάσσεσθε τοῖς ἰδίοις ἀνδράσιν, ὡς ἀνῆκεν ἐν Κυρίῳ.

19 Οἱ ἄνδρες, ἀγαπᾶτε τὰς γυναῖκας καὶ μὴ πικραίνεσθε πρὸς αὐτάς.

20 Τὰ τέκνα, ὑπακούετε τοῖς γονεῦσιν κατὰ πάντα, τοῦτο γάρ ἐστιν εὐάρεστον ἐν Κυρίῳ.

21 Οἱ πατέρες, μὴ ἐρεθίζετε τὰ τέκνα ὑμῶν, ἵνα μὴ ἀθυμῶσιν.

22 Οἱ δοῦλοι, ὑπακούετε κατὰ πάντα τοῖς κατὰ σάρκα κυρίοις, μὴ ἐν ὀφθαλμοδουλίαις ὡς ἀνθρωπάρεσκοι, ἀλλ᾽ ἐν ἁπλότητι καρδίας, φοβούμενοι τὸν Θεόν. 23 Καὶ πᾶν ὅ τι ἐὰν ποιῆτε, ἐκ ψυχῆς ἐργάζεσθε, ὡς τῷ Κυρίῳ καὶ οὐκ ἀνθρώποις, 24 εἰδότες ὅτι ἀπὸ Κυρίου λήψεσθε τὴν ἀνταπόδοσιν τῆς κληρονομίας· τῷ γὰρ Κυρίῳ Χριστῷ δουλεύετε. 25 (Ὁ δὲ ἀδικῶν κομιεῖται ὃ ἠδίκησεν, καὶ οὐκ ἔστιν προσωποληψία.)

4 Οἱ κύριοι, τὸ δίκαιον καὶ τὴν ἰσότητα τοῖς δούλοις παρέχεσθε, εἰδότες ὅτι καὶ ὑμεῖς ἔχετε Κύριον ἐν οὐρανοῖς.

2 Τῇ προσευχῇ προσκαρτερεῖτε, γρηγοροῦντες ἐν αὐτῇ ἐν εὐχαριστίᾳ, 3 προσευχόμενοι ἅμα καὶ περὶ ἡμῶν, ἵνα ὁ Θεὸς ἀνοίξῃ ἡμῖν θύραν τοῦ λόγου, λαλῆσαι τὸ μυστήριον τοῦ Χριστοῦ (δι᾽ ὃ καὶ δέδεμαι), 4 ἵνα φανερώσω αὐτό, ὡς δεῖ με λαλῆσαι. 5 Ἐν σοφίᾳ περιπατεῖτε πρὸς τοὺς ἔξω, τὸν καιρὸν ἐξαγοραζόμενοι. 6 Ὁ λόγος ὑμῶν πάντοτε ἐν χάριτι, ἅλατι ἠρτυμένος, εἰδέναι πῶς δεῖ ὑμᾶς ἑνὶ ἑκάστῳ ἀποκρίνεσθαι.

7 Τὰ κατ᾽ ἐμὲ πάντα γνωρίσει ὑμῖν Τυχικὸς ὁ ἀγαπητὸς ἀδελφὸς καὶ πιστὸς διάκονος καὶ σύνδουλος ἐν Κυρίῳ, 8 ὃν ἔπεμψα πρὸς ὑμᾶς εἰς αὐτὸ τοῦτο, ἵνα γνῷ τὰ περὶ ὑμῶν καὶ παρακαλέσῃ τὰς καρδίας ὑμῶν, 9 σὺν Ὀνησίμῳ, τῷ πιστῷ καὶ ἀγαπητῷ ἀδελφῷ, ὅς ἐστιν ἐξ ὑμῶν· πάντα ὑμῖν γνωριοῦσι τὰ ὧδε.

10 Ἀσπάζεται ὑμᾶς Ἀρίσταρχος, ὁ συναιχμάλωτός μου, καὶ Μᾶρκος ὁ ἀνεψιὸς Βαρνάβα (περὶ οὗ ἐλάβετε ἐντολάς· ἐὰν ἔλθῃ πρὸς ὑμᾶς δέξασθε αὐτόν), 11 καὶ Ἰησοῦς ὁ λεγόμενος Ἰοῦστος, οἱ ὄντες ἐκ περιτομῆς οὗτοι μόνοι συνεργοὶ εἰς τὴν βασιλείαν τοῦ Θεοῦ· οἵτινες ἐγενήθησάν μοι παρηγορία.

12 Ἀσπάζεται ὑμᾶς Ἐπαφρᾶς, ὁ ἐξ ὑμῶν, δοῦλος Χριστοῦ, πάντοτε ἀγωνιζόμενος ὑπὲρ ὑμῶν ἐν ταῖς προσευχαῖς, ἵνα στῆτε τέλειοι καὶ πεπληρωμένοι ἐν παντὶ θελήματι τοῦ Θεοῦ. 13 Μαρτυρῶ γὰρ αὐτῷ ὅτι ἔχει ζῆλον πολὺν ὑπὲρ ὑμῶν, καὶ τῶν ἐν Λαοδικείᾳ καὶ τῶν ἐν Ἱεραπόλει.

14 Ἀσπάζεται ὑμᾶς Λουκᾶς, ὁ ἰατρὸς ὁ ἀγαπητός, καὶ Δημᾶς. 15 Ἀσπάσασθε τοὺς ἐν Λαοδικείᾳ ἀδελφούς, καὶ Νυμφᾶν καὶ τὴν κατ᾽ οἶκον αὐτοῦ ἐκκλησίαν.

16 Καὶ ὅταν ἀναγνωσθῇ παρ᾽ ὑμῖν ἡ ἐπιστολή, ποιήσατε ἵνα καὶ ἐν τῇ Λαοδικέων ἐκκλησίᾳ ἀναγνωσθῇ, καὶ τὴν ἐκ Λαοδικείας ἵνα καὶ ὑμεῖς ἀναγνῶτε.

17 Καὶ εἴπατε Ἀρχίππῳ, "Βλέπε τὴν διακονίαν ἣν παρέλαβες ἐν Κυρίῳ, ἵνα αὐτὴν πληροῖς."

18 Ὁ ἀσπασμὸς τῇ ἐμῇ χειρὶ: Παύλου. Μνημονεύετέ μου τῶν δεσμῶν. Ἡ χάρις μεθ᾽ ὑμῶν. Ἀμήν.

8 Hierarchy

In chapter 2 I suggested that 'Hierarchy' is signaled by three organizing factors: constituent structure, taxis, and span. I further suggested that taxis seems to be the principal vehicle for expressing hierarchy above the sentence level, so I will begin with taxis and then treat constituent structure and span, in that order. After discussing the three factors, I offer three parallel outlines (sect. 8.4) showing the progressive refinements contributed by the successive factors. The reader may wish to consult the outlines while reading the following discussion.

8.1 Taxis. In presenting the evidence supplied by taxis, I will usually treat a whole verse as a unit even though the conventional verse breaks are not always as felicitous as they might be. In some cases the signal I adduce will not be just at the verse break but off to one side. The structural relationships are usually so obvious that I assume the reader will be able to make the necessary adjustments without inconvenience. My concern at this juncture is to highlight the basic tactic progression rather than treat the lower-level tactic relationships. So then, I state the tactic relationships verse by verse. First I give the signal involved, then the relationship signaled, and then the level or point to which the relationship attaches.

I offer a partial list of paratactic and hypotactic signals in Koine Greek (not all found in Colossians). The paratactic signals are: αλλα, αρα, δε, δια τουτο, διο, ἤ, και, νυν, ουν, τοινυν, asyndeton[42] and ellipsis.

---

[42] By *asyndeton* is meant the absence of a conjunction or other overt signal to link two sentences. The presence of an overt signal is normal in Koine Greek, so much so that the absence of such a signal has been given a name. Since the use of asyndeton is one of the options available to an encoder (in Koine Greek) and represents a choice on his part, asyndeton must be just as much of a signal as any of the sibling options would be. Since the effect of asyndeton is to juxtapose two units, I regard it as a paratactic signal.

The hypotactic signals are: γαρ, διοτι, εαν, ει, επει, ἵνα, ὅπως, ὅτι, ὡς, ὥστε, nonfinite verbs, relative pronouns, and prepositions. For a somewhat different listing see Grassmick (1974:86). I have concluded elsewhere (sect. 2.2) that tactic signals are unambiguously one or the other.

1:1 Start.
  2 Asyndeton, parallel to vs. 1 (actually 2b is parallel to 1).
  3 Asyndeton, parallel to vs. 1 (presumably, decision dictated by other factors).
  4 Participle, subordinate to participle in vs. 3.
  5 δια, subordinate to main verb in vs. 3.
  6 Participle, subordinate to last word in vs. 5.
  7 καθὼς και, parallel to προηκουσατε in vs. 5 or ηκουσατε in vs. 6.
  8 και, parallel to vs. 7b.
  9 δια τουτο και, parallel to something of higher level than previous verse.
  10 Infinitive, subordinate to πληρωθητε in vs. 9.
  11 Participle, subordinate to infinitive in vs. 10.
  12 Participle, subordinate to infinitive in vs. 10 or to main verb in vs. 9.
  13 Relative clause, subordinate to πατρι in vs. 12.
  14 Relative clause, subordinate to υἱου in vs. 13.
  15 Relative clause, subordinate to υἱου in vs. 13.
  16 ὅτι, subordinate to vs. 15.
  17 και, parallel to vs. 16b.
  18 και, parallel to vs. 17.
  18b Relative clause, subordinate to vs. 18a or to υἱου in vs. 13.
  19 ὅτι, subordinate to vs. 18b.
  20 και, parallel to vs. 19b.
  21 και, parallel to vs. 20.
  22b Infinitive, subordinate to main verb in vs. 22a.
  23 ει γε, subordinate to vs. 22b.
  24 νυν, parallel to vs. 9.

25 Relative clause, subordinate to last word in vs. 24.

26 μυστηριον is in apposition/subordinate to λογον in vs. 25.

27 Relative clause, subordinate to ἁγιοις in vs. 26.

28 Relative clause, subordinate to Χριστος in vs. 27.

29 Relative clause, subordinate to vs. 28b.

2:1 γαρ, subordinate to 1:29.

  2 ἱνα, subordinate to 2:1.

  3 Relative clause, subordinate to last word in 2:2.

  4 δε, parallel to 2:1?

  5 γαρ, subordinate to 2:4.

  6 ουν, parallel to 1:24.

  7 Participle, subordinate to main verb in 2:6.

  8 Asyndeton, parallel to 2:6.

  9 ὁτι, subordinate to 2:8.

  10 και, parallel to 2:9.

  11 Relative clause, subordinate to αυτω in 2:10.

  12 Participle, subordinate to 2:11.

  13 και, parallel to 2:8.

  14 Participle, subordinate to 2:13 or to 2:14b?

  14b και, parallel to (?).

  15 Participle, subordinate to 2:14.

  16 ουν, parallel to 2:8?

  17 Relative clause, subordinate to 2:16b.

  18 Asyndeton, parallel to 2:16.

  19 και, parallel to 2:18b.

  20 Asyndeton, parallel to 2:16?

  21 Quotation, subordinate to 2:20.

  22 Relative clause, subordinate to 2:21.

  22b κατα, subordinate to 2:20.

  23 Relative clause, subordinate to 2:22b.

3:1 ουν, parallel to 2:16?

  2 Asyndeton, parallel to main clause in 3:1 (repetition).

3 γαρ, subordinate to 3:2.

4 Asyndeton, parallel to 3:3.

5 ουν, parallel to 3:1?

6 Relative clause, subordinate to 3:5.

7 Relative clause, subordinate to 3:5.

8 δε, parallel to 3:5.

9 Asyndeton, parallel to 3:8.

10 και, parallel to 3:9b.

11 Relative clause, subordinate to νεον in 3:10.

12 ουν, parallel to 3:5?

13 Participle, subordinate to main verb in 3:12.

13b καθως και, parallel to (?).

14 δε, parallel to main verb in 3:12?

15 και, parallel to 3:12?

15b και, parallel to 3:15a.

16 Asyndeton, parallel to 3:15?

17 και, parallel to 3:15?

18 Asyndeton, parallel to 3:1.

19 Asyndeton, parallel to 3:18.

20 Asyndeton, parallel to 3:18 and 19.

21 Asyndeton, parallel to 3:18, 19, and 20.

22 Asyndeton, parallel to 3:18, 19, 20, and 21.

23 και, parallel to main verb in 3:22.

24 Participle, subordinate to main verb in 3:23.

25 δε, parallel to 3:24.

4:1 Asyndeton, parallel to 3:18, 19, 20, 21, and 22.

2 Asyndeton, parallel to 3:18.

3 Participle, parallel to participle in 4:2.

4 Relative clause, subordinate to μυστηριον in 4:3.

5 Asyndeton, parallel to 4:2?

6 Asyndeton, parallel to 4:5.

7 Asyndeton, parallel to 2:6.

8 Relative clause, subordinate to Τυχικος in 4:7.

9 συν, subordinate to 4:8.

9b Asyndeton, parallel to main clause in 4:7 (repetition).

10 Asyndeton, parallel to 4:7?

11 και, parallel to Μαρκος in 4:10.

12 Asyndeton, parallel to 4:10 (repetition).

13 γαρ, subordinate to 4:12.

14 Asyndeton, parallel to 4:10 and 12 (repetition).

15 Asyndeton, parallel to 4:10 and 7?

16 και, parallel to 4:15.

17 και, parallel to 4:16.

18 Asyndeton, parallel to (?).

8.2 **Constituent Structure**. The evidence from taxis makes it possible to posit tentative paragraphs—wherever a paratactic signal refers back or attaches to a point several verses (or more) removed from it, a paragraph break may be assumed. My discussion of constituent structure will go paragraph by paragraph.

Robert Funk (1966) and others[43] have demonstrated that it is a standard feature of Koine Greek epistolary genre to have three highest-level constituents: salutation, body, and sign-off. The salutation and sign-off are distinguished by nominal sentences. Colossians follows the pattern nicely, with the first two verses forming the salutation and the last verse the sign-off.

1:1-2. There are two nominal sentences of equal rank which form a paragraph.

1:3-8. I read παντοτε with the main clause rather than the participial phrase (vs. 3). I read vs. 4 as an aside, parenthetical, and subordinate to προσευχομενοι (vs. 3) rather than to the main verb. I take δια (vs. 5) as

---

[43] See, for example, Doty (1973), Funk (1967), Mullins (1968), Jack Sanders (1962), and White (1972).

subordinate to the main verb (vs. 3) [my text does not have εχετε in the preceding clause (vs. 4), but even if it did it would make poor sense to subordinate δια to it]. Without και, vs. 7 is probably subordinate to the finite verbs in the preceding clause, but my text has και which leads me rather to see εμαθετε as parallel to προηκουσατε in vs. 5. In any case, vss. 3-8 form a single sentence, and hence can be no more than one paragraph. I take it that these verses form a rapport-building paragraph preparatory to the business of the epistle.

1:9-23. As I adduced in section 2.4, no two points in a discourse outline may have the same beginning, even where the outline indents. The corollary to that is that a first subordinate point (e.g., A under II) cannot be strictly parallel to anything before it. In this case there is an obvious break at vs. 9 such that it is not merely parallel to vs. 8, i.e., it is a higher-level break (the signal is both paratactic and anaphoric), but there is no obvious point to which the paratactic signal may be tied. In this case the whole paragraph, vss. 3-8, is the signal that distinguishes the roman numeral rank from the capital letter rank. I see vs. 12 as subordinate to vs. 9 because my text reads ἡμας, whereas it would be subordinate to vs. 10 if the text read ὑμας. I take the relative clause in vs. 18 to be parallel to the similar structure in vs. 15, though it could be subordinate to the preceding clause. Vs. 21 begins a new sentence, but the thought seems to be a continuation of that in vs. 20.

1:24-2:5. I take it that νυν is not temporal here, but signals a new departure—it is accompanied by a main verb and a sudden shift in subject matter. This section pretty well has to be B, since A and III are already taken. I consider γαρ to be invariably a hypotactic signal, so that 2:1 is subordinate to 1:29 (unless it be to the whole passage 24-29, since vs. 24 does have a similar thought also). My text reads δε in vs. 4, which helps me to see it as parallel to vs. 1, although it could be even without the δε.

2:6-7. The use of ουν and the switch to imperative mode signal a major break, which pretty well has to be C. Vss. 6-7 form the signal that distinguishes the capital letter rank from that of the arabic numerals to follow.

2:8-15. I take it that the imperative in lead position opens a new paragraph. In vs. 13 I take και to be emphatic, working with the pronoun in emphatic position, so there is asyndeton between vs. 13 and vs. 12. Vs. 13 is a sentence, but the subject of the independent verb seems to be Θεου in vs. 12, so I do not see vs. 13 as beginning a new paragraph. The basic thought seems clearly to be a continuation of vs. 12. I take the participial clause in vs. 14a to be subordinate to the independent clause in vs. 14b. Again the και is emphatic, so there is asyndeton between vs. 14 and vs. 13. Because of its position, εξαλειψας is essentially parallel to χαρισαμενος in vs. 13. The independent verb in vs. 14 has the same subject as the independent verb in vs. 13. The structure of vs. 15 is similar to that of vs. 14, and again the same subject is involved, so it seems best to regard vs. 15 as being parallel to vs. 14.

2:16-19. The use of ουν and the switch to hortatory mode signal a major break. Is it parallel to 2:8 or 2:6? If 2:6-7 introduce a major section, the material in vss. 16ff is certainly appropriate to such a section. My inclination is to view vs. 16 as parallel to 2:8. Vss. 16 and 18 are parallel, so that the paragraph has two main constituents, with ουν as the introducer.

2:20-23. If one read ουν here, this paragraph would presumably be of the same rank as the preceding one [my text now does read ουν here, but I am leaving the discussion as it was]. However, my text does not have it, so I see 2:20-23 and 2:16-19 as together composing a section introduced by the ουν in vs. 16. That the subject matter of the two paragraphs is closely related lends support to this conclusion.

3:1-4. The use of ουν and the return to imperative (last seen in 2:8) signal a major break. Again, the material here is appropriate to the major section introduced by 2:6-7, so that I am inclined to view this paragraph break as parallel to those at 2:16 and 2:8. Because of the asyndeton the relationship of vs. 4 is not clear, but it does belong to this paragraph. I regard it as parallel to vs. 3. I consider this whole paragraph to be the signal that introduces the section 3:1-17, and distinguishes the arabic numeral rank from that of the lower case letters to follow (at 3:5 and 3:12).

3:5-11. The ουν signals and introduces the paragraph. The logical connection between this paragraph and the preceding one is so close that its inferior rank seems clear. It is dominated by the three imperatives (vss. 5, 8, and 9) which are essentially parallel, except that the last two are closely related semantically, and perhaps should be viewed as together forming a unit parallel to the first.

3:12-17. The ουν signals and introduces the paragraph, which is evidently parallel to the preceding one. Vss. 12 and 14 are parallel and form a unit (so that vs. 13b is included), and so for vs. 15a and vs. 15b. Is vs. 16 parallel to vs. 15b or to vs. 12? How is the absence of a και to be explained? I see two possibilities: either it divides the paragraph (or section) into two pieces, 3:12-15 and 3:16-17, or it makes vs. 16 an extension of vs. 15b, and in that case vs. 17 is parallel to vss. 15 and 12. If vs. 17 is also serving as closure for a larger section, 3:1-17, then the second alternative is preferable.

3:18-4:1. The asyndeton plus the vocatives suggests a new departure. The material here is appropriate to the major section introduced by 2:6-7, so I posit an arabic numeral rank rather than a capital letter one. The six vocatives can clearly be paired off, but I think it is the factor of span that helps us there, so I will not indicate that grouping yet. Vs. 23 is parallel to the imperative in vs. 22, but not to the vocative. My text has a γαρ in 24b and a δε at the beginning of vs. 25 (instead of γαρ). The most logical connection for vs. 25 is ληψεσθε in vs. 24.

4:2-6. The asyndeton plus the return to general imperative indicates another break. Since this material is also appropriate to 2:6-7, I see no motivation for positing a rank higher than arabic numeral. Vs. 5 opens with asyndeton, but the imperatives in vs. 5 and vs. 2 seem clearly parallel. It seems improbable that another high-level break is indicated; rather I consider the two sentences involved to be parallel constituents of a paragraph. I supply the present participle "being" in vs. 6a and consider it to be subordinate to vs. 5.

4:7-9. The change from imperative to indicative joins the asyndeton to indicate a break. From here on, the material is no longer appropriate to 2:6-7, but consists of scattered concluding remarks of a phatic nature. In retrospect 4:2-6 serves nicely as a winding down paragraph to close off the major section 2:6-4:6, so I assign a capital letter rank to this break. I take vss. 7-9 to form a paragraph which joins with two following paragraphs to make up the section D. At this point a refinement is required in my claim that no two points in a discourse outline may have the same beginning. The existence of two or more parallel constituents which combine to make up a unit forces the assigning to the first constituent a rank inferior than that to the unit—a part is not equal to the whole. Thus, vss. 7-9 form a constituent paragraph inferior in rank to the section which also begins at that point. One might say, however, that the almost complete lack of cohesion is the signal for the section rank, while the independent verb is the signal for the paragraph rank (in this case).

4:10-14. The triple occurrence of ασπαζεται clearly defines vss. 10-14 as a paragraph. Presumably it is parallel to 4:7-9.

4:15-17. That these three disparate sentences are tied together with "and" indicates that they are to be taken together, forming a paragraph parallel to the preceding two (presumably).

4:18. As already mentioned, the nominal sentences of this verse are typical of the sign-off in Koine Greek epistolary genre, so this verse represents the third constituent at the highest level.

I am conscious that in the foregoing discussion I probably was not consistent in confining my decisions to those that derive exclusively from evidence supplied by taxis and constituent structure; I probably imported some evidence from span. I beg the reader's indulgence. By way of extenuation I would note that such consistency is difficult to achieve and that it really is not necessary (except, perhaps, in a study such as this) since the total effect of all three factors is what an analyst is after.

8.3 **Span**. Person spans prove to be highly significant in Colossians. Defining a person span in terms of the independent verbs, we get sharply defined boundaries which correspond nicely with the capital-letter-rank breaks which I proposed on the basis of constituent structure. The crucial spans are 1:24-2:5, 1st sg.; 2:6-4:6, 2nd pl.; 4:7-14, 3rd sg.—they confirm sections B, C, and D. The only independent verb in section A, 1:9-23, is 1st pl. (vs. 9). There are some lesser spans—1:12-22, 3rd sg.; 1:16-20, 3rd pl.; 2:9-15, 3rd sg.; 3:5-8, 3rd pl.; 3:13-16, 3rd sg.; 4:15-17, 2nd pl.—which do not involve independent verbs, except for the last one. Some of them, at least, will be relevant and helpful at lower ranks.

Tense spans appear not to be very important in our text. One might speak of a present tense span in 2:3-10, 2:16-19, and 3:16-23, and an aorist span in 2:11-15, but they seem to have little bearing on the outline—2:16-19 is a paragraph and 2:11-15 may prove to be a subdivision. There are fourteen places where a tense occurs three times in a row and six places where a tense occurs four times, but they are probably fortuitous so far as the outline is concerned.

Voice spans are few and may have even less bearing on the outline of our text than does tense. One might speak of an active voice span in

2:13-18, 3:16-21, 4:7-10, and of a middle span in 3:6-13 (but it is not solid), but they do not seem to match any recognizable constituent.

There is one clearly significant mood span and another that may be. The imperative span in 3:18-4:1, which is coterminous with a vocative span, makes this section as well delineated as any in the book. 2:7-19 is heavy with participles and seems to correspond to a recognizable stretch. One might call 1:10-12 a participle span, 1:13-17 an indicative span, 1:19-23 a largely nonfinite span, 3:2-8 a finite verb span, as also 4:7-10 and 4:13-18, but they do not seem to contribute to the outline.

A few other grammatical spans might be mentioned. The relative pronoun span in 1:14-18 and the 3rd sg. masculine pronoun span in 1:16-18a may have a low-rank significance. 2:6-3:17 might be called a span of the conjunction ουν—there is a string of them at major breaks. The word does not occur anywhere else in the book, so the repetition here is probably significant. The repetition of any feature, especially if in parallel constructions, may be said to partake something of the nature of a span and will be relevant to the structure of the text at some level.

As for lexical spans, the several terms for deity pervade the book (Christ 26 times, God 22, Lord 13) presaged, perhaps, by the heavy concentration of them in the first three verses. The word πας occurs very frequently (39 times), mostly in the first chapter, notably in 1:15-20.

The 2nd pl. personal pronoun occurs very frequently, along with dependent verbs in the 2nd pl., and may be said to occur in spans. 1:2-10 is one such, wherein the pronoun does not occur in the nominative case. This span overlaps the boundaries of paragraph 1:3-8. The 2nd pl. is absent from 1:11-20. It recurs in 1:21-25, 27, 2:1, and then solidly in 2:4-8. It seems that Paul is concerned to overlap the major boundaries with the 2nd pl. (pronouns and dependent verbs) so that it serves a cohesive function.[44] It has previously been noted that 2:6-4:6 is a span wherein the independent verbs are in the 2nd pl. (the effect of the 3rd person imperatives in 2:16 and 18 is as if they were 2nd person). After virtually no pronouns in 3:18-4:5 there is a steady supply from 4:6 to the end, which includes the section 4:7-17 (like 1:3-8, it is mainly phatic).

Third person masculine singular pronouns, personal and relative, make 1:14-21 a span about the Son, which agrees well with the structure in that section. There is a span involving τα in 1:16-17 that also coincides with the structure.

1:24-2:5 is a clear 1st sg. span involving both verbs and pronouns (there are also a few 1st pl. forms, evidently editorial); they occur nowhere else except in the final section (4:7-17) and in the final clause of 1:23 (to provide cohesion). These verses clearly form a section which is largely about Paul.

2:6-15 form a span about Christ, signaled by the noun and both kinds of pronouns, with vss. 9-12 forming a solid core for the span. This agrees well with the outline.

2:16-23 seems to have some affinity to 2:8-15 in that the main verbs of both are in the nature of warning, but I am not sure how, or that, they should be joined. As for 16-19 and 20-23, I think there is sufficient evidence to join them. The imperative triplet in vs. 21 seems to hark back to the first triplet in vs. 16. That the main verb in vs. 21 is middle voice makes it very similar in effect to the 3rd person imperatives in vss. 16 and 18.

---

[44] Should it appear that I am using span in two ways, I remind the reader that a given signal or factor may function in more than one macrosystem simultaneously. However, where a span overlaps the boundaries of a section, I do not use it to define that section hierarchically.

3:1-17. Vss. 1-4 form a "Christ" span, signaled largely by the noun. Vss. 5-9 are a span about vice. Vss. 12-17 are a span about virtue. All of which agrees nicely with the outline.

3:18-4:1 form a span on family and social relationships and a "Lord" span. There are three parallel sets: a husband-wife span in 3:18-19, a parent-child span in 3:20-21, a master-servant span in 3:22-4:1.

4:7-18 form a proper-name span. Vss. 9-14 are a span defined by the triple occurrence of ἀσπάζεται. Vss. 15-17 are a span defined by verbs in the 2nd pl. (vs. 18 also has one).

8.4 **Outlines**. The first outline shows how much taxis (all by itself) can show us about the hierarchical structure of a text. The second outline shows the improvements that are possible when constituent structure is added to taxis. Finally by adding span we get the whole picture which is reflected in the third outline. The first two outlines are given side by side to facilitate comparison. In the first outline wherever a chapter number appears at the left margin, I posit a new paragraph. When a question mark appears immediately after a number, its rank is in doubt. Where a question mark appears by itself at the left of a number, it indicates a possible alternate rank—the precise position of the question mark is relevant.

Outline 1	Outline 2
Taxis	+ Constituent Structure
	I. Salutation 1:1-2
1: 1	1
2	2
	II. Body 1:2-4:17
1: 3	3
4	4

5		5	
6		6	
? 7		7	
8		8	
		A. 1:9-23	
1: 9?		9	
10		10	
11		11	
? 12		12	
13		13	
14		14	
15		15	
16		16	
17		17	
18		18	
? 18b		18b	
19		19	
20		20	
21?		21?	
22		22	
23		23	
		B. 1:24 – 2:5	
1: 24?		24	
25		25	
26		26	

27

28

29

2:1

2

3

4?

5

27

28

29

2:1

2

3

4

5

C. 2:6 – 4:6

2: 6?

7

6

7

1. 2:8 - 15

8?

9

10

11

12

13?

14?

14b?

15

8

9

10

11

12

13?

14

15?

2. 2:16-23

a. 2:16-19

2:     16

17

16

17

	18		18
	19		19
			b. 2:20-23
2:	20?		20
	21		21
	22		22
	22b		22b
	23		23
			3. 3:1-17
3:	1?		1
	2		2
	3		3
	4?		4?
			a. 3:5-11
3:	5?		5
	6		6
	7		7
	8		8
	9?		9
	10		10
	11		11
			b. 3:12-17
3:	12?		12
	13		13
	13b		

14?	14
15?	15
16?	16?
17?	17?
	4. 3:18-4:1
3: 18?	18
19	19
20	20
21	21
22	22
23	23
24	24
25?	25
4:1	4:1
	5. 4:2-6
4: 2?	2
3	3
4	4
5?	5
6	6
	D. 4:7-17
	1. 4:7-9
4: 7?	7
8	8
9	9

	9b			9b
				2. 4:10-14
4:	10?			10
	11			11
	12			12
	13			13
	14			14
				3. 4:15-17
4:	15?			15
	16			16
	17			17
				III. Sign-off 4:18
4:	18?			18

Outline 3 represents the outline that I am suggesting for Colossians. The headings are not an essential part of the outline and may be ignored. It will be observed that this outline illustrates the two qualities I claimed for discourse outlines in section 2.4: first, there may be solitary subdivisions; and second, no two beginning points may be precisely the same. The apparent exceptions in the outline are of two kinds: where the signal distinguishing rank is a conjunction, the beginning points are actually different, but the outline is not detailed enough to reflect it; where a unit is made up of parallel constituents, a difference in rank must be recognized between the whole and the first part, even though they share a beginning point.

The reader may wonder why some subdivisions are assigned a letter or number and others are not. In general I assigned a letter or number only where there was a sentence break. However, I wanted to highlight the more important parallel structures, even though it might involve only two relative clauses, so I included them in the outline without a letter or number. Further, I did not wish to assign the same rank to units that are not equal in the progression of the structure. Thus, if I assigned A to 1:1-2a and B to 1:2b, the value or significance of the capital letter rank would be distorted and obscured—1:2b does not represent a major step in the discourse in the way that 1:9-23, 1:24-2:5, etc., do.

Outline 3

+ <u>span</u>

I. Salutation 1:1-2
       1-2a
       2b
II. Body 1:3-4:17
       5b-6
       7-8
  A. Prayer and Praise 1:9-23
         9b-11
       12-23
           15-18a
           18b-23
              21-23
  B. Paul's Ministry 1:24-2:5
         2:1-5
         1-3
           4-5
  C. Christian Responsibility 2:6-4:6
    1. Warnings 2:8-15
          13-15
           14

15

2. More Warnings 2:16-23
   a. 2:16-19

      16-17

      18-19
   b. 2:20-23
3. Exhortations 3:1-17
   a. 3:5-11

      5-7

      8-11
   b. 3:12-17
      1) 12-14

         12-13

         14
      2) 15-16

         15

         16
      3) 17
4. Commands 3:18-4:1
   a. 3:18-19
      1) 18
      2) 19
   b. 3:20-21
      1) 20
      2) 21
   c. 3:22-4:1
      1) 22-25
      2) 4:1
5. Conclusion 4:2-6
   a. 4:2-4
   b. 4:5-6
D. Closing Remarks 4:7-17

8.5 Structural Diagram of Colossians. Although outlines are useful in their own way, I feel that a specialized structural diagram is the appropriate vehicle for displaying the hierarchical structure of a discourse in a precise manner. I say "specialized" because my diagram differs from other such diagrams that I have seen in two important ways. I have maintained the word order of the text (the few exceptions, mainly conjunctions, have an arrow pointing to their correct linear position). I have generally not diagrammed the internal structure of clauses except that an embedded clause is given its own line, and all coordinate structures are highlighted. My concern has been to facilitate the tracing of the discourse structure. What the diagram mainly shows is the contribution of hierarchy to that structure, but by retaining the word order, the prominence signals have not been skewed or obscured. The internal structure of a clause is usually obvious at a glance, and to diagram it in detail would clutter up the page and obscure the discourse structure (of course, more detail can be added if desired). In line with my concern, conjunctions are generally highlighted.

[Note to the reader: because this is being self-published, to include the structural diagram would be too complicated, so it has been omitted, along with the comments on it.]

9 Cohesion

In chapter 3 I suggested that cohesion is signaled by five organizing factors: grammatical agreement, phoric reference, conjunction, lexical association, and given information. Here, rather than discuss each factor singly, I will go paragraph by paragraph stating the combined contribution of all five factors to the cohesion within each paragraph (and between them).

9.1 Comments. The low-level concord, such as the case endings, is so obvious and so low level that I will only comment on unusual occurrences or where it operates across a clause boundary. (But it does contribute to the unity of the text in its way.) Any and all spans that have been noted have a cohesive function.

1:1-2. The proper names and "God" have exophoric reference to the culture, the experience common to author and addressee. They are a sort of given information. The repetition of the names is a case of anaphora. The nominal sentences and general content conform to the pattern of Koine epistolary genre. To the extent that such things are predictable, they contribute to Cohesion. "To you" and "our" in vs. 2 are anaphoric. The four occurrences of καὶ provide low-level cohesion.

1:3-8. "Our" in vs. 3 and "we", the subject of the main verb and elided subject of the participles at the end of vs. 3 and beginning of vs. 4, are anaphoric. "God", "father", "Lord", "our", "Jesus", and "Christ" are all repeated from the previous verse, but in a different arrangement. The individual words are anaphoric, but the new construct illustrates the organizing factor I call "given information". Thus, although (or perhaps because) there is a roman numeral rank break between vss. 2 and 3, there is a great deal of cohesion between them. The 2nd pl. personal pronoun in vs. 3 is anaphoric—there are six more in this paragraph, plus one elision of it, plus four verbs in the second person plural. They are all anaphoric and provide strong internal cohesion for this paragraph.

The participle in vs. 4 and δια plus accusative in vs. 5 are both causal and illustrate the organizing factor I call "conjunction". The verbs, προηκουσατε (vs. 5), ηκουσατε και επεγνωτε (vs. 6), and εμαθετε (vs. 7), are clearly related and illustrate the organizing factor I call "lexical association". Should we say that these verbs also illustrate person, tense, voice, and mood concord? An instance of case concord having at least clause-level relevance is furnished by the relative pronoun in vs. 5, since it controls the content in vss. 5b-8. (Any relative pronoun will illustrate concord operating above the lowest level.)

The lexical content of vss. 5 and 6 is closely knit: "the hope laid up in heaven", "the word of the truth of the gospel", and "the grace of God in truth" are related and furnish another illustration of lexical association. και occurs five times at phrase level and twice at clause level, adding its bit of cohesion. By the end of the paragraph (i.e., in vss. 1-8), the root word "brother" has occurred twice; and so for "holy", "grace", and "truth"; while "faith" and "love" have occurred three times; besides the repeated use of terms for deity. συνδουλου and διακονος in vs. 7 are lexical associates.

All in all there is no lack of cohesive signals in this paragraph. The first person plural pronouns in vss. 7 and 8 are anaphoric to vs. 3 and set up the transition to the next paragraph.

1:9-23. Δια τουτο serves as a high-level conjunction indicating result. "We", as free pronoun and subject of both verbs and elided subject of both participles (all in vs. 9), is anaphoric to vs. 8. There is close lexical association between ηκουσαμεν in vs. 9 and δηλωσας in vs. 8. The second person plural pronouns in vss. 9 and 10, the subject of the subjunctive verb in vs. 9, and the elided subject of the participles in vss. 10 and 11 are also anaphoric to vs. 8, so there is plenty of cohesion to bridge the high-level break between vss. 8 and 9. The repetition of "since the day . . . heard", vss. 6 and 9, is an instance of lexical association, and is cohesive. But "heard" in vs. 9 is anaphoric to "heard" in vs. 4, so "since the day we heard" in vs. 9 is an instance of given information with cohesive value. "Praying for you" in vs. 9 is a repetition of the almost identical expression in vs. 3. "His will" in vs. 9 is reminiscent of "God's will" in vs. 1; "his" is anaphoric to a prior paragraph, whichever referent is chosen.

"To pray" and "to ask" are close lexical associates, vs. 9. The ἵνα with subjunctive is a conjunction usually signaling purpose, but in this instance may be weakened to give the content of the asking. Such terms as "knowledge", "will", "wisdom", and "understanding" (vs. 9) are clearly lexical associates. The infinitive in vs. 10 serves the function of a purpose/result conjunction. Such terms as "worthily", "pleasing", and "good" are lexical associates (vs. 10). The repetition of words like καρποφορουντες and επιγνωσιν has some cohesive value. The three participles in vss. 10-11 illustrate concord of gender, number, case, and tense. "Strength", "strengthened", and "power" are lexical associates (vs. 11). ὑπομονην and μακροθυμιαν are related.

"Thanking the father" (vs. 12) is reminiscent of "we thank the . . . father" in vs. 3. The lead participle in vs. 12 is parallel to the participles in vs. 9 and shares their elided subject. There is concord of gender, number, case, and tense among the three participles—a concord that spans three verses. ἡμας in vss. 12 and 13 and the subject of the verb in vs. 14 are anaphoric, but at this point become inclusive (heretofore the first person has been exclusive). "Light" (vs. 12) and "darkness" (vs. 13) are opposites; the two clauses in vs. 13 are opposites; and terms like "inheritance", "delivered", "translated", "redemption", and "forgiveness" (12-14) are related; all of which illustrates lexical association. The third singular relative and personal pronouns in vs. 13 are coreferent and anaphoric to "father" in vs. 12. The third singular relative and personal pronouns in vss. 14-22 are all coreferent and anaphoric to "son" in vs. 13. There are seventeen of them, some in every verse, so the cohesion is massive.

The coreferential occurrences of τα παντα and τα in vss. 16-20 are very cohesive, along with other occurrences of the word "all". The doublets and quadruplets in vss. 16-17 are cohesive in themselves, besides the lexical association of their contents. ὅτι in vs. 16 is a causal conjunction. The final clause of vs. 16 is given information. The ἵνα in vs. 18 is a purpose conjunction, while the ὅτι in vs. 19 is causal. The "in heaven" and "on earth" at the end of vs. 20 is cohesive (see vs. 16), as well as the repetition of "by him". All in all, it is hard to imagine how there could be much more cohesion than is exhibited in vss. 15-20, precisely the verses that discourse upon the exalted position of God's Son.

After an absence of nine verses the second person plural reappears in vs. 21—the pronoun (here and in vss. 22, 24, 25, and 27) is anaphoric to vs. 10—and serves as subject for the two verbs in vs. 23. I take it that "you" (vs. 21) is intended as part of "all" (vs. 20) and is a hyponym (or synecdonym). The repetition of αποκαταλλασσω (vss. 21 and 20) is coreferential and cohesive. The subject of the finite verb in vs. 21 is the same as in vs. 19, and there is agreement in tense and voice as well. The infinitive in vs. 22 serves the function of a purpose conjunction. The triplet and doublets in vss. 21-23 are cohesive in themselves, besides the lexical association of their contents.

By this time a number of further terms have been used more than once: "gospel", "work", "hope", "body", and "authority"—but in the face of the strong cohesion otherwise provided, their contribution is slight. In vs. 23b, concord of case, gender, and number extends over two relative pronouns and a participle. "Which you heard" is given information. Throughout this paragraph και occurs ten times at phrase level and seven times at clause level, while ειτε occurs six times; all are cohesive. "Paul" and the first person singular pronoun are coreferential with vs. 1, but I take it that the reason they are introduced here is to set up cohesion across the major break between vss. 23 and 24.

1:24-2:5. The first person singular subject of the two verbs in vs. 24 is anaphoric to vs. 23, and the various first person forms (pronoun and verb) in vss. 24, 25, 28 (editorial "we"), 29, 2:1, 4, and 5 are coreferential and cohesive. The second person plural pronoun in vs. 24 (and vss. 25, 27, 2:1, 4, and 5) is anaphoric and also provides cohesion across the break. "His body . . . the church" in vs. 24 is reminiscent of "the body, the church" in vs. 18 and is given information. "My flesh" in vs. 24 is reminiscent of "his flesh" in vs. 22. εγενομην εγω διακονος (vss. 25 and 23) is clearly cohesive. "The word of God" in vs. 24 is reminiscent of "the word of truth" in vs. 5.

The unrelenting hypotaxis that characterizes vss. 24-29 is signaled by relative pronouns and participles which supply cohesion through coreference and concord. "Sufferings" and "afflictions" (vs. 24) are clearly related. The infinitive in vs. 25 has the function of a purpose conjunction. "The saints" in vs. 26 is a hyperonym of "you". "Hidden", "revealed", and "make known" (vss. 26-27) are lexical associates. The repetition of "the mystery" (vss. 27 and 26) is coreferential. "Proclaim", "warning", "teaching", and "present . . . complete" (vs. 28) are lexical associates. The triple repetition of "every man" is cohesive. Also in vs. 28, ἱνα is a purpose conjunction. εις ὃ in vs. 29 almost seems to serve as a conjunction of purpose, or as a coreferent to the prior one. κοπιω, αγωνιζομενς, ενεργειαν, ενεργουμενην, δυναμει in vs. 29 and αγωνα in 2:1 are lexical associates.

γαρ in 2:1 is a causal conjunction. The triplet in 2:1 is cohesive. ἱνα in vs. 2 is a purpose conjunction. The content of vs. 2 is internally cohesive. Sets of terms like "understanding", "knowledge" and "wisdom", and "mystery", "treasure" and "hidden" (vss. 2-3) are lexical associates. εις επιγνωσιν in vs. 2 seems to indicate purpose. "This" in vs. 4 is anaphoric—I consider its antecedent to be the content of 2:1-3. In vs. 4 ἰνα is purpose and in vs. 5 γαρ is causal. In vs. 5, the doublets and their contents are cohesive. The repetition of words such as "faith", "hope", "love", "glory", "wisdom", "knowledge", "riches", and "power" has some cohesive effect. Also, "God" occurs three times in this paragraph, and "Christ" five times. καὶ occurs eight times at phrase level and twice at clause level; δε occurs twice and αλλα once. Though not as massive as in the preceding section, the cohesion in this section is certainly ample.

2:6-7. ουν is a high-level inferential conjunction. "As you have received Christ Jesus the Lord" is given information, going back to the first few verses of the letter. The subject of the verbs in vs. 6 and elided subject of the participles in vs. 7 is anaphoric. "Him" (vs. 7) is anaphoric to vs. 6. "Walk in him" is reminiscent of 1:10. "Rooted", "built", and "established" (vs. 7) are lexical associates and are reminiscent of "steadfast" in 2:5 and "grounded and settled" in 1:23. More especially, "established in the faith" (vs. 7) is almost a repetition of the expressions in 2:5 and 1:23. There is concord of gender, number, and case among the four participles in vs. 7. "As you have been taught" is given information. The verb form of "thanksgiving" has occurred twice before. αυτη is anaphoric to "faith." καὶ occurs twice. In short, there is scarcely anything in these two verses that is not cohesive in some way.

2:8-15. The subject of the verb and personal pronoun in vs. 8 are anaphoric to 2:6, as is the second person plural wherever it appears (vss. 10, 11, 12, and 13). μη τις ὑμας in vs. 8 seems to be a deliberate repetition of the same words in 2:4 since the subject matter of both verses is very similar. μη . . . εσται seems to function as sort of a purpose/result conjunction. "For in him dwells all the fulness" in vs. 9 is given information (see 1:19). "You are complete in him" in vs. 10 almost seems like given information, considering 1:28 and 1:22. "Who is the head of all principality and power" in vs. 10 is also given information (1:15-16). "From the dead" in vs. 12 is reminiscent of 1:18.

There is good internal cohesion in vs. 8 supplied by lexical association. ὅτι (vs. 9) is a causal conjunction. "Him" (vs. 9) is anaphoric to "Christ" at the end of vs. 8. The three relative pronouns in vss. 10-12 are coreferent and anaphoric to "Christ". Vs. 11 has good internal cohesion supplied by lexical association, as does vs. 12. "Him" in vss. 11, 12, and 13 are coreferent and anaphoric to "Christ".

The similarities between 2:13 and 1:21 are too extensive and obvious not to have been deliberate. The emphatic καὶ ὑμᾶς occurs only in these two places in the epistle. In each case it is followed by a circumstantial clause, one referring to "sins" and the other to "wicked works". "Reconciled" is clearly related to "having forgiven . . . trespasses". But 2:13 is also very cohesive with the two verses just before it: the repetition of "dead", "trespasses" in vs. 13 and "sins" in vs. 11; "uncircumcision" in vs. 13 and "circumcision" in vs. 11; "flesh" in vs. 13 and in 11; συνεζωοποίησεν in vs. 13 and συνηγέρθητε in vs. 12. "Forgiving us all trespasses" in vs. 13 is virtually given information (see 1:14). The subject of the finite verbs and elided subject of the participles in vss. 13-15 is presumably the same and anaphoric to "God" in vs. 12. Although the subject matter of each verse (13, 14, 15) is quite distinct, they have in common that they are results of Christ's death and resurrection; and they are almost identical in structure: each of the three sentences has a circumstantial clause at both beginning and end. "Us" in vss. 13 and 14 is anaphoric to 1:13. The repetition of "principalities and powers" (2:15 and 10) is cohesive. καὶ occurs as a conjunction at phrase level five times and once at clause level.

2:16-23. οὖν is a high-level inferential conjunction. "You" in vss. 16 and 18 and as subject of the verbs in vs. 20 continues to be anaphoric and coreferent with the rest. The triplets in vs. 16 are cohesive, both in themselves and their content. The relative pronoun ties vs. 17 to vs. 16. "The body is of Christ" in vs. 17 is given information (1:18, 24). The repetition of "let no one . . . you" in vss. 18 and 16 is cohesive. The subject of the main verb in vs. 18 is also the elided subject of the three following present active participles, which also agree in gender, number, and case. "Head" and "body" in vs. 19 hark back to 1:18, and "body" was also repeated in 2:17. There is internal cohesion in vss. 16-18, although most of the words are *hapax legomena*. But there is clear lexical association between vs. 18 and 2:8 and 2:4.

"Since you have died with Christ from the rudiments of the world" in vs. 20 is given information (2:8 and 12). The repetition of "world" is cohesive. There is lexical association between vs. 21 and 2:16, and the triplet is cohesive. The relative pronoun ties vs. 22a to vs. 21. "The commandments and doctrines of men" in vs. 22b is synonymous with "the tradition of men" in 2:8. The relative pronoun ties vs. 23 to vs. 22b. The triplet is cohesive in form and content. The repetition of "humility" (vs. 23 and 2:18) is cohesive. "Flesh" in vs. 23 is almost coreferent with the occurrences of the word in 2:18, 13, and 11. και occurs six times at phrase level and once at clause level, η occurs four times, μηδε twice and δε once.

3:1-4. ουν is a high-level inferential conjunction. "Since you have been raised with Christ" is given information (2:12-13). The subject of the verbs in this paragraph and the second person plural pronouns continue to be anaphoric and coreferent. "Christ" occurs four times, is the subject of two verbs and a participle, and has one coreferential pronoun. τα ανω ζητειτε and τα ανω φρονειτε are so close as to be virtually synonymous. The opposition of ανω and γης is cohesive. γαρ (vs. 3) is a causal conjunction. "You have died" (vs. 3) is given information (2:20). The repetition of "life" and "be revealed" (vss. 3 and 4) is cohesive. "Our" is anaphoric to 2:14. "Hidden" (vs. 3) and "revealed" (vs. 4) are lexical associates. και occurs but once.

3:5-11. ουν is a high-level inferential conjunction. The subject of the verbs and masculine plural participles, and the second person plural pronouns continue to be anaphoric and coreferent. The repetition of τα επι της γης, in vss. 5 and 2, is cohesive. τα (twice), ἃ, οἷς and αυτοις in vss. 5-7 are coreferent. The list of vices in vs. 5 and vs. 8 furnishes lexical association. "Put to death" (vs. 5) and "put off" (vs. 8) are related, as emphasized by the use of και. μη ψευδεσθε (vs. 9) is related to vs. 8. "Having taken off the old nature with its deeds" in vs. 9 comes close to being given information (3:5). "Take off old" and "put on new" are in clear lexical association. The quadruple set of doublets in vs. 11 is cohesive. There is case concord in the lists in vss. 5 and 8, and in the doublets in vs. 11. και occurs four times at phrase level and once at clause level, δε occurs once and αλλα once.

3:12-17. oun is a high-level inferential conjunction. Whereas 3:5-11 may be viewed as an elaboration of 3:2b, 3:12-17 may be viewed as an elaboration of 3:2a, producing a chiastic effect (which is cohesive). "Put on" in vs. 12 is the opposite of "put to death" (3:5) and "put off" (3:8) and sets up a lexical association of opposites between the two paragraphs. The subject of the verbs in second person and of all the participles in this paragraph, the second person pronouns, and the reciprocal and reflexive pronouns, continue to be anaphoric and coreferent. "As elect of God, holy and beloved" is pretty well given information, even though the term "elect" has not been used before. The list of virtues furnishes lexical association and case concord. The doublet in vs. 13 is cohesive. "Even as Christ forgave you" in vs. 13 is given information (2:13). καθως και . . . οὑτως και is cohesive. "Love" in vs. 14 is a continuation of the list in vs. 12 and illustrates case concord spanning two verses. "The peace of God" in vs. 15 is given information (1:2). The relative pronoun in vs. 15 is anaphoric to "peace". "Be ye thankful" in vs. 15 is given information (2:7). "The word of Christ" in vs. 16 is reminiscent of "the word of God" in 1:25.

ἡ ειρηνη του Θεου βραβευετω εν (vs. 15) and ὁ λογος του Χριστου ενοικειτω εν (vs. 16) are cohesive. The doublet and triplet in vs. 16 are cohesive in content. The three participles in this verse agree in tense, voice, case, number, and gender. There is lexical association between vs. 17 and the rest of the paragraph. "In word" refers back to vs. 16 and "in deed" to vss. 12-14, producing a chiastic effect. The ellipsis of the main verb in vs. 17 is cohesive. "Giving thanks to God and Father" is given information (1:12).

καὶ occurs five times at phrase level, twice at clause level, and for the first time twice at sentence level, binding the separate sentences into a paragraph. δε and ἤ each occurs once. The use of words like "love", "grace", "peace", "wisdom", "body", "heart", "word", "work", and "thanks", all familiar by now, has some cohesive effect. "God" occurs three times, and "Christ" and "Lord" both twice in this paragraph. The use of "Lord" in vss. 16 and 17, for the first time since 2:6, is probably setting up cohesion across the major break between vss. 17 and 18, since "Lord" is prominent in the next section.

3:18-4:1. From this point on there are no paragraph-level conjunctions. The six sentences in this section are simply juxtaposed, but each begins with a vocative and has its main verb in the imperative, which provides good cohesion. All the verbs (except in vs. 25) are second person plural, but the subject in each case will be a "hyponym" (a part of the whole) of "you" as used up to this point. "Lord" occurs five times, including in the first sentence of each set, while "God" and "Christ" occur only once each. The imperatives in this section may be viewed as specific examples of the general command in vs. 17, another hyponymic relationship. There is close cohesion within each set: wives-husbands, children-parents, slaves-masters.

"Submit" in vs. 18 and "obey" in vss. 20 and 22 clearly have cohesive value. "Proper in the Lord" (vs. 18) and "pleasing in the Lord" (vs. 20) are clearly related. γαρ in vs. 20 is a causal conjunction and ἵνα in vs. 21 is a purpose conjunction. The repetition of μη in vss. 19 and 21 may be cohesive. Vss. 22-25 have internal cohesion (lying entirely within the unit in question, in this case a sentence) supplied by conjunctions and lexical association, but not much external cohesion (links to points lying outside the unit in question). "Knowing" in vs. 24 comes close to serving as a causal conjunction, and similarly in 4:1. "You have a Master in heaven" (4:1) comes close to being given information. καὶ occurs at phrase level twice in this section and at clause level three times, while δε and αλλα each occurs once.

4:2-6. The subject of the verb and participles in vs. 2 is anaphoric to the full "you" as it was before 3:18. If not precisely given information, vs. 2 is certainly reminiscent of 1:3, 1:9, and 2:7. The purpose usually expressed by ἱνα (vs. 3) is probably weakened here to be the content of the praying. "Us" in vs. 3 is exclusive and anaphoric to 1:28 (or 1:9). The "we" in 1:28 is probably editorial, but it may well be here in 4:3 also. "The mystery of Christ" in vs. 3 is given information (2:2), and "making it manifest" (vs. 4) almost is too (1:26). The infinitive in vs. 3 may function as a purpose/result conjunction. The third person pronouns in vs. 4 (relative and personal) are anaphoric to "mystery" in vs. 3. The subject of the verbs in vs. 4 and "me" are anaphoric to "Paul", last named in 1:23 and last referred to in 2:5. ἱνα (vs. 4) is a purpose conjunction. The repetition of "to speak" is cohesive.

περιπατειτε was the first main verb, in 2:6, of this major section (2:6-4:6) and is here, in 4:5, the last. Since these are the only places that this form occurs (the verb does occur in two other places with different inflections), the repetition may have been deliberate, and in that event we would have another "sandwich" (the two occurrences enclosing the contents and defining the limits of the section) with the resulting cohesion. But the repetition may be fortuitous, and in that event there is little cohesion since the first occurrence is quite distant.

Again, the subject of the verb and participle in vs. 5 and of the infinitives in vs. 6, and the pronouns in vs. 6 are anaphoric and coreferent. This is the first paragraph since the first chapter to contain first person singular and plural, and second person plural, all three. This is the first, and only, paragraph in the epistle without any coordinating conjunctions.

4:7-9. "Me" and "you" continue to be anaphoric as before. The contents of the triplet in vs. 7 are very similar to 1:7, and cohesive in itself, but not given information since it is about a different person. τουτο is cataphoric and part of a purpose conjunction. "Comfort your hearts" is reminiscent of 2:2. The description of Onesimus is cohesive with that of Tychicus. The last five words of the paragraph are given information and very similar to the first five words; together they form a 'sandwich'. και occurs three times at phrase level and once at clause level.

4:10-14. The triple use of ασπαζεται is cohesive. The occurrence of so many proper names is cohesive—there is case concord. ὁι, ὁυτοι, and ὁιτινες in vs. 11 are coreferent and anaphoric, and they show concord of gender, number, and case. "Kingdom of God" is cohesive with 1:13. In vs. 12, "Epaphras, who is of you, a servant of Christ" is given information (1:7). "Who is of you" is cohesive with the similar expression in 4:9. "Always struggling for you in prayers" in vs. 12 is reminiscent of 4:2, 2:1, and 1:3,9. The purpose clause in vs. 12 is reminiscent of 1:28. "The will of God" reminds us of the same expression in 1:1. "You" and "I" continue to be anaphoric. γαρ in vs. 13 is scarcely causal but is a hypotactic conjunction. "Laodicea" is anaphoric to 2:1. και occurs six times at phrase level.

4:15-17. The subject of the main verbs and the pronouns continue to be anaphoric and coreferent. That the three main verbs are aorist imperatives is cohesive. "The brothers in Laodicea" is given information. Vs. 16 is internally cohesive. The triple reference to Laodicea is cohesive. και occurs twice at phrase level, once at clause level, and twice at sentence level, thereby binding the three disparate sentences into a paragraph.

4:18. The references to the first and second person continue to be anaphoric. "Paul" forms a sandwich with "Paul" in 1:1 (although it also occurred in 1:23). A statement like "Grace be with you" is so predictable at the end of a letter as to be virtually given information. The occurrence of nominal sentences is predictable from the epistolary genre, and hence cohesive.

9.2 Summary. First, I wish to register my surprise at the sheer volume of cohesion that our text displays. I had not expected so much. But it is not distributed evenly throughout the text. There are some seeming tendencies or patterns that invite comment. In this connection an instrument for measuring cohesion would be most helpful. The Halliday-Hasan (1976) notion of counting "ties" is a step toward such an instrument, but I have experienced some difficulties in applying it. I have recognized five different organizing factors, or types of cohesive signal, and it is not at all clear to me that they are of equal value or weight. Nor am I sure how to go about assigning a quantifiable value to each type. Further, within a type, like "lexical association", the different signals seem to me to furnish varying degrees of cohesion—some are very strong; others are quite weak. Involved here is the statistical probability of an item occurring. Still, something must be done, so I have simply tried for a rough, subjective, general evaluation of the density and strength of the cohesive signals in each paragraph. After all, a hearer or reader does not count or measure such signals; what he gets is a general impression. (For that matter, the author probably does not count or measure them either; I assume he goes by the 'feel' of it.)

I have referred to the sheer volume of cohesion in our text. The interplay of cohesive signals throughout the book is such that I see no basis for doubting the integrity of the letter. It was presumably written by one person and at one time. There are two strands of reference that pervade the letter from beginning to end—over 100 each to deity and to the Colossians.

Person references have a major cohesive role. Aside from the second person plural which pervades the letter, other persons are manipulated with a view to providing cohesion. They are used to provide cohesion across major breaks in the outline. Thus, the first person plural occurs in the last line of 1:2 and in the first line of 1:3, bridging that break, then reoccurs in the last two lines of the second paragraph and the first two lines of the third (1:7-9), bridging that break. The first person singular occurs at the end of 1:23 and in 1:24-25, bridging that major break, and also occurs in 1:29 and 2:1, a low level break within the paragraph. The second person plural occurs with significant density in 2:4-5 and 2:6-8 (being sparse or absent for a ways on each side), bridging that major break. This device is used just once more beyond this point—"Lord" occurs in 3:16-17 (last used in 2:6) and in 3:18, 20, bridging that gap. The third person, singular and plural, is used to provide local cohesion within paragraphs here and there.

Now I will look at the section and paragraph breaks again to see what other cohesive signals operate to bridge the gaps. The proper names and nominal sentences link 1:1-2 to the culture. Besides "our" and "we", the break between 1:2 and 1:3 is bridged by "you" and the repetition of "God", "father", "our", "and", "Lord", "Jesus", "Christ" in the last and first lines respectively. So much cohesion so soon intrigues me.

Besides "us" and "we", the break between 1:8 and 1:9 is bridged by "you" and δηλωσας ἡμιν . . . ηκουσαμεν. Other signals providing cohesion but which reach back behind vs. 8 are δια τουτο, "since the day we heard it" (vs. 6) and "praying for you" (vs. 3).

Besides "I", the break between 1:23 and 1:24 is bridged by "you" and εγενομην εγω διακονος (1:23 and 25). Other signals providing cohesion but which reach behind vs. 23 are "his body . . . the church" (1:18), "my flesh" (1:22), and "the word of God" (1:5).

Besides "you", the break between 2:5 and 2:6 is bridged by "Christ" and το στερεωμα της εις Χριστον πιστεως ὑμων (2:5)-βεβαιουμενοι εν τη πιστει (2:7). Other signals providing cohesion are ουν, "as you have received Christ Jesus the Lord" (1:1-3), "rooted and built" (1:23), "as you have been taught" and μη τις ὑμας in 2:8 and 2:4. Because 2:8-15 is subordinate to 2:6-7, it seems to work with it for purposes of external cohesion. (It is hard to know where to stop here because 2:8-15 is heavy with given information reaching back to the first chapter.)

There are no immediate ties to bridge the break between 2:15 and 2:16. More remate signals providing cohesion are ουν, "you", and "the body is of Christ" (1:18, 24). Again, there are no immediate ties bridging 2:23 and 3:1. More remate signals are ουν, "you" and "since you have been raised with Christ" (2:12-13), and perhaps "you have died" (3:3 and 2:20). The only immediate signal linking 3:4 and 3:5 is "you". Others are ουν and τα επι της γης (3:5 and 2). There are no immediate ties between 3:11 and 3:12. Other ties are ουν, "you", "as elect of God, holy and beloved", plus the opposition between "put on" and the list of virtues on the one hand, and "put off" and the list of vices on the other, and perhaps "even as Christ forgave you" (3:13 and 2:13).

There are two immediate ties between 3:17 and 3:18, "Lord" and "you"; the only other tie is the possible hyponymic relationship between the commands in 3:18-4:1 and the general command in 3:17. The only immediate link between 4:1 and 4:2 is "you". Otherwise, the general content of vs. 2 is reminiscent of 1:3, 9, and 2:7, and there is "us", "I", and "the mystery of Christ" (2:2). "You" and "me" are the two ties linking 4:6 and 4:7. The same two ties link 4:9 and 4:10; 4:14 and 4:15 are linked by "you" and "Laodicea". Linking 4:17 and 4:18 there is "you", and to a lesser extent, "I" and "greeting" (occurs as a verb in 4:15, 14, 12, and 10).

For those interested in statistics, I include a chart (fig. 9) showing a rough computation of units of cohesion per line of text. I am not satisfied with the result. It goes counter to the impression I received before trying to count and weigh the "ties". I probably was not consistent in counting and weighing. The chart is divided by paragraphs, and for each paragraph I show internal cohesion (where a tie lies completely within the paragraph), external cohesion (where a tie reaches to some point outside the paragraph), and the total of both. The numbers represent "units of cohesion" per line of text. If the chart were in the form of a graph, it would move up and down in an erratic fashion. Before I tried to count ties, I had the impression that paragraph 1:9-23 was the most cohesive, and that from 3:18 on, the cohesion was noticeably less—impressions that the chart contradicts. In terms of internal cohesion alone, however, 1:15-20 has six units per line of text, making it easily the most internally cohesive 12-line block of text in the epistle. (Perhaps that colored my impression of the section, 1:9-23, that contains it.)

Beside figure 9 I have placed a second chart, figure 10, showing a rough evaluation of the cohesion operating across paragraph and section breaks. I counted only the signals which I felt could reasonably be said to have been deliberately introduced for that purpose, and I used a somewhat different value system than for figure 9; I believe there is a significant pattern. Both charts agree that 2:6 is a pivotal point in the letter. It is a regular feature of Paul's letters that he begins by setting out a propositional basis, and then makes practical applications that derive from that basis. In this letter, 2:6-7 is the hinge where he starts on the application. Up to this point the cohesion across paragraph breaks is uniformly strong. During the application it is uniformly moderate. From 4:7 on, the disparate concluding remarks of a phatic nature, it is uniformly light.

Paragraph	COHESION			Paragraph Juncture	Cohesion Quotient
	Internal	External	Total		
1:1-2	2.25	1.5	3.75		
				1:2/3	5
1:3-8	3.4	.85	4.25		
				1:8/9	7
1:9-23	4.3	.45	4.75		
				1:23/24	7
1:24-2:5	4.1	.4	4.5		
				2:5/6	9
2:6-7	3.75	3	6.75		
				(7/8)	(2)
2:8-15	3.33	1.33	4.66		
				2:15/16	3
2:16-23	4.4	.8	5.2		
				2:23/3:1	4
3:1-4	4.5	1.5	6		
				3:4/5	3
3:5-11	4.8	.7	5.5		
				3:11/12	5
3:12-17	4.7	1.7	6.4		
				3:17/18	4
3:18-4:1	4.35	.45	4.8		
				4:1/2	4.5
4:2-6	3.4	1.8	5.2		
				4:6/7	2
4:7-9	3.4	1.5	4.9		
				4:9/10	2
4:10-14	4	1.6	5.6		
				4:14/15	2
4:15-17	3.5	.75	4.25		
				4:17/18	3
4:18	1.5	3	4.5		

Figure 9   Figure 10

Looking at figure 9 again, I note that the internal scores hold fairly constant and that the more pronounced variation is in the external scores. The ebb and flow of external cohesion is probably significant, but I am not yet sure how.

10 Prominence

In chapter 4 I suggested that Prominence is signaled by three organizing factors: theme, focus, and emphasis. It will be well to briefly review my definition of these terms. *Theme* refers to the essential development of a discourse; it is signaled by the information that carries the discourse forward or contributes to the progression of the argument. Such information constitutes the theme line, which has both a linear and a hierarchical quality. The theme line pervades the discourse. *Focus* differs from theme in two essential ways: its domain will normally be a paragraph or section, rather than the whole discourse; it attaches only to a particular participant or event, or perhaps to a whole clause, and says in effect, "this is the central element in this stretch of text". *Emphasis*, in its turn, refers to any localized highlighting, whatever the encoder's purpose in so doing. The essential characteristic which distinguishes it from theme and focus is its domain, the extent of which is usually a single word or phrase.

In attempting to discern the Prominence structure of Colossians, a major concern will be to trace the theme line. The term theme line reflects my conviction that it must have a linear quality. Since Prominence is indispensable to communication, and since a discourse is encoded linearly, the decoder must perceive the prominence linearly, at least in part. (I have already argued that Prominence has a hierarchical quality as well.) So I start at verse one and work straight through the text. Having already analyzed the hierarchical structure, I use the paragraph breaks as reference points. My basic rule of thumb is that if a piece may be removed without disrupting the flow of the argument, then it is not thematic.[45] Since the first clause of a paragraph is usually independent and the topic clause for that paragraph, it will necessarily be in the theme line. Any steppingstones that are necessary to get to such a clause must be in the theme line also. (It may be pushing the analogy too far to suggest that if the steppingstones are too far apart the decoder may fall in and drown, but intuitively I feel that the analogy may have some validity.)

In a logical discourse like this one, signals of taxis and relation (conjunctions) are of the essence in tracing the argument. An independent clause will be in the theme line unless it is parenthetical. A purpose clause will usually be in the theme line, and a reason clause often will be. I use topic and comment to apply to whole phrases and clauses. A topic clause must be independent and will not be in comment relationship to another clause. Any other material will be comment, by which I simply mean that a comment must be semantically or grammatically linked to its topic and enlarge upon it in some (any) way. A clause that is a comment upon a topic clause may itself be the topic for a following comment, but I will not call it a topic clause—that technical term is reserved for the first type.

Under "Observations" below, I speak of focus as something distinct from the theme line. Focus is signaled by repetition and emphasis. Emphasis may also be used just for local color. I consider that emphasis is signaled in the following ways: foregrounding (in which I follow conventional wisdom); repetition, making an item the topic of one or more comments (appositives, relative clauses, etc.); dequotation (which emphasizes the item isolated by that process, not the dequoted item); use of synonyms; use of a form that is itself emphatic; and promotion.

---

[45] I am referring exclusively to the linguistic organization of the text. In applying this rule of thumb to Colossians, I am not implying that material not in the theme line is unimportant—a profound truth may be stated in an aside.

So far as I know, this device has not been recognized and described before (see sect. 4.3.2).

10.1 Observations. The following observations on Prominence in Colossians will proceed verse by verse (the verse numbers appear in the left margin). The paragraph breaks will be indicated by chapter numbers (they appear only at such breaks), and there will be a summary statement covering each paragraph following the verse by verse discussion. All three organizing factors: theme, focus, and emphasis will be treated together.

1:1 The material in apposition is phrase-level comment and out of the theme line, although it probably lends some emphasis to "Paul".

2 "In Colosse" is emphasized by foregrounding. "To you" is in dequotation and has the effect of emphasizing "grace".

Sentence one gives the two participants in the performative axis for the whole epistle. Sentence two is in comment relationship to one and presents two other major participants.

1:3 Although not in the theme line, "for you" is emphasized by foregrounding; "you" is in focus for the paragraph.

4 The whole verse is parenthetical, a comment on a comment, and out of the theme line.

5 The prepositional phrase (διὰ) is in "comment" relationship to the main clause in vs. 3. The relative pronoun introduces a comment upon "hope".

6 The whole verse is a comment on "gospel" (end of vs. 5) and out of the theme line, but lends some emphasis to "gospel".

7 The finite verb is controlled by the relative pronoun in vs. 5 and is a continuation of the comment upon "hope". The material in apposition is phrase-level comment and out of the theme line, but along with the following clause lends some emphasis to

"Epaphras". The relative clause is a comment on "Epaphras", but not in the theme line.

8 The participial clause is also a comment on "Epaphras", and in the theme line; it seems to lead into the next paragraph, so that to delete it would be awkward.

Although six clauses, in this paragraph (1:3-8), were judged not to be in the theme line, yet each one contributes to the reinforcing of "you" as the element in focus in this paragraph. Every clause in the paragraph, thematic or not, mentions "you" except for the independent clause at the beginning. Note that focus operates independently from theme.

1:9 "We" is emphasized by foregrounding (which involves using a free pronoun) and association with emphatic καί. It is further emphasized by the dequotation of the sentence adverb, "since the day we heard" (which is not thematic). "For you" is emphasized by foregrounding. The last prepositional phrase in vs. 9 and the first in vs. 10 are secondary comments, not in the theme line.

10 Although the three participial clauses in vss. 10-11 are important comments on the infinitive clause, I do not consider them to be in the theme line, but they do lend importance to the infinitive clause.

12 "Giving thanks" is the second branch of the main clause in vs. 9. "With joy" is emphasized by foregrounding. "Father" receives emphasis from the clauses that modify it. The second participial clause is a comment on "father", but not in the theme line.

13 Both the clauses in this verse are comments on "father" (vs. 12), and in the theme line.

14 The whole verse is a comment on "son" (vs. 13), but not in the theme line; however, this and the following clauses lend importance to "son".

15 The whole verse is a comment on "son" in vs. 13 and is in the theme line.

16 "In him" is emphasized by foregrounding. "All things" is emphasized by the repeated and detailed appositives even though they are phrase-level comment and out of the theme line. In the last clause, "they all" is emphasized by foregrounding; "by him and for him" also is foregrounded. All of this verse is thematic except for the appositives.

17 In the first clause, "he" is emphasized by initial position. In the last clause, "they all" is emphasized by foregrounding. Both are thematic.

18 In the first clause, "he" is emphasized by initial position. The sheer repetition of "he" and "all" is emphatic. "Who is the beginning" is parallel to "who is the image" in vs. 15. In the final clause, "all things" is emphasized by foregrounding; "he" is emphasized by use of a free pronoun. The whole verse is in the theme line.

19 "In him" is strongly emphasized. It is a phrase-level constituent but has been shifted to a position as if it were a sentence-level constituent (an instance of promotion). The whole verse is thematic.

20 "Through him" is slightly emphasized by foregrounding, but the repetition of "through him" strongly emphasizes it, and the appositive lends importance to the whole clause. The participial clause is a comment on the preceding clause, but not in the theme line, and so for the material in apposition.

21 "You" is strongly emphasized, by promotion as well as by association with emphatic καί. The concessive clause is a comment on "you" and out of the theme line.

22 The opening prepositional phrases are secondary comment. The infinitive clause is thematic.

23 The first two comments on "gospel" are secondary (nonthematic). "I" is emphasized by the use of a free pronoun, plus the proper

name. The last relative clause is in the theme line because it leads into the next paragraph.

The focus changes three times in this paragraph. In vss. 9b-11 the focus is on "you": it is introduced, slightly emphasized in the topic sentence and is reinforced in the first thematic comment. In vss. 12-14 the focus is on "father", introduced in the second branch of the topic sentence and reinforced by the three subsequent clauses. (In these clauses "father" is in the role of Agent, while "us" is in the role of Patient and may be in secondary focus.) In vss. 15-20 the primary focus is on "son", the topic of the controlling relative clauses and repeatedly emphasized. There is secondary focus on "all things", which is emphasized only a little less than "son". In vss. 15-18a the interplay between the two items is especially noticeable. In vss. 21-23 the primary focus is on "you"; the unusually emphatic και ὑμας is reinforced by the subsequent comments. It may be worth noting that vss. 15-20 are unusually solid, thematically (there is very little material that is not thematic). Also, there was heavy and repeated emphasis upon the items in primary and secondary focus. In terms of degree of theme, focus and emphasis, all three, vss. 15-20 may prove to be the most prominent in the epistle.

1:24 "In my flesh" is a secondary comment. "For his body" is not, since it is a necessary steppingstone to get to the following material.

25 "I" receives emphasis from the use of the free pronoun. The whole verse is steppingstone, and thus in the theme line.

26 The participial clause is a comment on "mystery" but not in the theme line (the argument moves along smoothly without it). The rest of the verse is steppingstone.

27 "The hope of glory" is phrase-level comment and not thematic. The rest is steppingstone.

28 "We" receives emphasis from the use of the free pronoun. The triple use of "every man" has an emphasizing effect, but I have

deleted one mention from the theme line. "In all wisdom" is a secondary comment. I assume that any statement of purpose will be thematic, unless it is off in some parenthetical corner.

29 The anarthrous participle introduces a comment on the finite verb but is out of the theme line.

2:1 Unless it is parenthetic, I assume that an independent clause will be in the theme line (at least in this genre). I take the effect of γαρ to be "I mention the above because" (much like the opening of 2:4), making 2:1 a comment on 1:29.

2 Even though "in love and" is part of a coordinate structure, I take it that the argument runs through the second element of the pair, and the first element may be deleted without damaging the theme line. I take "a knowledge of the mystery . . ." to be a necessary steppingstone to get to 2:4.

3 The relative clause is a comment on "Christ" (vs. 2) and not in the theme line (though it may lend some emphasis to Christ).

4 "This" is emphasized by foregrounding. The whole verse is thematic.

5 In all three of the coordinate structures in this verse, I trace the theme line through the second element only, even though the whole coordinate is a comment upon the immediately prior clause, in the first two cases. Since "your" is emphasized by foregrounding in the first element of the third pair, I transfer that emphasis to "your" in the second element.

Focus is less distinct in this paragraph than in the last. "You", "body", "church", "saints", "all men", and "those in Laodicea" might be said to work together so that we could call "the church" the focal item for the whole paragraph, but the first person has a better claim—there are fourteen references to it throughout the paragraph. The first person is the Agent in 1:28-2:5, a continuation of the role assignment in 1:24. Although most of the paragraph is in the theme line (but only by virtue of being steppingstone), there is little emphasis and weak focus, so that the Prominence of this paragraph is diffuse, in sharp contrast to the last one.

2:6   I take "Jesus, the Lord" to be in apposition to "the Christ", and thus a phrase-level comment. The rest of the verse is thematic. "In him" is emphasized by foregrounding.

7   The whole verse is in comment relationship to the main clause (vs. 6) and out of the theme line.

I do not see any focus, apart from the theme. This paragraph is simply the introduction to a large section, like 1:1-2, and lacks some of the characteristics of a fully developed paragraph.

2:8   "You" is emphasized by foregrounding. The two κατα phrases are in apposition. I have usually considered the second element to be a comment on the first and out of the theme line (being phrase-level comment). In this case, however, both could be left out of the theme line except that "Christ" is the antecedent for "him" in the purpose clause, so I have retained the second element of the apposition and excluded the first.

9   "In him" is emphasized by foregrounding. The whole verse is thematic.

10   "In him" is slightly emphasized by foregrounding, but also by the relative clause (which is a nonthematic comment).

11   All of the verse after the finite verb is comment on that verb and out of the theme line except for the participial clause, which smooths the transition to the continuation of the theme line.

12   The δια phrase is necessary because "God" is the subject of the following verbs (vss. 13-15). The appositive is not in the theme line.

13   "You" is heavily emphasized by promotion and by association with emphatic και. The concessive clause is a comment on "you" and out of the theme line.

14   The independent clauses in vss. 14 and 15 bother me because they are not connected directly to what precedes them, but they must

be retained in the theme line as steppingstones to vs. 16. Further, they do not strike me as being parenthetical, so their rank (independent) places them in the theme line. The last participle in both verses is nonthematic.

The focus in vss. 8b-12 is on "Christ", which is introduced in the first thematic comment and heavily emphasized throughout the passage. In the same verses "you" might be said to be in secondary focus. In vss. 13-15, "God" is probably in focus since it is the subject of the three main verbs and of all the participles except the first, even though "you" is heavily emphasized in vs. 13 (it does not occur in vss. 14 or 15).

2:16 "You" is emphasized by foregrounding. The list seems to me to be secondary, but it cannot very well be deleted from the theme line.

17 The whole verse is a comment on the list and not in the theme line.

18 I take the second participial clause to be in comment relationship to the first one and not in the theme line; the rest of the verse is.

19 The relative clause is a nonthematic comment on "head", but does lend some emphasis to "head".

20 The "as" clause is secondary; the rest of the verse is thematic.

21 The three imperatives plus their relative clause are in apposition to the main verb and not thematic, though they lend emphasis to it.

22 In the κατα phrase I take the coordinate nouns to be synonyms and so keep only the second for the theme line. But the synonym and all of vs. 23 (which is also nonthematic) do provide some emphasis on "teachings of men".

The focus in this paragraph is on the "teachings of men", or something of the sort. It is implied in the list in vs. 16, described in vs. 18, and stated specifically and with emphasis in vss. 20-23.

3:1 "Things above" is emphasized by foregrounding, as is the second occurrence of "Christ", slightly. I take the participial clause as a nonthematic comment on "above".

2 "Things above" is doubly emphasized now, by repetition as well as foregrounding. The use of a close synonym for "seek" has the effect of emphasizing the verbal idea as well.

4 This verse is parenthetical and out of the theme line.

"Christ" is in focus in this paragraph; it occurs in each comment and in the parenthetical sentence.

3:5 "Earthly" is emphasized by being placed in a separate phrase, as well as by the list. The relative clause is out of the theme line.

6 This relative clause is a comment on the list and not thematic.

7 This relative clause is also a comment on the list, but is necessary in order to lead to the "now" in vs. 8. The second clause in vs. 7 is secondary comment.

8 "You" is emphasized by the use of a free pronoun. Again, I do not see how to get rid of the list, even though it seems secondary.

9 Although an independent clause, I take vs. 9 to be in comment relationship to vs. 8 but in the theme line. The final prepositional phrase is secondary comment.

10 Everything after "new", including vs. 11, is a comment on it and out of the theme line, but does lend emphasis to "new". The participles that I include in the theme line are necessary steppingstones to get to vs. 12.

The focus in vss. 5-9 is on "earthly members" (which is a synonym for "old man" in vs. 9). The list in vs. 5 is the topic for the comments in 6 and 7. The list in vs. 8 is followed by the reference to "the old man with its practices" in vs. 9. In vss. 10-11 the focus switches to the opposite, the "new man", which is the topic for the comments in these verses.

3:12 The dequotation of the sentence adverb ("as . . . beloved") has the effect of emphasizing the verb and putting the adverb out of the theme line.

13 All the material in this verse is out of the theme line.

14 The relative clause is a comment on "love" and not thematic, but does lend emphasis to "love".

15 The relative clause is a comment on the main clause and not thematic, but the rest of the verse is.

16 I take the independent clause to be in comment relationship to "be thankful". The participles are comments upon the main clause and lend emphasis to it, but are not in the theme line.

17 I take "whatever you do" to be in comment relationship to the main clause, but quite emphatic. An expression like "whatever" is emphatic in itself, and the elision of the verb in the main clause lends importance to the subordinate clause since the main clause depends upon the subordinate one for its verb. "In word or work" is a secondary comment. "All" in the main clause is emphasized by foregrounding and repetition. The participial clause is a non-thematic comment.

Perhaps the best candidate for focus is the reciprocal relationship symbolized by "each other", but it is not clear. The occurrence of both αλληλων and ἑαυτοις vs. 13 (the first major comment, even though not in the theme line), the reciprocal notion latent in vss. 14 and 15, and the use of ἑαυτους again in vs. 16, may be adduced as evidence for the choice.

3:18 The use of the vocative is emphatic throughout the section. "As is becoming in the Lord" is a nonthematic comment.

19 I am inclined to exclude "and do not be bitter against them" from the theme line, but it is a finite clause in an independent sentence.

20 The dependent clause is nonthematic comment, I think.

21 I have elsewhere stated that I assume that a purpose clause will be thematic, but in this instance I am not sure.

22 "In everything" is emphasized by foregrounding. The coordinate prepositional phrases are nonthematic comment.

23 "From the soul" is emphasized by foregrounding.

24 "From the Lord" is emphasized by foregrounding. "The Lord Christ" is emphasized by foregrounding. A statement of reason will often be thematic, I believe, and the above are required to account for "also" in 4:1.

25 This verse is parenthetical and not in the theme line.

4:1 "Right and fair" is emphasized by foregrounding. "You" is emphasized by foregrounding as well as by association with emphatic καί.

The item in focus is "Lord", which occurs in almost every comment and is emphasized twice.

4:2 "Prayer" is emphasized by foregrounding. The participles (in vss. 2b and 3a) might be excluded from the theme line on the basis that they are not needed to get to vs. 5, logically, but I rather suspect that a large part of Paul's reason for giving the main exhortation is found in vs. 3. I include both purpose clauses.

4 The whole verse is secondary comment.

5 "Wisdom" is emphasized by foregrounding. The participial clause is a nonthematic comment.

6 I supply the participle "being" in the first clause—it is a nonthematic comment. I include the purpose clause in the theme line.

In verses 3 and 4 the focus seems clearly to be on the first person (the plural is probably editorial). If vss. 5-6 have a focal item, it is probably "those outside" to which "each one" in vs. 6 also refers.

4:7 "All my news" is emphasized by foregrounding. "Tychicus" is emphasized by the elaborate appositive, which, however, is not in the theme line.

8 The relative clause is a comment on "Tychicus" but a steppingstone to "Onesimus", which is necessary to account for the plural subject of the independent clause at the end of vs. 9. The rest of the material in vss. 8 and 9 I consider to be nonthematic.

I suppose "Tychicus" is in primary focus and "Onesimus" in secondary focus.

4:10 Everything in vss. 10 and 11, except for the basic topic clause, is nonthematic comment of one sort or another. The proper names receive some emphasis by virtue of the comments.

12 The relative clause and appositive are nonthematic comment which lend emphasis to "Epaphras". The rest of the verse I consider to be thematic, including the purpose clause.

13 The whole verse is out of the theme line.

14 The appositive is nonthematic but does make "Luke" more prominent than "Demas".

Focus here goes by sentence, attaching to the subject of the main verb in each case. In the second sentence "you" is also prominent.

4:15-17 With this string of short, disparate commands I have not excluded anything from the theme line. Nor is it meaningful to speak of focus.

4:18 Once Paul has signed off, the remaining comments are presumably secondary.

Having treated the three organizing factors together, I will now say something about them separately. As stated at the beginning of this chapter, the tracing of the theme line is a major concern. This will be done in the next section. The following section will be devoted to focus, emphasis, and the interaction of the three factors.

10.2. **Theme line**. The trace of the theme line should be read as follows. Verse numbers appear in the margin (some will be missing) but chapter numbers occur only at paragraph breaks. Only topic clauses begin at the left hand margin (with two exceptions which will be noted presently), and they are the only ones that do not appear between slant lines. I use parentheses for material that is not really comment, that I cannot really delete from the topic clause, but which still seems

187

secondary. If more than one line is needed for something, the continuation is single spaced and goes to the first indented position except for topic clauses, which go to the margin. A comment upon a clause will be indented five spaces from the beginning point of its topic. (All comments are between slant lines.) A comment upon a specific item, usually a noun, will begin directly below its topic. If a topic has two parallel comments, they will be shown as parallel. In the event that a topic item begins at the left margin, its comment will too (one of the exceptions mentioned above). Underlining indicates emphasis, of whatever sort. Double underlining indicates unusually strong emphasis, either of an item in isolation (usually by promotion) or to distinguish an emphasized item occurring in an emphasized clause. If a topic clause is an apodosis, its protosis will appear as a cataphoric comment which starts at the left margin (the other exception mentioned above).

In the following trace of the theme line, I have used an English gloss rather than the Greek text (but I did the analysis on the Greek text and it could be used for the trace without difficulty), for two reasons: the gloss makes it easier to identify certain exegetical choices, and I just wanted to see how it would work. I am not concerned to defend the gloss; I only tried for intelligibility, not elegance.

The Theme Line

1:1 <u>Paul</u> (and Timothy) to the saints <u>in Colosse</u> (and faithful brothers in Christ)

2 /<u>Grace</u> and peace to you from God our Father and the Lord Jesus Christ/

1:3 We thank the God and Father of our Lord Jesus Christ always

5 /because of the hope laid up for you in heaven/

/which you heard before in the word of the truth of the <u>gospel</u>/

7 /as also you learned from <u>Epaphras</u>/

8 /who informed us of your love in spirit/

1:9 Consequently, <u>we</u> actually do not stop praying for <u>you</u> (and asking)
   /that you be filled with the knowledge of his will/

10   /<u>so as to walk worthily of the Lord</u>/

12 . . . .[46] giving thanks to the <u>Father</u>
<u>with</u>   <u>joy</u>

13   /who rescued us from the authority of the
darkness/

                                             /and
translated us into the kingdom of the <u>son</u> of his love/

15   /who* is the image of the invisible God, firstborn
of all creation/

16   /for, <u>all things</u> were created <u>in him</u>

                              <u>they</u>   <u>all</u>   were
created <u>by him</u> and <u>for him</u>

17   and <u>he</u> is before   all

                              and <u>they all</u> exist
<u>in him</u>

18   and <u>he</u> is the head of the body/

                   /who*[47] is the   beginning,
firstborn from the dead/

                   /that   in   all   things   he   might   become
preeminent/

19   /for all the fullness was pleased <u>in Him</u> to dwell
and <u>through Him</u> <u>to reconcile the all to him</u>/

21   /<u>You too</u> he has now reconciled/

22   /to   present   you   holy   (and   unblamable   and
unaccusable) before him/

---

[46] The line of dots is intended to indicate that the opening words of 1:9, "Consequently, we actually do not stop", are to be understood here as well, so that vs. 12 is a continuation of the topic clause in vs. 9.

[47] The asterisks in vss. 18 and 15 indicate that the relative pronouns to which they are attached are co-referent and parallel.

23   /if you remain grounded and   firm in the faith and not removed from the hope of the gospel/

/of which I (Paul) have become a minister/

1:24 Now then, I rejoice in my sufferings for you and fill up the remainder of the afflictions of Christ for his body

/which is the church/

25   /of which I have become a minister/

/ac- cording to the dispensation of God/

/which was given to me for you/

/to complete the word of God/

26   /the mystery now revealed to his saints/

27   /to whom God wished to make known what is the glorious wealth of this mystery among the nations/

/which is Christ in you/

28   /whom we preach/

/admonishing   and teaching every man/

/that we may present every man complete in Christ Jesus/

29   /unto which I even toil/

2:1   /For I want you to know how great a struggle I have for you (and . . .)/

2   /that their hearts be encouraged/

/knit together unto all wealth of assurance of understanding/

/unto a knowledge of the mystery of the God and Father and of the Christ/

4   [48]/Now I say this so that no one deceive you with vain speech/

---

[48] 2:4 is parallel to 2:1.

5 /for I am with you in spirit/

   /beholding the firmness of <u>your</u> faith in Christ/

2:6 Therefore, /as you have received the Christ/ walk in <u>him</u>

2:8 Beware lest anyone capture <u>you</u> through philosophy and vain deceit

   /according to the principles of the world and not Christ/

9   /because <u>in him</u> all the fullness of the Godhead dwells bodily

    and you are complete in <u>him</u>/

11   /in whom you have also been circumcised/

        /buried with him in baptism/

12   /in whom you have also been raised/

        /through faith in the energizing of

  God/

13   /Yes <u>you</u> he made alive with him/

         /having forgiven us all trespasses/

14   /Having erased the written code of regulations that

  was <u>against us</u>/ he even removed it completely

15   /Spoiling principalities and powers/ he disgraced them

  openly

2:16 Therefore, let no one judge <u>you</u> (in food . . . sabbath)

18 nor let anyone cheat <u>you</u>

   /delighting in humility and worship of angels/

19 /and not holding fast the <u>head</u>/

20 /since you have died with Christ from the principles of the world/

  why are you subject to <u>rules</u>

22 /according to the <u>teachings of men</u>/

3:1 Therefore, /since you have been raised with Christ/ seek <u>things

  above</u> /where the <u>Christ</u> is/

2 <u>mind things above</u> (not things on the earth)

3 /for you have died and your life is hidden with Christ in God/

3:5 Therefore, mortify your <u>earthly</u> members (fornication . . . greed)

7   /in which <u>you</u> once walked/

8 But now <u>you</u> also put away all these (anger . . .) out of your mouth

9   /Do not lie to each other/

/having taken off the old man/

10   /and having put on the <u>new</u>/

3:12 Therefore, <u>put on</u> compassion . . . long-suffering, but above all

14   these <u>love</u>

15   And let the peace of God umpire in your hearts

and be thankful

16   /<u>Let the word of Christ dwell in you richly</u>/

17   And /<u>whatever you do</u>/ do <u>all</u> in the name of the Lord Jesus

3:18 <u>Wives</u>, submit to your own husbands

<u>Husbands</u>, love your wives (and do not be bitter against them)

<u>Children</u>, obey your parents in everything

21   <u>Parents</u>, do not tease your children /lest they be discouraged/

22   <u>Slaves</u>, obey your human masters <u>in everything</u>

23   and whatever you do, work at it <u>from the soul</u> /as to the

Lord and not men/

24   /knowing that you will receive the reward of the

inheritance <u>from the Lord</u>/

/for you serve <u>the Lord Christ</u>/

4:1   <u>Masters</u>, give to your slaves what is <u>right</u> and <u>fair</u>

/knowing that <u>you also</u> have a Master in heaven/

4:2   Be devoted to <u>prayer</u>

/watching therein with thanksgiving/

3   /at the same time praying for us also/

/that God would open to us a door for the word/

/to speak the mystery of Christ/

5   Walk <u>in wisdom</u> toward those outside

/that you may know how to answer each one/

4:7   <u>Tychicus</u> will tell you <u>all my news</u>

8   /whom I sent to you, with Onesimus/

9   they will tell you about everything here

4:10 Aristarchus, Mark, and Jesus greet you

12   <u>Epaphras</u> greets you

        /always laboring for you in prayers/

            /that you may stand perfect and complete in all the will of God/

14   Luke and Demas greet you

4:15   Greet the brothers . . .

        And /when the epistle has been read to you/ cause that it also be read in the assembly in Laodicea (and the one from Laodicea, that you also read)

        And say to Archippus, " . . . "

4:18   The salutation with my hand, Paul

10.3 Summary. According to the framework I am proposing, Prominence is signaled by three organizing factors: theme, focus, and emphasis. I believe this approach works nicely on Colossians. Though there is cooperation among the three factors, they are clearly distinct and often operate independently. Although I may be overlooking some further factors that contribute to prominence, I insist that we need at least these three.

I will begin by discussing the role of emphasis; only the places where it contributes to theme or focus will be mentioned. When I pass over an item underlined in the trace of the theme line above, the emphasis is merely providing local calor. In 1:1 "Paul" and "Colosse" are definitely thematic, the main participants in the discourse, and it is appropriate that they be emphasized. In the first comment in 1:3 (not in the theme line), "you" is emphasized and is the focal element in the paragraph. In 1:9 "we" is the Agent (subject) of the topic clause and is thematic; "you" is the focal element in 1:9b-11. In 1:10 "so as to walk worthily of the Lord" is thematic—it is an important point in the argument. In 1:12 "Father" is the focal element for 1:12-14. In 1:14 "son" is the focal item (primary focus) for 1:15-20, reinforced by the third singular pronoun in those verses; "all things" is in secondary focus for 1:15-20. In 1:20

"through him to reconcile them all to him" is thematic—a very important point in the argument—as well as containing the focal element. In 1:21 "you" is the focal element for 1:21-23. In 2:6 "him" is thematic by virtue of being in the topic clause, but since the focal element of 2:8-12 is "Christ", 2:6-7 might well be viewed as sharing that focal element, which would make "him" focal as well. In 2:8 "you" is thematic. In 2:9 and 10 "him" is focal. In 2:16 "you" is thematic, as in 2:18. "Rules" in 2:20 and "teachings of men" in 2:22 are focal. "Things above" in 3:1 and 2 is thematic; "Christ" is focal. In 3:5 "earthly" is both thematic and focal. In 3:8 "you" is thematic. In 3:10 "new" is focal. I think all the emphasized elements in 3:12-17 are thematic. The vocatives in 3:18-4:1 are thematic. "Lord" in 3:24 (twice) is focal. In 4:7 "Tychicus" is focal and thematic, and so for "Epaphras" in 4:12.

I am surprised at the degree of independence between focus and theme; they seem to be largely supplementary. In 1:3-8 the focal element, "you", is introduced in a nonthematic comment and repeated in five others, while being repeated in four thematic comments. The repetition also provides internal cohesion. The effect is to bind the paragraph together and to give it a certain density of prominence, pervading the paragraph. In 1:9-23 there is a split topic clause (in vss. 9 and 12) and four successive focal elements. The focal elements for 1:9b-11 and 1:12-14, "you" and "Father" respectively, are both introduced in the topic clause as Beneficiary (indirect object), and each becomes the subject of the following comment clauses, some of which are not in the theme line. The focal element for 1:15-20, "son", appears at the end of the third comment on "Father", but since it is the topic for the next twelve comments, there is no doubt as to its status. In these verses there is almost complete overlap or interaction of theme and focus (with a high incidence of emphasis). "All things" provides a strong secondary focus. In 1:21-23 "you" is the focal element; theme and focus work together to a lesser degree than in 1:15-20.

The paragraph 1:9-23 gives occasion for a digression on a possible correlation between focus and the notion of semantic paragraph, as distinct from grammatical paragraph. It is a commonplace of recent linguistics to recognize the possibility of a skewing between so-called deep structure and surface structure. Thus, although a proposition is normally encoded as a clause, it may be encoded as a phrase, or even a word. Similarly, a semantic paragraph may presumably be encoded in something less than a grammatical paragraph. I suppose that if a semantic paragraph is to be posited without reference (or contrary) to grammatical signals, it must be on the basis of unity of subject matter. In that event, focus could well be an important factor, even serve as the basis for positing more than one semantic paragraph within a grammatical one. In this instance one could posit four semantic paragraphs: vss. 9-11, 12-14, 15-20, and 21-23 within the single grammatical paragraph, 1:9-23. But I would resist the positing of a semantic paragraph that straddles a major grammatical paragraph break, e.g., joining 1:23 and 1:24-2:5 because "Paul" is mentioned. The first person is introduced in 1:23 to provide cohesion across the major break, and since cohesion is necessary for communication, it has a right to its own existence. It will not do to set up a semantic paragraph that obviates such cohesion.

I have suggested the first person as possibly the focal element for 1:24-2:5. In that case there is substantial overlap between theme and focus in this paragraph. This paragraph "feels" quite different from 1:3-8; there is less density of Prominence. In 2:8-15 the focal element of vss. 8-12 is "Christ", introduced in the first comment and mentioned in each subsequent clause (being the topic of three of them). Here focus is distinct from theme. In 2:13-15 "God" is focal, and since it is the subject of most of the verbal forms there is overlap with theme. In 2:16-23 the focal element "teachings of men" is distinct from theme.

In section 10.1 I suggested that "Christ" is the focal element of 3:1-4. It does occur five times, but "you" occurs six times and they are each emphasized at least once. They are both introduced in a comment, and in either case there is some independence from theme. In 3:5-9 "earthly members" is focal and there is overlap with theme, while in 3:10-11 (part of the same grammatical paragraph) the focal element is "new man", which is independent of theme. There is no clear focus in 3:12-17. In 3:18-4:1 the focal element, "Lord", is quite independent of theme. If 4:2-4 has a focal element, it is the first person and is quite distinct from theme. From 4:7 on, if there is any focus, it is on the proper names that serve as subject of the independent verbs, so that it is scarcely distinguishable from theme.

The varying degrees of focus with varying degrees of overlap with theme produce a shifting configuration of Prominence. Also involved are the incidence of emphasis and the ratio of thematic to nonthematic material. Taking an impressionistic reading of the four factors, 1:15-20 emerges as having far and away the highest Prominence quotient or density in the epistle; it is evidently the centerpiece in the author's argument. The rest of 1:9-23 has a good density. In contrast, 1:24-2:5 is diffuse, has low density. From 2:8 on, the density is back up to a good level. 3:1-4 and 3:18-4:1 are about even and have the highest density after 1:15-20 (but a good ways behind it), but they are quite different in flavor. It could be argued that they are strategic at their respective points in the argument of the book. I include a rough, impressionistic chart (fig. 11) of the four factors: degree of focus, degree of overlap between focus and theme, ratio of thematic to nonthematic material, and incidence of emphasis—mentioned at the beginning of the paragraph, but I do not know how to interpret it beyond what I have said.

I have not attempted to produce an abbreviated thematic outline, giving a single theme sentence for each paragraph and larger section.

Although such an outline has mnemonic value I regard it as something of an artificial abstract. It is not a legitimate statement of the prominence structure of a discourse. But such abstracted themes are useful (indeed necessary) as a translation tool for languages that require the stating of the theme at the beginning of each episode, section, or paragraph. I have yet to perceive the usefulness of what John Austing calls "core theme" (1977:8).

	degree of focus	overlap focus theme	ratio of theme	amount of emphasis
1:3-8	good	light	5-6	little
1:9-23			21-16	
9-11	fair	medium	3-5	some
12-14	fair	medium	3-3	little
15-20	<u>very good</u>	heavy	10-4	<u>much</u>
21-23	good	medium	5-4	little
1:24-2:5	poor	medium	18-8	little
2:7-8			2-4	little
2:8-15			14-9	
8-12	good	light		little
13-15	fair	heavy-		little
2:16-23	fair-	light	7-9	some
3:1-4	fair+	medium	6-3	much
3:5-11	fair		8-6	some
5-9		heavy		
10-11		light		
3:12-17	poor	?	7-9	much
3:18-4:1	fair+	light	12-7	much
4:2-6				
2-4	fair	light	5-3	little
5-6	poor	?	2-2	little

Figure 11

11 Style and Strategy

11.1 Style. At this point my choice of a piece of ancient literature as a corpus presents me with a difficulty: I do not have access to a native speaker of Koine Greek. From a careful study of all extant examples of Hellenistic Greek, it might prove possible to identify and correlate certain signals with certain registers and/or codes, but such a study might well qualify as a thesis in its own right and lies outside the scope of this work. However, a few brief and general observations may be made.

The author's codes would presumably remain constant in a corpus like Colossians, and thus make no further contribution to the discourse structure than the choices of lexicon and structure that might be dictated by those codes. If we knew what the code signals were, it might clear up an occasional question as to why a certain word or construction was used.

The register, or the factors contributing to it, would probably remain fairly constant also. Most commentators regard it as unlikely that Paul had personally visited the church in Colosse; the statements in 1:7 and 2:1 may be understood in this way. In such an event, the author would presumably be more formal than with people he knew, and would be reasonably polite so as to gain rapport. In fact, the first and last ten verses or so are quite phatic in nature. Only after establishing his authority in 1:24-2:5, which he does in a nice manner, does he begin to use the imperative. He starts slowly, but becomes increasingly direct, culminating in the vocatives in 3:18-4:1, after which the intensity declines rapidly. So then, I consider that there are at least three noticeable factors contributing to the register of Colossians: the author writes from a position of authority, is more or less formal, and is generally polite.

Although the question of the authorship of the various epistles within the traditional Pauline corpus lies entirely outside the scope of this study, I think my framework suggests an avenue of investigation which has not been sufficiently explored. Not only must the purpose and subject matter of an epistle be considered, but also its code(s) and register(s). By way of illustration, the style (as the term is used in biblical studies) of the pastoral epistles is apparently distinct from that of the other letters in the Pauline corpus. Nigel Turner seems to quote P.N. Harrison with approval.

> P.N. Harrison, in his notable work, thus summarizes the genuine Pauline style with its irregularities and abruptness: "the tendencies to fly off at a tangent, the sudden turns and swift asides, the parentheses and anacolutha" (_The Problem of the Pastoral Epistles_, Oxford 1921, 41). The style of the Pastorals, on the other hand, is said to be "sober, didactic, static, conscientious, domesticated," lacking Paul's energy and impetus, intellectual power, and logic (1976:101).

Turner goes on to characterize the style of the pastorals in the following way.

> The arguments are not sustained as long as they are in Paul, and in place of Paul's reasoned pleas comes assertion. Compared with Paul's, it is rather an ordinary style, lacking his energy and versatility; it is slow, monotonous and colourless; it is abstract with fewer concrete images (1976:101).

I suspect that the crucial difference is one of register. Before enlarging on this point I wish to cite a statement by F.F. Bruce.

> In general the situations with which Paul's letters deal, the people to whom he refers . . . , the incidents which he briefly recalls—all these were matters of common knowledge to his readers and himself, and the merest allusion was sufficient to show them what he had in mind. But we have to reconstruct those situations as best we may . . . (1965:11).

If we but remember that Paul and Timothy were intimate, that Timothy was fully instructed in Paul's theology, knew how he felt on almost any issue, the differences become predictable. There is no need for sustained argument, reasoned plea, or asides to head off possible objections. Paul knew that Timothy was at one with him; they had discussed all these things before. Free from the pressure of a critical audience, Paul would use precisely "an ordinary style". When uncertain of his audience, and writing polemically, Paul's style might well become "ragged" (Thompson 1967:106). Predictably there would be a substantial difference in register between a letter written to Timothy and one written to the Colossians. This difference in register would result in a completely different flavor in the two books.

I have no evidence that Paul changed dialects anywhere in the epistle, so "dialect" is not a factor here. Nor have I identified any feature that can be excluded as "idiolect".

11.2 **Strategy**. In chapter 6 I suggested that Strategy is signaled by five organizing factors: content, genre, information rate, modality, and sincerity. They will be considered in that order.

11.2.1 Content. I have limited content (as an expression of Strategy) to overt reference. Thus, the content of Colossians is the referential value of the wording with which the text presents us. What we have is the result of the author's choice of what to encode overtly. From a decoding perspective and with a piece of ancient literature (so that we have no intimate knowledge of the situational context for the epistle), it is difficult to say much of anything about information that the author may have decided not to encode. But we can attempt to perceive the author's purpose as reflected in the content, which will involve some reading between the lines.

Commentators upon Colossians are generally agreed that the author's basic purpose was to combat an incipient 'heresy' of some sort, although their characterizations of that heresy vary considerably. I will content myself with working through the text and making some general observations as I go.

The author gives the doctrinal setting in the first two verses by relating both himself and his addressees to God the Father and the Lord Jesus Christ. By way of building rapport, Paul compliments the Colossians upon the good things he has heard about their progress in the faith. He only mentions good things, but by citing Epaphras as his source, who as an officer in their assembly (1:7) would know all about them, he lets it be known that he probably would also have heard any unfavorable information. We may reasonably conclude that Paul's decision to make overt reference only to complimentary information (in 1:3-8) is an expression of his strategy.

The content of his prayer for them in 1:9-11 gives overt expression to Paul's concern: he wants them to really know God's will and to conduct themselves accordingly. In the process of praying for the Colossians and thanking the Father (1:9-14), Paul enlarges the doctrinal setting. It would seem that by using the article with the first mention of concepts like "knowledge of God", "power of his glory", "share of the inheritance", "authority of the darkness", "kingdom of the son", "redemption", and "forgiveness of sins" he is treating them as given information and acting as though the Colossians share his understanding of them (the concepts).

It has already been observed that 1:15-20 have the highest density of both Cohesion and Prominence of any similar block of text in the epistle. Looking at the content of these verses, it is hard to imagine what more Paul might say by way of affirming and reiterating the preeminence of the "Son". The coincidence of such density of cohesion, prominence, and content points to these verses as being central to the author's purpose. Evidently the Colossians had been exposed to notions concerning "God's Son" that did not do him justice. To judge from Paul's energetic response, he considered the situation to be serious. From the use of the phrase παν το πληρωμα, it is usually understood that there were probably gnostic elements in the heresy Paul was combating. To persons exposed to gnostic teaching such a phrase would be suggestive.

Having presented a propositional base, Paul turns the focus upon the Colossians in 1:21-23, making some initial applications. Then, in 1:24-2:5 he establishes his authority in a low-key way and affirms his concern for their welfare, which includes his concern that they have a full understanding of the mystery of God and Christ (in whom are hidden all wisdom and knowledge) and not be deceived by vain words. He closes this section on a complimentary note.

As previously noted, 2:6-7 seems to be the hinge where Paul turns to practical application, appealing to the propositional basis he has already adduced. Some of the things said about Christ in 2:8-15 are reminiscent of 1:15-20, but the emphasis is upon the benefits that have accrued to them as believers in Christ. Verse 10 makes a good summary statement: "ye are complete in him". This affirmation, along with the warning against philosophy and vain deceit which derive from human tradition, may give further insight into the heresy Paul was combating. A phrase like τα στοιχεια του κοσμου would presumably be suggestive to anyone familiar with gnostic teaching. The repeated references to Christ's supremacy over "principalities and powers" are leading up to the next paragraph.

In 2:16-23 the negative side of Paul's concern finds maximum expression. The Colossians were evidently in danger of falling prey to legalism and an undue concern with outward form on the one hand, and an improper attitude toward the spirit world on the other. It is the latter danger that Paul combats with his insistence upon Christ's supremacy over principalities and powers.

I take it that by 3:1 Paul has finished combating heresy, as such, and turns to some exhortations based on their position in Christ with a view to improving their Christian experience, which would also be part of his purpose. The direct commands in 3:18-4:1 are also a reflection of this purpose. In 4:3 Paul gives a personal request: he wants them to pray for him. He then goes into the concluding remarks which are largely of a rapport-building nature.

To really set out the content of Colossians would involve a conventional exegesis of the text, and to do so would increase the bulk of this discussion unduly without a commensurate contribution to its purpose; besides, many published exegeses are already available. This would also be the place to display the propositional structure of the text, should one wish to. Although such a display is useful as a translation tool, it seems to me that it distorts the discourse structure to a certain extent. I prefer to use a structural diagram as the basic vehicle for displaying the discourse structure of a text (see chap. 12).

11.2.2 Genre. Reference has already been made to Koine Greek epistolary genre and some of its characteristics. Colossians is an unambiguous example of this genre. Among the constraints imposed by the genre are a salutation and sign-off expressed in nominal sentences, at least three parts to the salutation: sender, addressee, and greeting; a "thanksgiving" or prayer formula following the salutation, and a logical orientation.

11.2.3 Information Rate. One of the advantages of the written medium is that the decoder can go back and try again; the rate of information injection is not so sensitive as in spoken medium. As one might expect from the medium, there are few if any "fillers" (words carrying zero information). Many of the signals contributing to Cohesion are also relevant here: any expression of grammatical agreement, phoric reference (except cataphora), or given information (as defined in section 3.5) will qualify as given information in the somewhat wider sense used here. In many of the coordinate structures, the second (or third or fourth) unit will be a synonym of the first, or otherwise be fairly predictable; such material, though not actually given, places less strain on a decoder than information that is really new.

Aside from the first two verses whose content is almost entirely predictable, I would say that the mean ratio of new to given information throughout the letter is around 50/50. 2:6-7 may go as low as 25/75, while 3:18-4:1 may go as high as 75/25, but most of the paragraphs have a more nearly even ratio.

11.2.4 Modality. Although I have discussed my framework from a decoding perspective, it is clear that Strategy relates mainly to the encoding process. An analyst does need to know the range of factors that may be involved, but there will not always be a great deal to say about one factor or another. Modality in Colossians is a case in point. The text seems to me to be quite straightforward with reference to the sorts of signals that contribute to modality. I would say that the choice of mood and of a finite verb, versus a participle or infinitive, relates mainly to Hierarchy, while the choice of voice relates mainly to Prominence. A good majority of the verbal forms are in the active voice, and a similar majority of finite verbs are in the indicative mood; most of the subjunctive forms follow either ἵνα or ἐαν, and there are no optative forms. The author transmits considerable emotional involvement, while being generally polite, complimentary, positive, and serious. He does not indicate any uncertainty about what he is trying to communicate.

11.2.5 Sincerity. I see no evidence of insincerity in the author's use of the discourse system.

12 The Discourse Structure of Colossians

How may we characterize the discourse structure of Colossians as a unified whole? Having discussed the several macrosystems with their organizing factors individually, I will now address the problem of bringing them all together in a single display. As already mentioned (sect. 11.2.1), I will use a specialized structural diagram as the basic vehicle for displaying the discourse structure of our text. In section 8.5 I discussed the mechanics of such a diagram, including one feature that is essential to my present purpose: the correct word order is maintained (and the entire text is reproduced).

By putting the discourse outline in the margin of the structural diagram, we get a complete and precise display of the hierarchical structure of the text (to whatever level of detail one may choose—I have generally stopped at the clause level). By retaining the correct word order, the Prominence signals are not skewed or obscured, but the diagram must be modified in some way if we are to do justice to the prominence structure of the text. By reproducing the complete wording of the text, all the signals for Cohesion, Style, and Strategy are available, but something more will have to be done for each of these macrosystems.

12.1 As mentioned above, Hierarchy is completely taken care of by the diagram (plus the outline). I propose the following modifications to give an adequate account of Prominence. To show the theme line, topic clauses will be placed between asterisks, and thematic comments will be placed between slant lines; material not enclosed by asterisks or slant lines is out of the theme line. Since the hierarchical quality of the theme line coincides with the diagram, the topic of each comment should be apparent. An item in focus will be enclosed in brackets (some other symbol may be used if preferred). Emphasis will be indicated by underlining, and extraordinarily strong emphasis by double underlining.

12.2 To acknowledge overtly every cohesive tie would clutter the diagram beyond recognition, even if we had the means to distinguish the type and degree of cohesion relevant to each signal (tie). Since the internal cohesion is fairly constant throughout the text, perhaps nothing need be done beyond making a statement to that effect in a footnote to the diagram (an exception like 1:15-20 could also be mentioned there). (Of course, a complete discussion of the cohesive signals, such as is given in section 9.1, can be appended to the diagram.) The one facet of Cohesion which I feel should be reflected in a modified diagram is the external cohesion whose function is to bridge paragraph and section breaks. I will use the cohesion quotients given in figure 10, placing the appropriate quotient within parentheses and just above the beginning of the paragraph.

12.3 What is to be done for Style? Where register, code, and dialect remain constant throughout a discourse, all that is needed is a note to that effect. Where there is a change in one of these factors, I suggest putting a descriptive term above the line of text at the point where the change begins. For example, if the encoder switches from a formal to a casual register, I would put "casual" at the appropriate spot, and then if there is a change back again, I would put "formal" at that spot. Similarly, if there is a change from male to female code, I would put "female" above the point of change, and so on. The last mentioned register(s) and code(s) are understood to continue in force until a change is specified.

It may have been noticed that in chapter 11 comparatively little space was given to the discussion of Style in Colossians and that here I propose to account for it very simply and briefly. It should not be assumed from this that Style is unimportant. Style is to discourse what seasoning is to food—a little goes a long way. In quantity, a half-teaspoon of salt may seem insignificant alongside a pound of potatoes, but to vary the ratio very much in either direction will produce an unpalatable result. The use of nutmeg or chili powder instead of salt would produce a dramatic (traumatic?) result. Similarly, an unexpected shift in register or code may have dramatic consequences, even though the shift may be characterizable by a single word.

12.4 As for Strategy, the several organizing factors contributing to it will require separate treatment. In section 11.2.1, I have discussed the problem of just how to set out the content of a text. By supplying the complete wording and in the correct order, we have everything except a spelling out of the referential value of the text. I see no way of incorporating a statement of the referential value into the diagram and still retain the actual wording of the text. One thing that can be done is to specify the relation obtaining between each comment and its topic: this can be done in the right margin opposite each comment. For the rest, the exegesis or commentary will have to be in a separate statement, i.e., not in the diagram, unless an attempt is made to translate the diagram into another language. If I were to attempt to display the discourse structure of Colossians entirely in English, this would involve translating the text, which would allow me to give an unambiguous indication of many exegetical choices (but probably not all). This would result in improved incorporation of content into the display of the discourse structure (if the translation were done skillfully), but would represent a loss for virtually all other factors. In my view, the loss would be so great that I would not consider the result to be an adequate representation of the discourse structure of the text. However, such a translated display would be a useful translation tool for speakers of English without a knowledge of Koine Greek (in the case of a corpus like Colossians) since for them the loss referred to is more or less unavoidable.

With reference to the genre of a discourse, it simply needs to be identified. If there is a change of discourse type along the way, this should be noted—a note above the beginning point of the change would be sufficient.

The information rate and the signals contributing to modality are readily recoverable from the displayed text, since it is all there. If there are any patterns deserving of special comment, a note may be appended. The sincerity of the encoder may be assumed. Any exception may be marked by putting "insincere" above the relevant material and indicating the linear extent in some way.

12.5 Rather than reproduce the whole structural diagram of Colossians incorporating the sorts of modifications discussed above, I will just take a sample paragraph to illustrate what the full-orbed display of the discourse structure of a text will look like. The choice of paragraph was dictated by considerations of space. The "(4.5)" above the paragraph is the external cohesion quotient bridging the gap between this and the prior paragraph. The terms "authoritative", "adult", and "polite" illustrate how I would indicate relevant codes and registers. The "personal involvement (vs. 4)" illustrates how I would handle an intrusion of modality requiring mention; the "(vs. 4)" indicates the extent. I follow Beekman and Callow in giving the relations in upper case (I owe to them the whole idea of handling relations in this way).[49]

---

[49] Since my purpose is to illustrate the application of my framework, I have taken no notice of alternative analyses. I make no special claims for the analysis I have used.

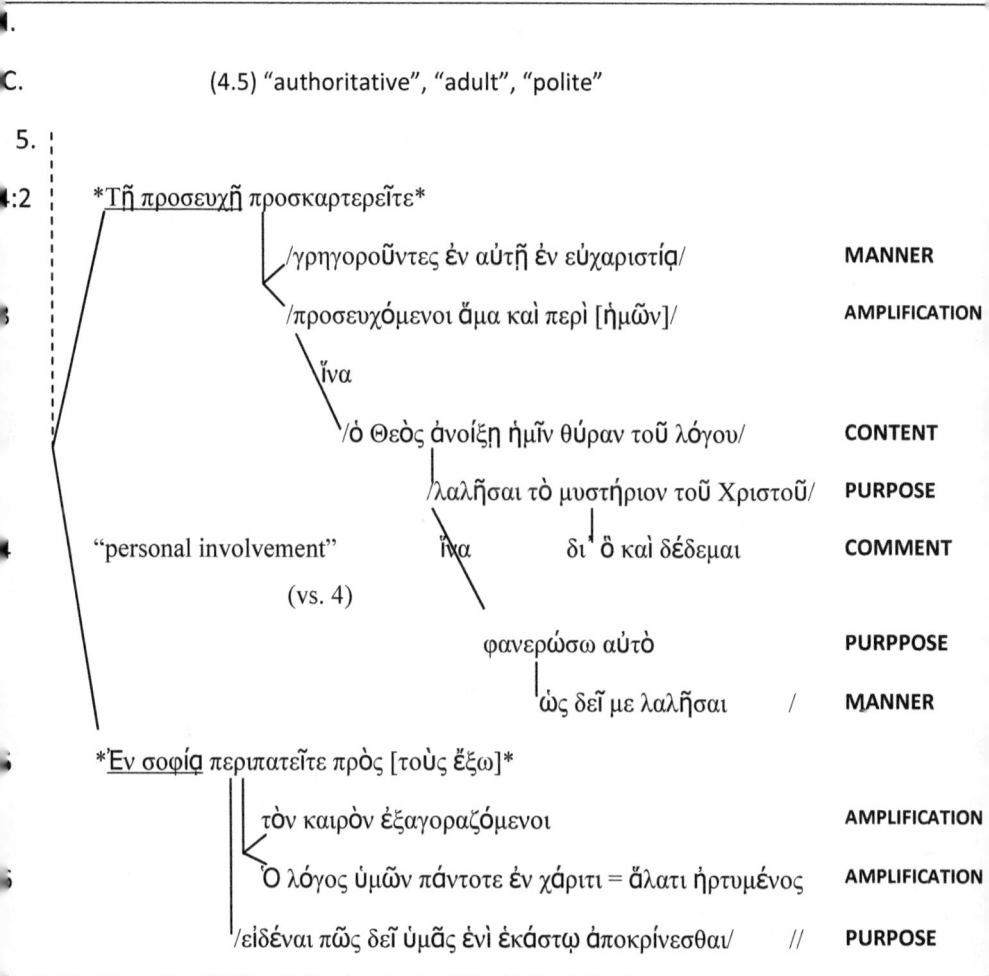

I.

C.   (4.5) "authoritative", "adult", "polite"

5.

:2   *Τῇ προσευχῇ προσκαρτερεῖτε*

           /γρηγοροῦντες ἐν αὐτῇ ἐν εὐχαριστίᾳ/   **MANNER**

          /προσευχόμενοι ἅμα καὶ περὶ [ἡμῶν]/   **AMPLIFICATION**

          ἵνα

          /ὁ Θεὸς ἀνοίξῃ ἡμῖν θύραν τοῦ λόγου/   **CONTENT**

             /λαλῆσαι τὸ μυστήριον τοῦ Χριστοῦ/   **PURPOSE**

  "personal involvement"   ἵνα   δι' ὃ καὶ δέδεμαι   **COMMENT**

       (vs. 4)

               φανερώσω αὐτὸ   **PURPPOSE**

                ὡς δεῖ με λαλῆσαι   /   **MANNER**

  Ἐν σοφίᾳ περιπατεῖτε πρὸς [τοὺς ἔξω]

         τὸν καιρὸν ἐξαγοραζόμενοι   **AMPLIFICATION**

        Ὁ λόγος ὑμῶν πάντοτε ἐν χάριτι = ἅλατι ἠρτυμένος   **AMPLIFICATION**

       /εἰδέναι πῶς δεῖ ὑμᾶς ἑνὶ ἑκάστῳ ἀποκρίνεσθαι/   // **PURPOSE**

Figure 12

13 Conclusion

13.1 **Contribution**. I will begin by listing and summarizing the elements in this discussion that are original (to my knowledge) and therefore represent a contribution to our discipline. First, and most important, is the framework itself (fig. I and PART I). It is more inclusive than any other approach I have seen except one,[50] and to my mind the organization of the factors is the most satisfactory that has so far been proposed. Involved is the distinct characterization of the five macro-systems and the roster of organizing factors that define each macro-system. Prominence is the only macrosystem with its roster of organizing factors that I borrowed 'as is' from someone else (K. Callow 1974), and even there my treatment of the details contains some original elements. I will mention such original elements in their turn.

Next in importance, I believe, is the material in section 7.2 and figure 8. Although the essential insights came from three sources (see note 39), the formulation given in figure 8 is original. This formulation satisfies my intuitions about language to an extent that no other formulation has. I am now able to make a clear distinction between discourse structure and propositional structure. The discourse structure of a text is determined by the interplay of all the factors in my framework. The propositional structure of a text is part of the factor I call 'content' and is a specific and selective combination of the lexicon of the language involved and the semantic hierarchy.

I will now work through the thesis from the beginning and mention the original elements as I come to them. The particular formulation of grammar as a form-meaning composite given in section 2.1.1.1 is new.

---

[50] Ilah Fleming has a scheme that includes at least as many factors as mine, but since it is part of a doctoral dissertation that has not yet been submitted, I do not feel at liberty to discuss it. I will simply say that I prefer my organization to hers.

Although Longacre said it first (1967a), I had come to regard "role" as being part of grammar before seeing his statement. I am not aware that anyone else has proposed including relation in grammar as well.

The characterization of a discourse outline given in section 2.4 is new; of special note is the claim that with but one exception (see sect. 8.2, 4:7-9) no two beginning points may be precisely the same. Similarly, the specialized structural diagram for displaying discourse structure is new. Its salient features are the reproduction of the whole text (with no changes) in the proper word order and an organization such that the text may be read unambiguously.

Although my discussion of Cohesion owes much to Halliday, there are some original ingredients. The notion that grammatical agreement and given information contribute to Cohesion is my own. Similarly the inclusion of exophora (reference to situation and culture) and synecdonym and metonym in a discussion of Cohesion is my own.

The germ idea of 'dequotation' I owe to Hockett (I have retained the term in deference to him), and several futher ideas I owe to Gleason, but much of my discussion of dequotation is original, including the characterization and the notion of levels. I believe that what I have called promotion is genuinely a new discovery.

The identity and composition of the organizational perspective that I call Style is a new formulation. The same thing may be said for Strategy. The discussion of content, information rate, and modality with reference to the encoder's strategy contains some original elements.

Part II contains some procedures that are original with me. There are also a few minor modifications of my discussion of the framework in Part I. The specialized structural diagram is new. The discussion of external and internal cohesion and the role of cohesion in bridging major breaks in the outline contains new elements. The notion of steppingstone in tracing a theme line is mine. The thoughts on a possible correlation between focus and semantic paragraph are mine. Figures 9, 10, and 11, though tentative and unsatisfactory, represent insights into the use of Cohesion and Prominence which I believe further research will render significant—they are new.

Finally, the discussion in chapter 12 is new. I believe that figure 12 represents an advance over the various ways that have heretofore been used to display the discourse structure of an expository discourse. I see no reason why it cannot be adapted for use with other types of discourse as well.

13.2 **Implications**. I will mention a few possible implications of this thesis for the future of the linguistic discipline, including some directions for further study.

If the view of language expressed in figure 8 (sect. 7.2) commends itself to others as valid, some of the confusion that has characterized past research and thinking in linguistics can be avoided in the future: the confusing of that which is language specific with that which is discourse specific; the confusing of lexicon with grammar on the one hand, and with the semantic hierarchy on the other; the confusing of logical system (universal) with logical structure (discourse specific).

I am well aware that the framework for discourse analysis which this thesis proposes is not definitive, but it is, I think, a significant step in the right direction. In whatever ways grammar has been defined in the past, in the future it must be understood in terms of discourse system. The roster of organizing factors discussed here will certainly be enlarged, and a better way of organizing them may well be forthcoming, but I believe my framework points the way toward the new paradigm that our discipline needs if we are to increase our understanding of the workings of human language—real language, as used by real people in real situations. A sentence grammar paradigm can no longer meet our needs.

As mentioned in the Introduction, my concern has been to be suggestive rather than exhaustive. It follows that virtually every topic that I treated could be profitably discussed in greater detail. Of course many of them already have been, but by and large from different perspectives than that suggested here. From my point of view, the area most urgently requiring further research is that of exophoric reference and implied information—information in the situation and culture that the encoder treats as given.

I am not satisfied with our understanding of Prominence and the organizing factors that contribute to it; much more work needs to be done in this area. Similarly, our understanding of register and code may fairly be classified as incipient. The whole area of an encoder's strategy has received minimal attention so far—I expect this macrosystem to be revised first and most. Each of the organizing factors contributing to Strategy requires more research. More needs to be done with the several factors I treated under modality. The procedure presented in chapter 12 for displaying the discourse structure of a text can no doubt be improved, both in its own right and as modified for other discourse types.

Narrowing the focus a little, there are some lesser matters that I would like to see developed further. The notion of levels of dequotation and their function would reward further study, I believe—and if there are levels of hypertaxis, there should be levels of hypotaxis with their functions. Promotion needs to be explored further. More work needs to be done on a way to measure or quantify Cohesion, as well as on the significance of variation in internal and external cohesion throughout a text. With reference to ancient literature, more attention needs to be given to the bearing of Cohesion upon the integrity of a text and of register upon its authorship. The significance of varying levels of Prominence and the interplay among the organizing factors that contribute to it needs elucidating.

In the introduction, I quoted Grimes' opinion to the effect that our knowledge is exceeded by our ignorance. I am not prepared to dispute his dictum, but it is safe to say that the ratio is changing in our favor. It is my sincere hope that this discussion will contribute to accelerating that rate of change.

REFERENCES

Abbott, T.K. 1897. *A Critical and Exegetical Commentary on the Epistles to the Ephesians and the Colossians*. Edinburgh. T. & T. Clark.

Aland, Kurt. 1965. The Significance of the Papyri for Progress in New Testament Research. *The Bible in Modern Scholarship*. J.P. Hyatt, ed. New York: Abingdon Press.

Aland, Kurt; Matthew Black; Bruce Metzger; and Allen Wikgren, eds. 1966. *The Greek New Testament*. New York: American Bible Society.

Anderson, Nels, ed. 1969. *Studies in Multilingualism*. Leiden: E.J. Brill.

Arndt, W.F. and F.W. Gingrich. 1957. *A Greek-English Lexicon of the New Testament and Other Early Christian Literature*. Chicago: The University of Chicago Press.

Austing, John. 1977. Introduction and Overview of II Corinthians. *Notes on Translation* 66:2-19.

Austing, June. n.d. Omie Discourse. *Unpublished MS.*

Bach, Emmon and Robert Harms, eds. 1968. *Universals in Linguistic Theory*. New York: Holt, Rinehart & Winston.

Bailey, C.J.N. 1973. *Variation and Linguistic Theory*. Center for Applied Linguistics.

_____ and R.W. Shuy, eds. 1973. *New Ways of Analyzing Variation in English*. Washington, D.C.: Georgetown University Press.

Ballard, D.L.; R.J. Conrad; and R.E. Longacre. 1971. The Deep and Surface Grammar of Interclausal Relations. *Foundations of Language* 7:1.70-118.

Becker, Alton L. 1965. A Tagmemic Approach to Paragraph Analysis. *College Composition and Communication* 16:5.237-42.

Beekman, John and John Callow. 1974. *Translating the word of God*. Grand Rapids: Zondervan.

_____ 1976. The Semantic Structure of Language. *Unpublished course notes*.

_____ 1977. The Semantic Structure of Written Communication. *Unpublished course notes*.

Bernstein, Basil. 1966. Elaborated and Restricted Codes: An Outline. *Explorations in Sociolinguistics*. Stanley Lieberson, ed. The Hague: Mouton, pp. 126-33.

_____, ed. 1973. *Class, Codes and Control II: Applied Studies towards a Sociology of Language*. London: Routledge and Paul.

Bickerton, Derek. 1971. Inherent Variability and Variable Rules. *Foundations of Language* 7:457-92.

Bloomfield, Leonard. 1933. *Language*. New York: Henry Holt and Co.

Bloomfield, Morton W. and Einar Haugen, eds. 1974. *Language as a Human Problem*. New York: W.W. Norton and Company.

Black, Robert A. 1967. Hopi Rabbit-Hunt Chants: A Ritualized Language. *Essays on the Verbal and Visual Arts*. MacNeish, June Helm, ed. Seattle: University of Washington Press, pp. 7-11.

Bogoras, Waldemar. 1921. Chukchee. *Handbook of American Indian Languages*. Franz Boas, ed. Washington, D.C.: Smithsonian Institution, Part 2:631-897.

Brend, Ruth M., ed. 1974. *Advances in Tagmemics*. Amsterdam: North-Holland.

Brennan, P.W. 1968. The Structure of Koine Greek Narrative. *Unpublished Ph.D. dissertation*, The Hartford Seminary Foundation.

Bruce, F.F. 1965. *The Letters of Paul*. Grand Rapids: Wm. B. Eerdmans.

Callow, Kathleen. 1974. *Discourse Considerations in Translating the Word of God*. Grand Rapids: Zondervan.

Carrington, John F. 1969. *Talking Drums of Africa*. New York: Negro Universities Press.

Carson, H.M. 1960. *The Epistles of Paul to the Colossians and Philemon*. Grand Rapids: Wm. B. Eerdmans.

Chafe, Wallace. 1970. *Meaning and the Structure of Language*. Chicago: The University of Chicago Press.

_____ 1974. Language and Consciousness. Language 50:111-33.

Chao, Yuen Ren. 1956. Chinese Terms of Address. *Language* 32:217-41.

Christensen, Francis. 1965. A Generative Rhetoric of the Paragraph. *College Composition and Communication* 16:3.144-56.

Clements, Paul. 1976. The Effects of Staging on Recall from Prose. *Unpublished Ph.D. dissertation*, Cornell.

Conklin, Harold C. 1956. Tagalog Speech Disguise. *Language* 32:136-39.

_____ 1959. Linguistic Play in Its Cultural Context. *Language* 35:631-36.

Cowan, George M. 1948. Mazateco Whistle Speech. *Language* 24:280-86.

Cromack, Robert E. 1968. *Language Systems and Discourse Structure in Cashinawa*. Hartford: Hartford Seminary Foundation.

Crowell, Thomas H. 1973. Cohesion in Borôro Discourse. *Linguistics* 104:15-27.

Dahl, Östen. 1974. *Topic and Comment, Contextual Boundness and Focus*. Hamburg: Helmut Buske.

_____ 1976. What Is New Information? *Report on Text Linguistic Approaches to Word Order*. N.E. Enkvist, ed.

Daneš, F., ed. 1974. *Papers on Functional Sentence Perspective*. Prague: Academia.

Deibler, Ellis W. n.d. Discourse Structure of Gahuku. *Unpublished MS.*

Derwing, Bruce L. 1973. *Transformational Grammar as a Theory of Language Acquisition*. Cambridge: Cambridge University Press.

Dijk, Teun A. van. 1972. *Some Aspects of Text Grammars*. The Hague: Mouton.

Dik, Simon. 1968. *Coordination: Its Implications for the Theory of General Linguistics*. Amsterdam: North-Holland.

Doty, William G. 1973. *Letters in Primitive Christianity*. Philadelphia: Fortress Press.

Duff, Martha. 1973. Contrastive Features of Written and Oral Texts in Amuesha. *Notes on Translation* 50:2-13.

Ellis, Dean S. 1967. Speech and Social Status in America. *Social Forces* 45:431-37.

Emeneau, Murray B. 1958. Oral Poets of South India—the Todas. *Journal of American Folklore* 71:312-24.

Enkvist, Nils E. 1964. On Defining Style: An Essay in Applied Linguistics. *Linguistics and Style*. John Spencer, ed. London: Oxford University Press, pp. 173-79.

Ferguson, Charles A. 1959. Diglossia. *Word* 15:325-40.

_____ 1971. *Language Structure and Language Use*. Stanford: Stanford University Press.

Fillmore, Charles. 1972. On Generativity. *Goals of Linguistic Theory*. Stanley Peters, ed. Englewood Cliffs: Prentice-Hall, pp. 1-19.

Firbas, Jan and Eva Golková. 1976. *An Analytical Bibliography of Czechoslovak Studies in Functional Sentence Perspective*. Brno: Univerzita Jana Evangelisty Purkyne.

Fishman, J.A., ed. 1968. *Readings in the Sociology of Language*. The Hague: Mouton.

Forster, Keith. 1977. The Narrative Folklore Discourse in Border Cuna. *Discourse Grammar: Studies in Indigenous Languages of Colombia, Panama, and Ecuador, Part 2*. R.E. Longacre, ed. Dallas: Summer Institute of Linguistics and University of Texas at Arlington, pp. 1-23.

Frake, Charles D. 1961. The Diagnosis of Disease among the Subanun of Mindanao. *American Anthropologist* 63:113-32.

Frantz, Donald G. 1971. *Toward a Generative Grammar of Blackfoot*. Norman: Summer Institute of Linguistics.

Frederiksen, Carl H. 1975. Representing Logical and Semantic Structure of Knowledge Acquired from Discourse. *Cognitive Psychology* 7:371-458.

Friedrich, Paul. 1966. Structural Implications of Russian Pronominal Usage. *Sociolinguistics*. Wm. Bright, ed. The Hague: Mouton, pp. 214-59.

Fries, Peter H. 1974. Some Fundamental Insights of Tagmemics Revisited. *Advances in Tagmemics*. Ruth M. Brend, ed., Amsterdam: North-Holland Publishing Co., pp. 23-34.

Funk, Robert W. 1966. *Language, Hermeneutic, and Word of God*. New York: Harper and Row.

_____ 1967. The Form and Structure of II and III John. *Journal of Biblical Literature* 86:4.424-30.

Gieser, Richard. 1972. Kalinga Sequential Discourse. *Philippine Journal of Linguistics* 3:15-33.

Gill, H.S. and H.A. Gleason, Jr. 1963. *A Reference Grammar of Panjabi*. Hartford: Hartford Seminary Foundation.

Gleason, H.A., Jr. 1961. *An Introduction to Descriptive Linguistics*. New York: Holt, Rinehart & Winston.

_____ 1964. The Organization of Language: A Stratificational View. *Monograph Series on Languages and Linguistics, No. 17*. Washington: Georgetown University, pp. 75-95.

_____ 1965. *Linguistics and English Grammar*. New York: Holt, Rinehart & Winston.

_____ 1968. Contrastive Analysis in Discourse Structure. *Monograph Series on Languages and Linguistics, No. 21*. Washington: Georgetown University, pp. 39-63.

_____ 1976. Continuity in Linguistics. *The Second LACUS Forum 1975*. Peter A. Reich, ed., Columbia, S.C.: Hornbeam Press, pp. 3-16.

_____ 1977. Realization, Transformations, and Filters. *The Third LACUS Forum 1976*. R.J. DiPietro and E.L. Blansitt, Jr., eds. Columbia, S.C.: Hornbeam Press, 1:486-94.

Grassmick, John D. 1974. *Principies and Practice of Greek Exegesis*. Dallas: Dallas Theological Seminary.

Grimes, Joseph E. 1972. Outlines and Overlays. *Language* 48:3:513-24.

_____ 1975. *The Thread of Discourse*. The Hague: Mouton.

_____ and Naomi Glock. 1970. A Saramaccan Narrative Pattern. *Language* 46:2.408-25.

Gumperz, John J. and Dell Hymes, eds. 1972. *Directions in Sociolinguistics*. New York: Holt, Rinehart & Winston.

Gundel, Jeanette M. 1974. The Role of Topic and Comment in Linguistic Theory. *Unpublished Ph.D. dissertation*, University of Texas at Austin.

Gunter, Richard. 1966. On the Placement of Accent in Dialogue: A Feature of Context Grammar. *Journal of Linguistics* 2:2.159-79.

Gutwinski, Waldemar. 1976. *Cohesion in Literary Texts*. The Hague: Mouton.

Haas, Mary R. 1944. Men's and Women's Speech in Koasati. *Language* 20:142-49.

_____ 1951. Interlingual Word Taboos. *American Anthropologist* 53:338-44.

Hale, Austin, ed. 1973. *Clause, Sentence, and Discourse Patterns in Selected Languages of Nepal*, Vol. I. Norman: Summer Institute of Linguistics.

Halliday, M.A.K. 1967. Notes on Transitivity and Theme in English, Parts I and 2. *Journal of Linguistics* 3:37-81, 199-244.

_____ 1968. Notes on Transitivity and Theme in English, Part 3. *Journal of Linguistics* 4:179-215.

_____ 1970. Functional Diversity in Language as Seen from a Consideration of Modality and Mood in English. *Foundations of Language* 6:322-61.

_____ 1973. *Explorations in the Functions of Language.* London: Edward Arnold.

_____ 1975. *Learning How to Mean—Explorations in the Development of Language*. London: Edward Arnold.

_____ and Ruqaiya Hasan. 1976. *Cohesion in English*. London: Longman.

Hasan, Ruqaiya. 1973. Code, Register and Social Dialect. *Class, Codes and Control II: Applied Studies towards a Sociology of Language*. Basil Bernstein, ed. London: Routledge & Paul, pp. 253-92.

Haugen, Einar. 1972. *The Ecology of Language*. Stanford: Stanford University Press.

Herzog, George. 1934. Speech Melody and Primitive Music. *Musical Quarterly* 20:452-66.

_____ 1945. Drum Signaling in a West African Tribe. *Word* 1:217-38.

Hockett, Charles F. 1963. The Problem of Universals in Language. *Universals of Language*. J.H. Greenberg, ed. Cambridge, Mass.: The M.I.T. Press, pp. 1-22.

_____ 1968. *The State of the Art*. The Hague: Mouton.

Hollenbach, Bruce. 1975. Discourse Structure, Interpropositional Relations, and Translation. *Notes on Translation* 56:2-21.

Huisman, Roberta D. 1973. Angaataha Narrative Discourse. *Linguistics* 110:29-42.

Hyatt, J.P., ed. 1965. *The Bible in Modern Scholarship*. New York: Abingdon Press.

Hymes, Dell. 1968. The Ethnography of Speaking. *Readings in the Sociology of Language*. J.A. Fishman, ed. The Hague: Mouton, pp. 99-138.

_____ 1972. Models of the Interaction of Language and Social Life. *Directions in Sociolinguistics*. John J. Gumpers and Dell Hymes, eds. New York: Holt, Rinehart & Winston, pp. 35-71.

_____ 1974. Speech and Language: On the Origins and Foundations of Inequality among Speakers. *Language as a Human Problem*. Morton Bloomfield and Einar Haugen, eds. New York: W.W. Norton and Company, pp. 45-71.

_____ ed. 1964. *Language in Culture and Society*. New York: Harper and Row.

Joos, Martin. 1962. The Five Clocks. Indiana University Research Center in Anthropology, Folklore, and Linguistics, Publication 22. *International Journal of American Linguistics* 28:2 (Part V):9-62.

Kiefer, Ferenc. 1966. Some Semantic Relations in Natural Language. *Foundations of Language* 2:228-40.

Kingston, Peter K.E. 1973. Repetition as a Feature of Discourse Structure in Mamaindé. *Notes on Translation* 50:13-22.

Labov, William. 1969. Contraction, Deletion, and Inherent Variability of the English Copula. *Language* 45:715-62.

_____ 1973a. The Linguistic Consequences of Being a Lame. *Language in Society* 2:1.81-115.

_____ 1973b. The Boundaries of Words and Their Meanings. *New Ways of Analyzing Variation in English*. C.J.N. Bailey and R.W. Shuy, eds. Washington, O.C.: Georgetown University Press, pp. 340-73.

_____ and Joshua Waletzky. 1976. Narrative Analysis: Oral Versions of Personal Experience. *Essays on the Verbal and Visual Arts*. June Helm MacNeish, ed. Seattle: University of Washington Press.

Larson, Mildred. 1975. *A Manual for Problem Solving in Bible Translation*. Grand Rapids: Zondervan Publishing House.

Lenski, R.C.H. 1964. *The Interpretation of St. Paul's Epistles to the Colossians, to the Thessalonians, to Timothy, to Titus and to Philemon*. Minneapolis: Augsburg Publishing House.

Levinsohn, Stephen H. 1975. Functional Sentence Perspective in Inga. *Journal of Linguistics* 11:13-37.

Lewis, Ronald K. 1972. Sanio-Hiowe Paragraph Structure. *Pacific Linguistics*, series A, 31.

Li, Charles N., ed. 1976. *Subject and Topic*. New York: Academic Press, Inc.

Lightfoot, J.B. 1959. *St. Paul's Epistles to the Colossians and to Philemon*. Grand Rapids: Zondervan Publishing House. Reprint of 1879 edition.

Lockwood, David G. 1972. *Introduction to Stratificational Linguistics*. New York: Harcourt Brace Jovanovich, Inc.

Longacre, Robert E. 1968. *Philippine Languages: Discourse, Paragraph and Sentence Structure*. Santa Ana: Summer Institute of Linguistics.

_____ 1970a. Hierarchy in Language. *Method and Theory in Linguistics*. Paul Garvin, ed. The Hague: Mouton, pp. 173-95.

_____ 1970b. Sentence Structure as a Statement Calculus. *Language* 46:783-815.

_____ 1972. *Hierarchy and Universality of Discourse Constituents in New Guinea Languages: Discussion*. 2 vols. Washington, D.C.: Georgetown University Press.

_____ 1976a. *An Anatomy of Speech Notions*. Lisse: Peter de Ridder Press.

_____ ed. 1976b. *Discourse Grammar: Studies in Indigenous Languages of Colombia, Panama, and Ecuador*, Part I. Dallas: Summer Institute of Linguistics and University of Texas at Arlington.

_____ ed. 1977. *Discourse Grammar: Studies in Indigenous Languages of Colombia, Panama, and Ecuador*, Parts II and III. Dallas: Summer Institute of Linguistics and University of Texas at Arlington.

Lowe, Ivan. 1969. An Algebraic Theory of English Pronominal Reference. *Semiotica* 1:2.397-421.

_____ 1972. On the Relation of Formal Sememic Matrices with Illustrations from Nambiquara. *Foundations of Language* 8:360-90.

McCarthy, Joy. 1965. Clause Chaining in Kanite. *Anthropological Linguistics* 7:5.59-70.

Mcleod, Ruth. 1974. Paragraph, Aspect, and Participant in Xavánte. *Linguistics* 132:51-74.

Mel'Čuk, I.A. and A.K. Žolkovskij. 1970. Towards a Functioning 'Meaning-Text' Model of Language. *Linguistics* 57:10-47.

Meyer, Bonnie J.F. 1974. The Organization of Prose and Its Effect on Recall. *Unpublished Ph.D. dissertation*, Cornell.

Miller, George A. 1956. Human Memory and the Storage of Information. *I.R.E. Transaction on Information Theory* IT;2:129-37.

Moulton, W.F. and A.S. Geden. 1963. *A Concordance to the Greek Testament*. Edinburgh: T. & T. Clark.

Mullins, T.Y. 1968. Greeting as a New Testament Form. *Journal of Biblical Literature* 67:418-26.

National Council of Teachers of English. 1966. *The Sentence and the Paragraph*. Champaign: National Council of Teachers of English.

Nestle, Erwin and Kurt Aland. 1960. *Novum Testamentum Graece*. 24th edition. Stuttgart: Privilegierte Wurttembergische Bibelanstalt.

Newman, John F. 1978. Participant Orientation in Longuda Folk Tales. *Papers on Discourse*. J.E. Grimes, ed. Dallas: Summer Institute of Linguistics and University of Texas at Arlington, pp. 91-104.

Nida, Eugene A. 1949. *Morphology*. Ann Arbor: University of Michigan Press.

_____ 1964. *Toward a Science of Translating*. Leiden: E.J. Brill.

_____ 1974. *Exploring Semantic Structures*. Munich: Fink Verlag.

_____ 1975. *Componential Analysis of Meaning*. The Hague: Mouton.

_____ and Charles R. Taber. 1969. *The Theory and Practice of Translation*. Leiden: E.J. Brill.

Ortony, Andrew. 1975. Why Metaphors Are Necessary and Not Just Nice. *Educational Theory* 25:1.45-53.

Pickering, Wilbur N. 1977. *The Identity of the New Testament Text*. Nashville: Thomas Nelson.

Pike, Kenneth L. 1964a. Discourse Analysis and Tagmeme Matrices. *Oceanic Linguistics* 3:1.5-25.

_____ 1964b. Beyond the Sentence. *College Composition and Communication* 15:129-35.

_____ 1967. *Language in Relation to a Unified Theory of the Structure of Human Behavior*. The Hague: Mouton.

_____ 1970. *Tagmemic and Matrix Linguistics Applied to Selected African Languages*. Norman: Summer Institute of Linguistics.

_____ and Ivan Lowe. 1969. Pronominal Reference in English Conversation and Discourse—A Group Theoretical Treatment. *Folia Linguistica* 3:68-106.

_____ and Evelyn G. Pike. 1977. *Grammatical Analysis*. Dallas: Summer Institute of Linguistics and University of Texas at Arlington.

Pitkin, Willis L., Jr. 1977a. Hierarchies and the Discourse Hierarchy. *College English* 38:648-59.

_____ 1977b. X/V: Some Basic Strategies of Discourse. *College English* 38:660-75.

Platt, John T. 1971. *Grammatical Form and Grammatical Meaning*. Amsterdam: North-Holland.

Postal, Paul. 1972. The Best Theory. *Goals of Linguistic Theory*. Stanley Peters, ed. Englewood Cliffs: Prentice-Hall, pp. 131-70.

Propp, Vladimir. 1958. *Morphology of the Folktale*. Translated by Lawrence Scott. Indiana University publications in anthropology, folklore, and linguistics, No. 10.

Reich, Peter A. 1969. The Finiteness of Natural Language. *Language* 45:831-43.

Ruegsegger, Manis. 1966. Reduplication and Redundancy. *Notes on Translation* 22:1-4.

Sanders, Gerald A. 1970. On the Natural Domain of Grammar. *Linguistics* 63:51-123.

Sanders, Jack T. 1962. The Transition from Opening Epistolary Thanks-giving to Body in the Letters of the Pauline Corpus. *Journal of Biblical Literature* 81:4.348-62.

Sankoff, David. 1971. Dictionary Structure and Probability Measures. *Information and Control* 19.

Sapir, Edward. 1949. *Selected Writings of Edward Sapir in Language, Culture, and Personality*. David G. Mandelbaum, ed. Berkeley: University of California Press.

Saussure, Ferdinand de. 1959. *Course in General Linguistics*. Translated by Wade Baskin. New York: McGraw-Hill.

Schank, Roger C. 1975. *Conceptual Information Processing*. New York: American Elsevier Publishing Co.

Schegloff, Emanuel. 1972. Sequencing in Conversational Openings. *Directions in Sociolinguistics*. J.J. Gumperz and Dell Hymes, eds. New York: Holt, Rinehart & Winston, pp. 346-80.

Sheffler, E. Margaret. 1978. Mundurukú Discourse. *Papers on Discourse*. J.E. Grimes, ed. Dallas: Summer Institute of Linguistics and University of Texas at Arlington, pp. 119-42.

Shell, Olive A. 1957. Cashibo II: Grammemic Analysis of Transitive and Intransitive Verb Patterns. *International Journal of American Linguistics* 23:179-218.

Simpson, E.K. and F.F. Bruce. 1957. *Commentary on the Epistles to the Ephesians and the Colossians*. Grand Rapids: Wm. B. Eerdmans.

Sinclair, J.McH. and R.M. Coulthard. 1975. *Towards an Analysis of Discourse*. London: Oxford University Press.

Spencer, John Walter, ed. 1967. *Linguistics and style*. London: Oxford University Press.

Stennes, Leslie. 1969. *Participant Identification in Adamawa Fulani*. Hartford: Hartford Seminary Foundation.

Stockwell, R.P., P. Schachter and B.H. Partee. 1973. *The Major Syntactic Structures of English*. New York: Holt, Rinehart & Winston.

Stout, Mickey and Ruth Thomson. 1971. Kayapó Narrative. *International Journal of American Linguistics* 37:4.250-56.

Taber, Charles R. 1966. *The Structure of Sango Narrative*. Hartford: Hartford Seminary Foundation.

Thompson, G.H.P. 1967. *The Letters of Paul to the Ephesians, to the Colossians and to Philemon*. Cambridge: Cambridge University Press.

Trail, Ronald L., ed. 1973. *Patterns in Clause, Sentence, and Discourse in Selected Languages of India and Nepal*, Vol. I. Norman: Summer Institute of Linguistics.

Turner, Nigel. 1976. *Style*. Vol. IV of *A Grammar of New Testament Greek*. J. H. Moulton. Edinburgh. T. & T. Clark.

Twaddell, W.F. 1976. *The Hildebrandlied*. Private printing.

Ullmann, Stephen. 1964. *Language and Style*. Oxford: Blackwell.

Vachek, Josef. 1966. *The Linguistic School of Prague*. Bloomington: Indiana University Press.

Wallis, Ethel. 1971. Discourse Focus in Mezquital Otomi. *Notes on Translation* 42:19-21.

Watters, David. 1978. Speaker-Hearer Involvement in Kham. *Papers on Discourse*. J.E. Grimes, ed. Dallas: Summer Institute of Linguistics and University of Texas at Arlington, pp. 1-18.

Weinreich, Uriel. 1963. *Languages in Contact*. The Hague: Mouton.

Welch, Betty. 1977. Tucana Discourse, Paragraph, and Information Distribution. *Discourse Grammar: Studies in Indigenous Languages of Colombia, Panama, and Ecuador*, Part II. R.E. Longacre, ed. Dallas: Summer Institute of Linguistics and University of Texas at Arlington, pp. 229-52.

Wells, Rulon S. 1947. Immediate Constituents. *Language* 23:81-117.

Wheatley, James. 1973. Pronouns and Nominal Elements in Bacairi Discourse. *Linguistics* 104:105-15.

White, John L. 1972. *The Form and Function of the Body of the Greek Letter*. Missoula: University of Montana Press.

Williams, Raymond. 1973. *The African Drum*. Highland Park, Mich.: Highland Park College Press.

Winograd, Terry. 1971. *Procedures as a Representation for Data in a Computer Program for Understanding Natural Language*. Cambridge: Massachusetts Institute of Technology.

Wise, Mary Ruth. 1971. *Identification of Participants in Discourse: A Study of Aspects of Form and Meaning in Nomatsiguenga*. Norman: Summer Institute of Linguistics.

_____ and Ivan Lowe. 1972. Permutation Groups in Discourse. *Georgetown University School of Languages and Linguistics: Working Papers* 4:12-34.

Young, R.E.; A.L. Becker; and K.L. Pike. 1970. *Rhetoric: Discovery and Change*. New York: Harcourt, Brace and World.

Other books by the author:

The Greek New Testament, According to Family 35
> *The only significant line of transmission, both ancient and independent, that has a demonstrable archetypal form in all 27 books; plus a totally new critical apparatus that gives a percentage of manuscript attestation to the variant readings, and that includes six competing published editions*

The Sovereign Creator Has Spoken, Objective Authority for Living
> *New Testament Translation with Commentary (over 4,000 footnotes)*

The Identity of the New Testament Text, IV
> *The theoretical explanation for* The Greek New Testament

Internet sites with further works by the author:
> www.walkinhiscommandments.com
> www.prunch.org